AND THEN YOU WIN

A Startup's Untold Story of G
Grind, and Glory

AND THEN YOU WIN

A Startup's Untold Story of Grit, Grind, and Glory

How a Bitcoin Venture Overcame
All Odds and Lived to Tell About It

GEORGE KIKVADZE

ethos
collective

Printed in the United States of America

Published by Igniting Souls
PO Box 43, Powell, OH 43065
IgnitingSouls.com

LCCN: 2025911721

Paperback ISBN: 978-1-63680-531-3
Hardback ISBN: 978-1-63680-532-0
eBook ISBN: 978-1-63680-533-7

Available in paperback, hardcover, e-book, and audiobook.

Cointelegraph is a media partner.

COINTELEGRAPH

To my sons Luca and David—may you always believe
that impossible is nothing.

ჩემს ვაჟებს ლუკასა და დავითს—შეუძლებელი
არაფერია.

The entire proceeds of my portion of this book
will be directed towards further funding
Bitcoin and Lightning Network development.

TABLE OF CONTENTS

PHOTO GALLERY

PART III: THEN THEY FIGHT YOU

PART IV: AND THEN YOU WIN

FOREWORD

There's a scene in *Star Trek III* where the Genesis Project unleashes a sweeping wave of transformation, rejuvenating an entire lifeless planet. It's a climactic revival—like a massive desert bloom after a rainstorm—powerful enough to bring Spock back from the dead after he sacrificed himself to save his companions. When I think of the incredible journey of Bitfury and the entrepreneurs who created it, I think of this scene.

My background in tech startups and venture capital spans decades. I've been fortunate to participate in the creation of foundational companies across wave after wave of technologies, dating back to the early commercialization of silicon. In my early years, I joined Wilf Corrigan, former CEO of Fairchild, at LSI Logic—a seminal Silicon Valley company where Jensen Huang, who would later found NVIDIA, was among our teammates, alongside future CEOs and GMs of Altera, Xilinx, and Broadcom. After LSI Logic, I went on to help develop a business plan for TSMC in Taiwan—now a trillion-dollar tech giant—where I was issued badge #A001 in the planning phase of its incorporation.

After becoming a venture capitalist in the early 1990s, I began assembling startup teams across sequential technology waves: silicon, communications equipment, Internet networks, P2P distributed systems, mobile applications, and later machine learning and Cloud/ SaaS—where I became the first backer of Zoom Video and a catalyst for Canva's formation. These waves of technology would later lead to my interest in P2P currency and ultimately inspire me to provide start-up capital to the founders of Bitfury.

Two specific experiences, coupled with my interest in economics, would be foundational in my interest in the peer-to-peer currency we now call Bitcoin. In 2000, I founded a company whimsically named Eyefrog.com—with Linus Torvalds as an advisor[1]—which developed a peer-to-peer file storage system that rebranded as AVVENU and was later acquired by Nokia to be their peer-to-peer, cloud-based user content portal for their smart phones called "Files by Ovi."[2]

In parallel, in 2003, I became a contributor to the creation of one of the world's first "free-floating" digital currencies called the Linden Dollar, and the resultant "digital economy" in *Second Life*, where my avatar name is, and was, Alan Greenspan Golum. These experiences set the stage for me to have an epiphany in 2010 to send a note into the "Twittersphere," seeking to build a community around what might become a new reality.[3] Working primarily in Silicon Valley for decades, where the environment is gushing with technical talent, ideas, and capital, can give one a strong sense of self-confidence and the belief that anything can work.

Silicon Valley's "company creation ecosystem" operates like Hollywood's studio system in pumping out movies: starting with a script and trailer (akin to a business idea and prototype), one can cast a lead actor (proven CEO), add studio-level distribution (portfolio relationships for customers and funding), and get projects off the ground with speed and strong momentum. Projects that gain traction can draw massive capital from the hundreds of venture funds within thirty miles of Sand Hill Road. It's a well-understood formula that works reliably.

For decades, I'd helped catalyze over twenty public companies that would reach more than $1 trillion in aggregate value by working to this formula: focusing on known risks, staying local, and assembling teams as one would in creating blockbuster movies.

It may have been a false sense of security that gave me the courage to step up to personally write a seven-figure check to back the raw startup of Bitfury and later to commit what would grow to a nine-figure sum to keep the company going through a downturn. Looking back, this was not an obvious bet; Bitfury's founding team was scattered across Ukraine, Georgia, Latvia, and Finland. They had no physical headquarters and no background in "deep tech," diving into a plan that would center on designing and building silicon compute chips, compute servers, and data centers around the world. These elements would become the key components of the foundational infrastructure needed to run the protocols underlying the emerging "industry" of Bitcoin at a massive scale. These characters—Valery Vavilov, George Kikvadze, "X," and Niko Punin—would create from scratch a foundational part of the world's most prominent open-source distributed database we now call Bitcoin, in a company called Bitfury.

None of my well-learned Silicon Valley lessons applied here. Because the founding team had no prior experience in deeply ingrained traditional methods for designing silicon, servers, or data centers, they were able to think "out of the box" and cut through layers of overhead to deliver incredibly creative solutions that worked with levels of efficiency traditional teams and methods were unable to achieve. Through sheer grit, energy, integrity, intelligence, and the success of their products, Bitfury rapidly grew to over one thousand team members across sixteen countries, operating hundreds of megawatts in data centers across Iceland, Eurasia, and Canada. At times, Bitfury machines powered data centers running over forty percent of the world's Bitcoin mining infrastructure, having developed pioneering technologies in custom silicon, ultra-dense compute servers, immersion cooling, and portable data centers.

This book chronicles tales so wild they're hard to imagine actually happening. While I believe that history repeats itself, this chapter of digital history—the journey to create an industrial-strength foundational infrastructure for one of the world's most revolutionary open-source technologies—won't be repeated. It's remarkable to think this scrappy team from outside Silicon Valley could build the infrastructure for the world's modern currency system.

George's title, *And Then You Win*, perfectly captures this decade-long journey across financing deserts, ups and downs of extraordinarily volatile price cycles for Bitfury's hardware products, as well as the productive output of the company's data centers, the crossing of raging rivers of regulatory uncertainty, and the intensity of competing with "China." There were scant moments when victory felt expected, followed by many moments when all hope seemed lost—and then another win.

After collaborating with Niko Punin in 2013, he introduced me to George and Val around 2014. These three and "X" would create and lead this amazing Bitfury team. At the time, Bitcoin traded around $400. Unsurprisingly, it was dismissed at the time by Wall Street icons like Warren Buffett as "rat poison squared" and later by Nassim Nicholas Taleb as "digital tulips without the aesthetics." Despite the controversy, I was already a believer in the underlying P2P technology and, having previously built up a position in gold derivatives going into the 2008–2010 financial crisis, I was willing to step up for this team. While "the equation" did not fit the traditional Silicon Valley model I described previously, something about these entrepreneurs struck me—not just their vision, but their unshakeable conviction and ability to just get things done—they *knew* they were building infrastructure for a new financial reality.

After my initial funding, I tried to get "traditional" Silicon Valley VCs to join me. I should have been able to predict the response: 100 percent rejections. Most couldn't see past the geographic distribution of the team or the nascent and uncertain nature of the Bitcoin ecosystem. I suppose it didn't help that our core technical asset, our CTO, named "X," refused to have a name or photo in the presentation deck. All we were allowed to use to represent his commitment to this effort was a photo of an anonymous man in a motorcycle helmet. Bitfury's ultimate success without any traditional Silicon Valley funding highlights the fact that Silicon Valley is not the only place to start and build world-class companies, and that the Silicon Valley ecosystem can be an echo chamber amplifying whatever's hot, sometimes completely missing opportunities that don't fit established patterns.

This creates an opportunity for the right entrepreneurs. George and Val and the team possessed both a global perspective and what I call "infinite patience with infinite urgency"—the ability to think in decades while executing in days and weeks. They understood that building the world's Bitcoin infrastructure wasn't just about compute and hash power or energy costs. They were building the picks and shovels for the gold rush into the world's new digital economy that most people couldn't see coming.

But this book is more than a business story. It's about what it takes to succeed against impossible odds—the grit to lead teams through brutal bear markets, the agility to pivot when core technology fails, the humility to know that luck and timing are silent partners in every victory. George tells this with the unflinching honesty of someone with scars to prove it.

From Wall Street boardrooms to CNBC chip demonstrations to building the world's largest mining operations, George and Val's journey embodies entrepreneurial dreams realized through pure determination. The sleepless nights during semiconductor crises. Painful decisions to lay off hundreds during crypto winter. The moment-by-moment choice to continue building when every rational indicator suggested quitting.

Bitfury's transformation from Bitcoin mining startup to diversified technology incubator reflects a deeper truth: successful entrepreneurs don't just adapt to change—they anticipate it. When chip development became unviable, they pivoted to infrastructure. When mining faced environmental criticism, they pioneered sustainable solutions. When crypto markets crashed, they doubled down on fundamental technology.

Perhaps most remarkably, they maintained a commitment to education throughout. The Necker Blockchain Summits we co-hosted weren't just networking opportunities—they were laboratories where digital finance's future was debated and designed. Watching the team passionately present Bitcoin's potential to everyone from Richard Branson to Buddhist monks to former prime ministers, I witnessed how technological evangelism accelerates adoption. Bitfury's offspring from our summits are far reaching across the industry, ranging from significant industry trade organizations such as the Global Blockchain Business Council, to publicly listed entities worth many $Billions of USD that evolved from Bitfury's operational footprint such as Hut 8 Corp (NASDAQ: HUT) and Cipher Mining (NASDAQ: CIFR), to a newly listed company, appropriately named "American Bitcoin" (NASDAQ: ABTC), partially owned by entities affiliated with the family of the President of the United States, which marks an inflection point with respect to positive regulatory acceptance for the industry.[4]

As I write this, Bitcoin has achieved the $100,000 milestone that once seemed fantastical, and the technology is now so well accepted that mainstream institutions like BlackRock and other institutions have launched numerous Exchange Traded Fund (ETF) products that now hold Bitcoin in aggregate worth hundreds of billions valued in USD. But the real triumph isn't in price charts—it's in the robust infrastructure making such prices sustainable. Bitfury built the foundation enabling institutional adoption, regulatory acceptance, and mainstream integration.

On that note, the technology is rapidly going mainstream. As of the time of this writing, Bitcoin ETFs are so mainstream that anyone with a brokerage account can now buy Bitcoin—the ease of purchase and sale of ETFs through well established stock brokerage channels is so low friction that even I no longer hold any Bitcoin directly (sacrilegious to many of the OG's in the segment!) as I can have exposure without having to go outside of my normal stock brokerage channels or deal with passwords.

The world needs more stories like this one. In an era of overnight success and social media hype, Bitfury's journey, captured in *And Then You Win*, is a testament to old-fashioned virtues: endurance, loyalty, and relentless pursuit of visions others deem impossible. It's a field manual for entrepreneurs daring to build the future, reminding us that the greatest rewards go not to those who are first, but to those who last.

This isn't just a startup memoir—it's a blueprint for building something the world doesn't understand yet. It's a reminder that real returns come when you bet on visionaries before the world believes.

I'm proud to have backed them. I'm prouder still to call them friends.

Now read on. If you've ever been laughed at for chasing a crazy idea, this book's for you.

—Bill Tai
Venture Capitalist; Early Backer and Board Director of Bitfury

PROLOGUE

THE SPARK

I definitely didn't expect my short-lived career at a glamorous hedge fund to end in under a year. But by October 31, 2008, the writing wasn't just on the wall. It was scrawled in red across the global economy. The financial system was unravelling. Lehman Brothers had collapsed. AIG was in cardiac arrest. And York Capital, the fund I had just joined, was shutting down its operations in the region.

As I was wrapping up my final day, Jamie Dinan, York's legendary founder, took me out for drinks at Cipriani and left me with a single line: "Think of the next big thing and position yourself for it." That advice hit harder than any investment memo I'd written. Not because it was comforting, but because it was exactly what I needed to hear.

I didn't know it then, but on that very same day—October 31, 2008—a pseudonymous figure named Satoshi Nakamoto published a nine-page paper titled, "Bitcoin: A Peer-to-Peer Electronic Cash System." I didn't read it. Nobody around me did. But it would go on to change the world. As Victor Hugo once said, "Nothing is more powerful than an idea whose time has come." Well, he could have been talking about Bitcoin.

It would take me another four years to finally cross paths with this "magic Internet money." That happened in Kyiv, Ukraine, where I met a jolly crew of Latvian and Ukrainian entrepreneurs. Even then, Bitcoin felt as distant as stars in the sky. It was trading at $20, a fraction of what it would become, but already hinting at its potential. To most people, including me, it sounded like fantasy—Internet money conjured from complex math problems. What could be more abstract?

But there was something different about Val, the founder of Bitfury—one of the pioneer Bitcoin miners and industry leaders. His sharp energy, bold vision, and piercing blue eyes left a mark. When he spoke about Bitcoin, it wasn't with the detached enthusiasm of a speculator. He talked with revolutionary fervor about decentralization, about returning power to individuals, about building a system where you wouldn't need to trust banks or governments—just math and cryptography. The way he described it transformed Bitcoin from a curious digital token into something profound: a tool for freedom.

As a lifelong lover of mathematics, that struck a chord. I thought of Galileo, who once wrote: "The book of nature is written in the language of mathematics." He believed natural laws followed mathematical truths. That idea stuck with me. Perhaps money, too, could be reduced to mathematical certainty, freed from the whims of central bankers and politicians.

The weeks after meeting Val, I couldn't shake the feeling that I'd glimpsed something important. I kept thinking about what Jamie had told me back at Cipriani: "Think of the next big thing." What if this was it? What if this strange digital currency was the kind of paradigm shift that happens once in a generation?

By 2013, as Bitcoin's price kept rising, I began to take it more seriously. I dove into research, reading everything I could find. The more I learned, the more convinced I became. This was more than speculative mania. This was the beginning of something transformative. And then I made a decision that would change everything: I went all in.

I joined Val's wild, underdog startup, Bitfury. We weren't just early; we were prehistoric by crypto standards. In an industry that barely existed, we were building the picks and shovels for a digital gold rush most people didn't even believe was real. Our official motto? "Impossible is nothing." It wasn't branding. It was a survival strategy.

What followed was a blur. We were building the plane while learning to fly it. We launched mining data centers in scores of countries, some in places so remote they were barely on Google Maps. We mined hundreds of thousands of Bitcoins when the entire network was still young. We incubated publicly listed companies over vodka shots in steamy banyas. We held strategy sessions in Necker Island jacuzzis with billionaires and visionaries who were just beginning to grasp what we already knew. And in the process, we incubated three unicorns, two of which—Cipher Mining and Hut 8—are publicly listed on Nasdaq, with three others: Axelera AI, Liquidstack, and Crystal Intelligence still in the works. And yes, we had many failures and heartbreaks along the way.

We dealt with everything from skeptical royals to curious FBI agents, suspicious oligarchs, and enthusiastic tech investors. We flew on private jets one month and worried about making payroll the next. We came within inches of complete wipeout more than a few times, saved by nothing but stubborn conviction and occasional strokes of impossible timing.

Had I known how insane this journey would be, would I still have jumped in? Absolutely. Because this wasn't just about Bitcoin. It was about building something against all odds. It was about belief when no one else believed. It was about doing hard things for the right reasons, with the right people, and refusing to quit, even when every rational indicator said we should.

This story you're about to immerse yourself in is real. It's raw. It's probably unbelievable to most people, but every word in this book is true. And the witnesses? Bitcoin OGs. VCs. Angels. Presidents. Oligarchs. Sheikhs. FBI Agents. Hackers. Buddhist monks. They lived it too.

Yes, this is a startup story. But it's also a story about life, chaos, courage, and how one idea introduced into this world by a mystery figure has triggered one of the wildest rides of our lives. It's about what happens when you stop asking how to build something and start asking if you're willing to pay the price to build it. Because in the end, that's all that matters—not the billion-dollar valuations, not the accolades, not the exits. What matters is whether you can survive the journey. Whether you can endure the cost. Whether you can find the resilience to keep going when everything inside you wants to quit.

This is that story.

PART I
FIRST THEY IGNORE YOU

ნაწილი I: თავიდან შენ არ გამჩნევენ

CHAPTER 1

MEETING VAL

What you seek is seeking you.

—Rumi

My journey into the world of Bitcoin began not with a sudden revelation, but as a culmination of experiences that had shaped my worldview long before Satoshi Nakamoto penned his white paper. The seeds were sown in the turbulent spring of 1991 in Tbilisi, Georgia. The air, deceptively fresh with the promise of a new season, carried an undercurrent of profound anxiety. I remember the aroma of strong Georgian coffee brewing in my mother's kitchen, mingling with the urgent, somber tones emanating from our television set. The Soviet Union, the monolithic entity that had defined our lives, was visibly crumbling, and with it, the foundations of everything we knew.

Growing up under the shadow of Soviet power instilled in me a deep-seated lesson, one that would echo through my later life: never entrust your future entirely to centralized authority. The collapse was a political event and a personal catastrophe. My parents, both respected doctors, had dedicated years of labor to building their savings, only to watch all of it transform into worthless paper almost overnight. The hyperinflation that ensued was a cruel farce, marked by a parade of rapidly devaluing currencies—coupons that lost purchasing power between breakfast and dinner. This experience etched a permanent skepticism onto my psyche regarding the trustworthiness of governments and central banks.

The hyperinflation that followed the Soviet Union's collapse wasn't just an economic event; it was a lived experience that shaped an entire generation's relationship with money and trust. In Georgia, currencies became worthless between breakfast and dinner. The "coupons" that replaced rubles lost purchasing power so rapidly that people would rush to spend them the moment they received them. For a young mind witnessing this chaos, the lesson was clear: centralized authorities, no matter how powerful they seem, can fail catastrophically.

"George," my father's voice was heavy one evening, the newspaper reporting yet another economic downturn resting in his lap. "You need to leave. You must go to the United States."

His words startled me. "Go to America? How?"

"It will become very difficult here," he continued, his surgeon's hands, usually steady, trembling slightly as he gestured towards the window, towards the uncertainty outside. "This country… it will take decades to find its footing. Your future lies elsewhere."

During these chaotic times, mathematics became my refuge. Numbers offered a logic and consistency starkly absent in the collapsing economy around me. They followed immutable rules. They didn't lie or change value capriciously like the rubles disintegrating in our hands. I found solace in their predictability, a stark contrast to the failed economic planning that had led to our predicament.

The relationship between mathematics and money would prove prophetic in my Bitcoin journey. While currencies around me shifted and collapsed, mathematical principles remained constant. This early appreciation for mathematical certainty would later make Bitcoin's cryptographic foundations deeply appealing. For those who've experienced monetary collapse, the idea of money governed by mathematical rules rather than political whims represents a profound shift.

As if the universe itself were conspiring to fulfill my father's wish, I stumbled upon an announcement for a high school exchange student competition just days later. With little to lose and a future to gain, I threw myself into preparation, studying by candlelight during frequent power outages. The competition was intense. Hundreds of students from across Georgia were vying for just five coveted spots in the American program. When my name was announced as one of the winners, the tears in my parents' eyes were not of sorrow, but of profound relief. They knew this was an escape route, a chance at a different life.

This twist of fate transported me from the economic wreckage of post-Soviet Georgia to the verdant landscapes of Gold Beach Union High School in Oregon. America opened doors I hadn't even known existed, leading me eventually to the University of Oregon, then the prestigious halls of Wharton, and finally to Johns Hopkins for graduate studies. My affinity for mathematics only deepened, providing a framework for understanding the world.

These formative experiences—witnessing the fragility of a centralized economy, developing a healthy distrust of unchecked authority, and learning the value of self-reliance—were unknowingly forging the mindset that would later draw me to a nascent digital revolution, one poised to challenge the very foundations of centralized finance.

The Path to Kyiv

My connection to Ukraine, and ultimately to Bitfury, began through my friendship with Marat Kicikov, whom I met in 2008 during my investing days in Kyiv with York Capital. Marat possessed a sharp mind and an invaluable ability to navigate the intricate and often opaque Ukrainian business landscape. We quickly bonded, sharing hours-long conversations that ranged from potential ventures to deeper life philosophies.

After the global financial markets imploded in late 2008, I stepped away from the hedge fund world, taking 2009 as a sabbatical. My then-fiancée, Dina, and I spread out a world map, marking destinations we'd always dreamed of visiting. Leaving our beloved pug, Feya, with family, we embarked on an adventure that saw us summiting Mount Kilimanjaro, where I proposed to Dina against the backdrop of an African sunrise, celebrating Carnival in Brazil, exploring the unique ecosystems of the Galapagos, and finally returning to Georgia for a week-long, one-hundred-guest, traditional wedding celebration. Marat was there, serving as a key toastmaster, a testament to our close bond. Later, we joined Marat and his wife, Asja, for travels through Italy and his serene seaside hometown of Jurmala, Latvia.

One evening after finishing dinner at the iconic 36 Line Grill Restaurant, with Chef Lauris showering us with endless grappa shots, we wandered out into the Jurmala night. The Baltic shore was calm, the air heavy with salt and silence. The orange sun was setting across the sea, the horizon awash in fire and glass. I bent down, picked up a flat stone, and skipped it across the water's still surface. Marat walked beside me in silence before asking the question that lingered. "So, what's next, George? Back to the hedge fund grind?"

I exhaled, watching the ripples fade. "Honestly, Marat, I'm not sure. The crisis… it exposed the cracks in that system. I'm searching for something different," I confessed. "Something with more substance, more impact." Little did I realize how prophetic those words would become, or how this seaside conversation would eventually lead me toward Bitcoin.

It wasn't until 2012, however, that Marat first uttered the word "Bitcoin" to me. By then, the nascent digital currency had already weathered its first volatile cycles, surging from fractions of a cent to nearly $30, only to crash back down to $2 before beginning a tentative climb. We were having dinner in Kyiv, the lamplight casting long shadows.

"George, you need to look into this… Bitcoin," he said, swirling his wine. "It's trading around $10 right now. I have a feeling it's going to be huge."

I chuckled, dismissing it as another fleeting tech fancy. "Another digital payment experiment? We've seen plenty of those fizzle out."

Marat leaned in, his usual intensity amplified. "No, this is fundamentally different. It's decentralized. No government, no bank controls it. It's pure mathematics—your favorite subject."

Bitcoin's early price history was marked by extreme volatility that would seem tame by later standards. In 2011, Bitcoin rose from under $1 to nearly $32, only to crash back to $2 by late 2011. These wild swings earned Bitcoin a reputation for instability, but also attracted attention from early adopters who recognized the significance of the underlying technology. Each boom-bust cycle brought new participants and gradually built the infrastructure that would support future growth.

I gave a noncommittal nod, my mind already drifting. Marat, ever the entrepreneur, was always exploring new frontiers. He mentioned he knew Valery Vavilov—Val—the founder of a company called Bitfury, through mutual connections in Latvia. Throughout 2012, Marat persistently brought up Bitcoin, his enthusiasm unwavering despite my initial scepticism.

Then, in early 2013, his call came with a new urgency. "It's time, George," he urged, his voice cutting through the phone static. Bitcoin was now hovering around $20. "You have to meet Val in Kyiv next week. He's building something truly revolutionary."

The Kyiv air bit through my coat as I stepped out of the car for the meeting. The cold was sharp, the kind that makes you second-guess your choices. "Remind me again, what does this Val guy actually do?" I'd asked Marat.

"He mines Bitcoin," Marat had replied simply.

"Mines? Like, with shovels and pickaxes?" I pictured digital prospectors in some virtual Klondike.

"Just meet him," Marat insisted.

So we met at Arena, a popular spot in Kyiv where the city's entrepreneurial pulse throbbed. Cafés like these, buzzing with conversation and the aroma of strong coffee, were the real boardrooms of Ukraine, far removed from sterile corporate offices.

I remember the day clearly. Bitcoin was trading near $20. Across the table sat Valery Vavilov. He spoke with a quiet intensity about decentralization, the future of money, and the concept of a digital store of value. The focused energy in his eyes captivated me, even as the technology he described bordered on the fantastical.

Val wasn't the stereotypical brash tech founder. He was more reserved, thoughtful, speaking with the precision of a coder but with flashes of visionary zeal. "This isn't just about digital payments, George," he stated, leaning forward. "This is about freedom. It's about shifting power away from central banks and empowering individuals."

My inherent scepticism, honed by witnessing Georgia's economic collapse, surfaced. "People have tried creating alternative currencies for years," I countered. "What makes Bitcoin different?"

Val grabbed a napkin and, with surprising clarity, began sketching the architecture of the blockchain. Boxes and arrows materialized under his pen. "Because, for the first time, we've solved the double-spending problem without needing a trusted central party. Do you realize the implications of that?"

The double-spending problem was a fundamental challenge in digital currency design before Bitcoin. In the physical world, if you hand someone a dollar bill, you no longer have it. But digital information can be copied infinitely. How do you prevent someone from spending the same digital coin twice? Previous attempts at digital money required a central authority to keep track of transactions. Bitcoin's breakthrough was solving this problem through cryptographic proof and distributed consensus, eliminating the need for trusted intermediaries.

At the time, my professional focus was on agricultural investments, seemingly worlds away from digital currencies. Yet, as Val spoke, I found myself drawing an unexpected parallel. The value of land, a core asset in agriculture, stems fundamentally from its scarcity. And here was Val, describing a digital asset engineered with absolute, verifiable scarcity, mathematically capped at 21 million units, forever.

That number—21 million—resonated strangely. I was born on the 21st, a number that seemed to pop up coincidentally throughout my life. It felt like a subtle nudge from the universe, a signal to pay closer attention.

The Cyprus Catalyst

In March 2013, the global financial system shuddered as the Cyprus banking crisis erupted. Banks slammed shut for nearly two weeks, capital controls were imposed, and ordinary citizens found themselves locked out of their own accounts while the government scrambled for a bailout. The fragility of the traditional system was laid bare.

> The Cyprus banking crisis of 2013 was a watershed moment for Bitcoin adoption. When the Cypriot government announced plans to impose a tax on bank deposits, essentially seizing a portion of citizens' savings, panic ensued. Banks closed for nearly two weeks, and strict capital controls were imposed. This event demonstrated how quickly traditional financial systems could freeze, trapping ordinary citizens' wealth. For Bitcoin advocates, Cyprus became a powerful real-world example of why decentralized, censorship-resistant money might be necessary.

Watching the events unfold, my conversations with Val took on a new weight. Bitcoin, previously an intriguing concept, suddenly seemed like a potential lifeboat in a sea of institutional failure. During this period, Bitcoin's price began a noticeable ascent, breaking through $30, then $40, reacting, it seemed, to the very real fears gripping depositors in Cyprus and beyond.

"We build the machines," Val explained during one meeting amidst the Cyprus turmoil, clarifying Bitfury's role. "Specialized computers—ASICs—designed solely to solve the complex mathematical problems that secure the Bitcoin network and, in the process, mint new coins. The more computational power, or hashrate, we contribute, the more secure the network becomes, and the more Bitcoin we earn as a reward."

Bitcoin mining secures the network through a competitive process where miners solve complex mathematical puzzles to validate transactions and earn rewards. At the heart of this system are ASICs (Application-Specific Integrated Circuits)—specialized computers designed solely to solve the complex mathematical problems that secure the Bitcoin network. Unlike general-purpose computers, these machines dedicate all their processing power to mining, achieving maximum efficiency while consuming less energy. This specialized hardware transformed Bitcoin from a hobby into a professional industry, providing the computational backbone that keeps the network secure and decentralized.

He spoke of the technical hurdles with the passion of a true believer, but the business model still felt nascent, the risks immense.

Then, in early April, Marat's text message arrived: "Bitcoin just crossed $200. Still think it's just a game?"

I stared at the screen. $200. From $10 when he first mentioned it less than a year prior, and $20 just weeks ago during my first meeting with Val. The rate of appreciation was staggering. The mathematician in me couldn't dismiss the exponential curve. The Cyprus crisis hadn't just highlighted Bitcoin's conceptual appeal; it seemed to be actively driving its value proposition in the real world.

Val explained that Bitfury was already a significant player in the mining space, but it operated largely on a cash basis. He envisioned "Bitfury 2.0" as a professionally managed, properly capitalized company adhering to Western standards of governance, auditing, and investor relations. He needed someone to bridge the gap between their Eastern European technical prowess and the demands of global capital markets.

Marat had convinced Val that my background of straddling post-Soviet realities and Western finance, with degrees from Wharton and Johns Hopkins and connections in US and European markets, made me the ideal candidate to spearhead this transformation.

Deep Dive Due Diligence

As Bitcoin surged past $300 in the following weeks, my curiosity solidified into serious consideration. I began my due diligence, diving deeper into this unfamiliar territory. My first calls were to my Wharton network on the West Coast, a network that was ingrained in tech.

I connected with Travis Katz, a successful entrepreneur and the founder of Trip.com, plugged into the Silicon Valley ecosystem, and Hardeep Walia, founder of the innovative FinTech platform Motif Investing. Both confirmed that Bitcoin was generating significant buzz, though opinions were divided about its legitimacy.

They suggested I speak with Divesh Makan, another Wharton classmate of ours whose firm, ICONIQ Capital, discreetly managed the fortunes of many tech billionaires. Pacing my Kyiv apartment, the rain drumming against the windows overlooking Shevchenko Park, I reached Divesh.

"George, you're onto something significant," he stated unequivocally after I outlined the Bitfury opportunity. "Some of the smartest, wealthiest tech investors in the world are quietly accumulating Bitcoin."

"Who?" I pressed.

"Can't name names," he replied, "but trust me. They see it as digital gold, a hedge against the traditional system."

ICONIQ Capital was founded in 2011 to serve as the family office for Facebook founder Mark Zuckerberg, but it quickly expanded to manage wealth for other tech luminaries. The firm's client list reportedly includes Jack Dorsey, Reid Hoffman, and other Silicon Valley elite. When Divesh mentioned that sophisticated tech investors were quietly accumulating Bitcoin, he was referring to a trend that would later become public as mainstream adoption accelerated.

This was a pivotal insight. Sophisticated investors, people who understood technology deeply, weren't dismissing Bitcoin; they were strategically acquiring it. Soon after, another classmate, Ty Jagerson, connected me with two influential figures in the Bitcoin space: Wences Casares and Micky Malka.

Wences, an Argentinian entrepreneur, founded the wallet company Xapo and was renowned in Silicon Valley for introducing countless tech leaders to Bitcoin. Micky, a Venezuelan investor, ran Ribbit Capital, a VC firm already making significant bets in the crypto landscape.

My call with Wences felt less like a business meeting and more like a meeting of minds shaped by similar experiences.

"You grew up in Soviet Georgia during the collapse?" he asked, his interest piqued.

"Yes. I saw the system fail firsthand," I replied.

"That's why we get it," Wences declared, leaning closer to the camera. "People who've lived through hyperinflation, seen savings vanish... we understand Bitcoin instinctively. It's not just tech; it's insurance against state failure."

Wences Casares became known as Bitcoin's "Patient Zero" in Silicon Valley for his role in introducing numerous tech leaders to cryptocurrency. Born in Argentina, he experienced firsthand the country's recurring monetary crises, including hyperinflation and currency devaluations. He and Micky Malka had previously co-founded Patagon, an online brokerage in Latin America that was acquired by Banco Santander in 2000 for around $750 million. This background gave him unique credibility when explaining Bitcoin's value proposition to wealthy Americans who had never experienced monetary instability. His Xapo wallet company would later store billions of dollars worth of Bitcoin in underground vaults.

His words resonated deeply. For those of us scarred by monetary collapse, Bitcoin represented monetary sovereignty.

Micky Malka offered a more pragmatic perspective. "Bitfury's tech looks strong," he acknowledged, "but mining is brutal. Hardware becomes obsolete fast. Timing and execution are everything. A slight delay can wipe out your margins."

His assessment was sobering but realistic. The mining industry was an arms race. Yet it also implied that operational excellence and technological leadership—areas where Bitfury seemed strong—could create a winning formula.

Armed with these insights, I immersed myself in understanding Bitcoin's fundamentals, devouring online courses on Khan Academy.

The Decision Point: Burning the Ships

My meetings with Val continued. His technical acumen was undeniable, but it was his unwavering conviction in Bitcoin's world-changing potential that truly captivated me. He envisioned Bitfury as a foundational infrastructure provider for a new financial paradigm.

Bitfury already had established mining operations in Iceland and Finland, leveraging cheap geothermal and hydro power. Their mining pool, Ghash.IO, was actually what Val called "a friends and family pool"—created by tech enthusiasts to help Bitfury manage its growing computational power, with Bitfury serving as the sole provider of hashing power. The operation was profitable, generating substantial cash flow, but Val yearned for legitimacy, for structure, for the transition to Bitfury 2.0.

"Most people see Bitcoin as digital money," Val explained during one meeting. "But it's more fundamental. It's a revolution in trust. Transactions without intermediaries... think about what that enables."

Coming from a place where trust in institutions was a luxury, I understood. The potential was immense, transformative.

Yet I knew the transition Val envisioned was fraught with peril. Before committing, I needed one final, crucial conversation. We met at a café in Kyiv's Premier Palace Hotel. Outside, the political climate was heating up; demonstrators were gathering in the Maidan, the seeds of the revolution being sown. Discussing a financial revolution against the backdrop of a political one felt strangely appropriate.

> The Maidan protests, also known as the Revolution of Dignity, began in November 2013 when then-President Viktor Yanukovych suspended preparations for an association agreement with the European Union. What started as peaceful demonstrations grew into a broader movement against corruption and authoritarianism. The timing of our Bitcoin discussions against this backdrop was prescient. Both represented challenges to centralized power structures, one political, the other financial.

Bitcoin had recently experienced its first major bull run, rocketing towards $1,150 in late November 2013, fueled by growing media attention and speculation. But the euphoria was short-lived. In early

December, the People's Bank of China prohibited financial institutions from handling Bitcoin transactions. The news sent shockwaves through the market, and the price tumbled, eventually settling around $600 to $700 by the time of our meeting. This volatility, however, didn't seem to rattle Val. His focus remained steadfastly on building the underlying infrastructure.

I looked him directly in the eye. "Val, transforming Bitfury from a cash operation to a Western-style company demands immense sacrifice. Governance, transparency, audits—everything changes. It requires a complete shift in mindset. Are you truly ready for that?"

I recounted the story of Hernán Cortés, who, upon arriving in the New World, supposedly burned his ships, signaling to his men that there was no turning back. "That's the level of commitment required, Val. Are you ready to burn the ships?"

> The story of Cortés burning his ships is likely apocryphal. Historical evidence suggests he scuttled them rather than burned them, and for practical rather than symbolic reasons. However, the metaphor of "burning the ships" has become synonymous with total commitment to a course of action, eliminating the possibility of retreat. For entrepreneurs, this concept represents the mindset needed for transformational change.

He met my gaze, the weak winter sunlight illuminating his thoughtful expression. This would be a fundamental change in identity. After a long moment, a slow smile spread across his face. "Absolutely."

In that instant, any lingering doubts evaporated. If he was truly ready for that leap, then so was I. I would commit fully—my time, my energy, my resources—to making Bitfury 2.0 a reality.

It felt like more than a career move; it was a philosophical alignment. The principles forged in the crucible of Soviet collapse, including skepticism of central control, belief in individual agency, and respect for mathematical certainty, all converged on Bitcoin.

As we shook hands, the weight of the decision settled in. We were simultaneously joining a company and enlisting in a revolution. And revolutions, as my childhood in Georgia taught me, are inherently messy, unpredictable, and profoundly transformative.

"We need to move fast," Val stated, breaking the silence. "This industry waits for no one."

"I'm ready," I replied. "I am all in."

That was the moment. The moment I stepped fully into the Bitfury story, joining Val to build what would become a cornerstone of the Bitcoin ecosystem. Looking back, every twist and turn—from Tbilisi to Oregon, from mathematics to finance, from Kyiv to that café— seemed to have led inexorably to this point. The universe, it seemed, had been preparing me for Bitcoin all along.

The adventure ahead would prove wilder, more challenging, and ultimately more rewarding than I could have ever imagined.

CHAPTER 2

THIS THING MINES BITCOIN?

Well, maybe it started that way.
As a dream, but doesn't everything?

—Roald Dahl

The Kyiv winter of early 2014 was charged with the electric tension of impending change. While Maidan Square simmered, cultivating a revolution born from exhaustion with endemic corruption, Val and I found ourselves in a peculiar juxtaposition. Our cozy office, warmed by the persistent hum of Bitfury's prototype mining rigs and cluttered with circuit boards, became an incubator for Bitfury 2.0. Outside, Ukraine teetered on the brink. Inside, we meticulously charted a course through the uncertainty, plotting the transformation of a nascent mining operation into a global technology player.

While Val and I charted the ambitious future of Bitfury amidst the political turmoil of Kyiv, the company's true foundation lay in its remarkable technical talent. The core team wasn't assembled from Silicon Valley or MIT. They were brilliant minds from Ukraine and Latvia who had mastered cutting-edge technology largely through self-determination and raw intellect.

Bitfury's technical team represented a new breed of innovators emerging from Eastern Europe in the 2010s. Unlike their Western counterparts, who often had access to established semiconductor industry networks and formal training programs, these engineers were largely self-taught, learning complex chip design from textbooks and online resources. This unconventional background gave them a unique advantage: they approached problems without preconceived notions about what was "impossible" or "impractical."

Valerii Nebesnyi, whom everyone simply called "X," epitomized this spirit. A Ukrainian genius with no formal semiconductor training, X had taught himself the intricacies of chip fabrication and full custom design purely from textbooks. While established chip designers had the luxury of decades of industry experience, X approached the problem with fresh eyes and remarkable intuition. He meticulously studied how semiconductor fabs worked, absorbing knowledge that typically required years in specialized institutions, and engineered Bitfury's first revolutionary 55 nm chip, a breakthrough that would establish our technological edge in the mining space.

Working alongside X was his right-hand man, Vlad, another brilliant Ukrainian who played a pivotal role in all things chip-related. While X conceived the architectural innovations, Vlad translated them into implementation reality, ensuring that X's theoretical brilliance became practical computing power. Together, they formed an innovative chip design powerhouse operating far from traditional semiconductor hubs.

The hardware ecosystem extended beyond the chips themselves. Malex, yet another Ukrainian technical virtuoso, was the mastermind behind integrating these chips onto boards and designing the actual mining servers. His expertise in hardware architecture and thermal management enabled Bitfury to maximize performance while maintaining operational stability—critical factors in the competitive mining landscape where efficiency determined profitability.

Supporting these efforts was Niko Punin, Finland's Bitcoin OG, who had been involved with many early Bitfury product designs. His deep understanding of Bitcoin's technical requirements and early ecosystem dynamics provided crucial insights that shaped our hardware development approach.

Rounding out this core team was the infamous Alex Petrov, a.k.a. "Sysman," our chief security officer. A Bitcoin OG and Latvian national like Val, Sysman brought over twenty-five years of IT and cybersecurity experience to the table. In a domain where security breaches could mean instant financial ruin, his seasoned perspective proved invaluable. Sysman approached Bitcoin's novel security challenges with both the wisdom of traditional information security and an intuitive grasp of blockchain's unique paradigms.

This Ukrainian-Latvian-Finnish crew constituted the brain trust of Bitfury when I first encountered them. They were brilliant, resourceful, and operating largely under the radar of the Western tech establishment. My task was clear but daunting: capitalize this exceptional technical talent and transform their innovations into a global enterprise.

The Eastern European tech scene of the early 2010s was characterized by exceptional technical talent that often remained hidden from Western investors and partners. Countries like Ukraine and Latvia had strong educational traditions in mathematics and engineering, but limited access to venture capital or established tech networks. This created a generation of entrepreneurs who were technically sophisticated but often struggled to scale globally without Western partnerships and capital.

Bitfury, in those early days, was undeniably raw. It possessed groundbreaking technology but lacked the structure and polish required for the global stage. Inspired by my admiration for Steven Spielberg, who famously mapped out his film endings first, I proposed a similar approach during a strategy session.

"Let's define Bitfury's ultimate destination," I suggested, "and then reverse-engineer the path to get there."

Our vision crystallized during intense discussions, often held in the steamy, birch-scented confines of a traditional Kyiv banya. We envisioned Bitfury not just as a miner, but as the premier technology company underpinning the entire Bitcoin ecosystem. Mining was the foundation, but the ambition stretched further to encompass developing the essential hardware and software—the picks and shovels—for this burgeoning digital gold rush.

"What's the endgame, Val?" I asked, wrapped in a towel, the banya's heat flushing our faces and freeing our minds.

"A full-stack Bitcoin company," he declared, wiping sweat from his brow. "Mining is just the beginning. We build the infrastructure, the security, the software. Everything."

"And the benchmark for success?"

Val took a sip of uzvar, a traditional dried fruit kompot, and smiled with quiet confidence. "When governments and central bankers start hoarding Bitcoin."

His ambition was audacious and almost defiant. We were aiming to disrupt centuries of monetary convention. Yet the reality was that Bitcoin remained largely ignored, misunderstood, or dismissed by the mainstream. This realization brought another crucial insight: our mission was largely educational. We had a responsibility to evangelize, to explain this complex technology to policymakers, investors, law enforcement, and the public. Ignorance was a significant barrier. We couldn't just build our business; we had to build understanding, becoming both architects and advocates for the ecosystem itself.

As we plotted strategy in the banya, I couldn't help but reflect on the unlikely nature of our team. While tech giants recruited from prestigious universities and established semiconductor players, we were powered by self-taught innovators from Eastern Europe who had bootstrapped their expertise through determination and raw intellectual horsepower. This unconventional genesis story was, I believed, our hidden advantage—we approached problems differently because we came from different backgrounds.

The Bitfury I envisioned would marry this technical brilliance with global business acumen and capital access. But I never wanted to lose the innovative spirit that X, Vlad, Malex, Niko, and Sysman embodied—the willingness to challenge conventional wisdom and find solutions where others saw only obstacles.

To achieve this, we needed allies, particularly in the West. The United States, with its deep capital pools, influential regulatory bodies, and vibrant tech scene, represented the ultimate proving ground. Convincing America's investors, regulators, and innovators was key to global acceptance.

During our flight to New York, I found myself leafing through the thick stack of research notes and clippings that formed my personal archive of early Bitcoin discourse. One piece jumped out: Goldman Sachs' Top of Mind report from 2014.

Buried in it was an interview with Daniel Masters, former head of commodities at JPMorgan. He framed Bitcoin not as a currency or tech fad, but as a commodity priced on flow, not stock. That was yet another aha moment for me.

Daniel Masters' insight about Bitcoin being priced on "flow, not stock" was a crucial early understanding of Bitcoin economics. Traditional commodities, such as gold, are valued based on their total existing supply (stock) relative to new production (flow). But Bitcoin's predetermined supply schedule and halvings mean that new supply (flow) has an outsized impact on price dynamics. This was one of the first sophisticated institutional analyses of Bitcoin's unique monetary properties.

Masters explained that markets don't move based on how much of something exists, but on how much new supply is hitting the market. And then it dawned on me that Bitcoin's built-in supply halving was a perfect trigger for this supply shock, propelling the price appreciation.

I knew a thing or two about commodities, and that was another powerful connecting dot for me. Bitcoin wasn't just scarce. It was a precision-engineered scarcity machine, with a countdown clock hardwired into its code.

"Val," I said, showing him the report. "Masters sees Bitcoin as a commodity with a predictable supply shock every four years."

Val glanced over with interest. "So the halving—"

"Is like OPEC announcing a fifty percent production cut, but guaranteed by math, not politics," I nodded.

"We need to be the most efficient miners when that happens," Val said decisively. "That's our edge."

The CNBC Bombshell

We arrived in New York over a weekend, the city's vibrant energy a stark contrast to the tense atmosphere of Kyiv. The sheer scale of Manhattan, the relentless pace, felt like stepping onto a different planet.

Through a fortunate coincidence, Michelle Caruso-Cabrera, a prominent CNBC anchor whom I met at the YPO Global Summit in Istanbul earlier on, was based in New York. I hadn't spoken to her in months, but Bitcoin's recent surge had put cryptocurrency on the mainstream media's radar.

> YPO (Young Presidents' Organization) is a global leadership community of chief executives and company leaders. At the time, I was a founding member of the Kyiv chapter. With over thirty-five thousand members in more than one hundred fifty countries, YPO provides a confidential space for peer learning and idea exchange among accomplished entrepreneurs and business leaders.

Trying to sound casual, I sent her a message: "Hey Michelle, in NYC for a bit, let's grab coffee. By the way, I'm involved with this Bitcoin mining company, Bitfury. We're leaders in the space, here meeting investors."

Her reply came astonishingly fast. "George, great timing! Bitcoin is red hot. Any chance you guys could come on *Squawk Box* Monday morning?"

My pulse quickened. *Squawk Box* wasn't just any morning show. It was the pre-market ritual for every serious investor, fund manager, and Wall Street trader. And I suspected it was live, unedited. This was a colossal opportunity. "Absolutely," I typed back immediately. "We'd be thrilled. Send the details. We're at the W Hotel.'

Michelle's assistant followed up swiftly. Just like that, we were scheduled to open the show at 7:30 a.m. Monday.

Now came the delicate task of informing Val. I found him in the hotel bar, calmly sipping green tea, an oasis of serenity amidst the city's buzz.

"Val," I began, trying to mirror his calm, "so the conference starts Monday, but before that... an old friend, Michelle, she works for CNBC... she suggested we appear on their morning show, *Squawk*

Box. It's quite influential. Reaches a lot of business leaders, investors. Our chance to introduce Bitfury directly to Wall Street."

I saw his eyes widen slightly. His English was functional but still developing. The idea of live American television was clearly daunting.

"Live TV?" he asked, his voice betraying a hint of anxiety. "In English? How many people watch?"

"Oh, you know, a fair few," I replied, suddenly finding the abstract art on the wall intensely interesting.

"George. How many?" he pressed.

"Well, maybe a few hundred thousand?"

Val visibly anxious. "Few hundred thousand?"

CNBC's *Squawk Box* was the flagship morning program for financial television, regularly drawing two hundred thousand to three hundred thousand viewers during its peak morning hours. While not massive by broadcast TV standards, its audience consisted almost entirely of financial professionals, institutional investors, and business decision-makers. An appearance on *Squawk Box* could reach more potential Bitcoin investors and partners in three hours than months of traditional outreach.

Observing the shift in his expression, I quickly downplayed it, ordering myself a double gin and tonic for fortification. "Don't worry! We have the whole weekend to prepare. We'll rehearse talking points. It'll be great exposure, exactly what we need." I conveniently omitted the confirmation that it was, indeed, entirely live.

My next call was to my classmate Hardeep, a veteran of CNBC appearances.

"Hardeep!" I practically shouted into the phone, pacing my hotel room. "We're going on *Squawk Box* Monday! What do we do?"

Hardeep, ever cool, offered crucial advice. "George, relax. Just nail two or three key messages. Repeat them. And tell Val to bring the chip. Something tangible. Americans love gadgets. It gives him something to hold, something to focus on besides the cameras."

Armed with Hardeep's wisdom, Val and I spent the weekend strategizing. We divided the talking points, anticipated questions, and rehearsed answers. We refined our narrative over dinner at Cipriani, the city lights twinkling outside. We were as prepared as we could be.

Showtime: "This Thing Mines Bitcoin"

Monday, April 9th, 2014, arrived crisp and clear. Surprisingly, I wasn't overly nervous. An early morning run around Union Square helped center me, the rhythmic pounding of my feet a counterpoint to the whirlwind ahead. Memories of late nights debating business ideas with Wharton classmates in nearby bars flooded back, youthful ambition unknowingly rehearsing for this very moment.

A black limo picked us up at 6:00 a.m. and transported us across the Hudson to the CNBC studios in New Jersey, the Manhattan skyline receding like a dream.

"You okay?" I asked Val. He was quiet, staring out the window.

"Got the chip. I'm fine," he nodded, patting his jacket pocket.

The studio was a blur of lights, cameras, and bustling crew members. Michelle greeted us warmly. Soon we were seated under the intense studio lights, facing Michelle and the main anchors, Andrew Ross Sorkin, and Joe Kernen. The makeup felt foreign, the earpiece hissed. There was a palpable tension, but also a sense of readiness. We exchanged a look in silent acknowledgment of the moment's significance.

The interview started broadly. I delivered my prepared points, referencing Milton Friedman's prescient vision of peer-to-peer electronic cash, emphasizing libertarian principles, and highlighting Bitcoin's potential. Crucially, I mentioned our engagement of top-tier law firm White & Case and our plans to pursue a public listing within eighteen months, signaling our commitment to legitimacy.

Milton Friedman's 1999 prediction of Internet-based electronic money was remarkably prescient. In an interview, the Nobel Prize-winning economist said, "I think that the Internet is going to be one of the major forces for reducing the role of government. The one thing that's missing, but that will soon be developed, is a reliable e-cash, a method whereby on the Internet you can transfer funds from A to B without A knowing B or B knowing A." This quote became a rallying cry for Bitcoin advocates, as it seemed to perfectly describe what Satoshi Nakamoto would create nearly a decade later.

Then came the pivotal moment. Andrew Ross Sorkin, leaning forward with genuine curiosity, asked the simple question that would define everything: "So what is it you guys actually do? Show me. What is mining?"

Val, who had been mostly silent, sprang to life. This was the moment Hardeep's advice paid off. He reached into his pocket and produced a small, intricate piece of silicon: Bitfury's prototype 55-nanometer ASIC chip that would be responsible for mining hundreds of thousands of Bitcoins.

In semiconductors, nanometer (nm) measurements refer to the size of the smallest features on a computer chip. A nanometer is one billionth of a meter. Smaller nanometer processes allow more transistors to fit in the same space, making chips faster and more efficient. Bitfury's 55 nm ASIC represented cutting-edge Bitcoin mining technology, delivering unprecedented computational power in a compact design.

He held it up for the cameras, pinching it between his thumb and forefinger, his pride unmistakable. "This," he announced clearly, "is the Bitfury mining chip. It's a full custom design. It does only one thing—processing Bitcoin transactions."

Andrew peered at the tiny object, bewildered. "This thing can mine Bitcoin?" he asked, incredulous. "Come on."

Val, seizing the moment, delivered the perfect, simple reply, a slight smile playing on his lips: "Oh, yes. This thing mines Bitcoin."

A beat of silence hung in the air, then a flurry of follow-up questions. But the soundbite had landed. The abstract concept of mining suddenly had a physical, albeit tiny, representation. "This thing mines Bitcoin" instantly became our unofficial slogan, a concise, memorable explanation for a complex process.

Interestingly, Joe Kernen remained relatively quiet throughout. Perhaps, as I like to think, he was absorbing the information, the seeds being planted for his later transformation into a vocal Bitcoin advocate. Looking back, that morning might have been the beginning of Joe's orange-pilling journey from skeptical anchor to one of mainstream media's most prominent Bitcoin believers.

"Orange-pilling" refers to the process of convincing someone of Bitcoin's value proposition, drawing from the Matrix movie reference to taking the "orange pill" (Bitcoin's brand color) to see the truth about money and financial systems. The term became popular in Bitcoin communities to describe successful evangelism efforts.

The impact was immediate and profound. We hadn't just talked about mining; we had "shown" it, demystifying the process. As an industry insider later remarked, "That moment humanized Bitcoin mining for millions."

After the Splash

The *Squawk Box* appearance exceeded all expectations. By the time we arrived at the Jacob Javits Center for the conference later that day, the clip was already viral within the crypto community. The buzz was specifically about Bitfury, Val, and the chip.

Val's entrance into the conference hall was akin to a rock star's arrival. People swarmed him, not just with congratulations, but with gratitude. "Thank you! You always delivered!" echoed through the crowd. This was a revelation. I knew Bitfury had a solid reputation, but witnessing this outpouring of trust was powerful. In an industry already notorious for scams and broken promises, Bitfury had built its reputation on reliability, often conducting business purely through digital messages and Bitcoin payments, sight unseen. Our Bitfury tiger logo t-shirts, worn that day, became instant identifiers, symbols of dependability.

The early Bitcoin mining industry was plagued by companies that took pre-orders for mining equipment but failed to deliver on time or at all. Butterfly Labs, one of the most notorious examples, collected millions in pre-orders but shipped products months or years late, by which time they were often obsolete. In this environment, Bitfury's reputation for reliability and on-time delivery was extraordinarily valuable. Customers trusted them enough to send Bitcoin payments before receiving hardware, a level of trust that was rare in the industry.

The conference itself became a whirlwind of connections. We met key figures who would become long-term allies and friends. There was Matt Roszak, an early Bitcoin investor with the calm demeanor of a seasoned VC; Brock Pierce, once a Disney star in films like *The Mighty Ducks* and *First Kid*, would later make headlines with a presidential bid and a new identity as a crypto visionary; Harry Yeh, already establishing himself as the go-to broker for large, institutional Bitcoin trades through Binary Financial; and David Carlson, whose Giga Watt facility in Washington State, powered by Bitfury chips, was becoming America's largest mining operation.

"You guys are building something real," Matt told us over drinks, the clinking of glasses a soundtrack to nascent deals. "Most miners are fly-by-night. You're building to last."

During a panel discussion later that day, I watched from the audience as Val fielded technical questions with remarkable clarity. When someone asked about Bitcoin's energy consumption—already a contentious topic—Val didn't defensively dismiss the concern as many might have.

"Bitcoin's energy use is its security feature, not a bug," he explained calmly. "What we're doing at Bitfury is making that process as efficient as possible while exploring ways to utilize renewable energy sources. We see mining as an energy transformation business—converting electricity into digital gold through mathematics and cryptography."

The skeptical questioner appeared to consider the response seriously, moving beyond the typical talking points. Each thoughtful exchange like this helped advance the conversation about Bitcoin's environmental considerations.

Energized by our New York success, the path forward was clear. We needed a physical presence in the heart of the tech world. It was time to head west, establish a San Francisco office, recruit American talent, and begin assembling the board of directors who would guide Bitfury 2.0.

As our plane climbed out of JFK, the setting sun casting Manhattan in gold, I glanced at Val. He was scrolling through a flood of meeting requests triggered by the CNBC appearance.

"So," I grinned, "still nervous about American TV?"

He chuckled, mimicking his own now-famous line. "This thing mines Bitcoin. Simple is best."

He was right. Amidst the noise and complexity, clarity had cut through. We had taken a calculated risk, stepped onto the biggest stage, and emerged not just unscathed, but amplified. Bitfury was no longer a name known only to insiders. We had become a recognized leader in a rapidly evolving industry.

The plane banked westward, towards Silicon Valley, towards the next chapter. The simple phrase, born under the bright lights of a TV studio, would become our calling card, echoing long after the cameras stopped rolling.

CHAPTER 3
STALIN'S BIRTHPLACE

It always seems impossible until it's done.

—Nelson Mandela

The transition from the charged atmosphere of New York to the sun-drenched optimism of California was jarring. As we stepped out of the San Francisco Airport, the sheer brightness felt almost alien after months shrouded in the grey pallor of Eastern European winter and the lingering tension of Kyiv. Val squinted beside me, marveling at the ubiquitous palm trees, symbols of a world seemingly untouched by the geopolitical and economic anxieties we carried.

We had arrived in Silicon Valley, the fabled heartland of technological innovation, ready to establish Bitfury's American beachhead. Bitcoin, having weathered the immediate aftermath of the Mt. Gox implosion, had found a fragile stability, trading in the $450 to $500 range during mid-year. While a far cry from its $1,150 peak just six months prior, this level still represented astonishing growth from its early days and provided a shaky foundation upon which to build.

Mt. Gox was once the world's largest Bitcoin exchange, handling approximately 70 percent of all Bitcoin transactions at its peak. In February 2014, the exchange filed for bankruptcy after revealing that hackers had stolen 850,000 Bitcoins (worth about $450 million at the time) over several years. The collapse sent shockwaves through the Bitcoin ecosystem, wiping out billions in market value and creating a crisis of confidence that took years to recover from. The incident highlighted the risks of centralized exchanges and sparked calls for better security practices across the industry.

Our entry into the world of venture capital was propelled by a stroke of serendipity. Antti Pennanen, founder of Finnish fintech startup MONI and fellow entrepreneur from Finland, was friends with our Niko Punin and had a unique connection: he had kite surfed with none other than Bill Tai, the legendary venture capitalist and angel investor, on Necker Island. That bond opened a vital door. Bill was a high-profile investor who also brought deep semiconductor expertise and, remarkably, had tweeted about Bitcoin as early as 2010, well before most took it seriously: "This P2P thing, Bitcoin is quite fascinating. Exciting times ahead."

"Wait, this guy is a top angel investor and a semiconductor expert?" I asked Niko incredulously as we set up our Spartan new office in Spear Tower, the panoramic vista of the San Francisco Bay stretching out before us. The combination seemed almost too perfect, a uniquely Silicon Valley blend of extreme sports and deep tech.

Niko smiled, taping a makeshift Bitfury logo to the wall. "Just wait till you meet him."

Bill Tai represented a unique breed of Silicon Valley investor who combined deep technical expertise with unconventional interests. His background included being employee number one at TSMC's precursor company and leading IPOs for major semiconductor companies at Alex Brown & Sons. His early recognition of Bitcoin's potential, demonstrated by his 2010 tweet, showed the kind of technological intuition that made him legendary in VC circles. The fact that he was also a world-champion-level kite surfer embodied the Valley's culture of pursuing excellence in multiple domains.

We met Bill at Ozumo, a sleek sushi restaurant buzzing with tech industry chatter. He arrived clad in the quintessential Valley uniform, a casual shirt and jeans, his energy immediately infectious. He possessed none of the stuffiness sometimes associated with high finance; instead, he radiated genuine curiosity.

"So you guys did your first chip tape-out *without* risk wafers?" Bill asked early in the conversation, his eyes wide with a mixture of disbelief and respect as he deftly handled a piece of sashimi. "That's audacious. Like performing brain surgery without practice. Incredibly brave, possibly foolish, probably both."

"We put everything we had into it—our life savings, about $1 million," Val replied simply. "We had no choice but to go all in. And it worked."

Bill was visibly impressed. Having made his fortune backing semiconductor pioneers, he understood the immense risks involved in silicon design. The fact that Bitfury's founders, essentially self-taught from textbooks, had successfully executed a complex ASIC design on their first attempt, betting everything on the outcome at Taiwan's UMC foundry, resonated deeply with his own entrepreneurial journey.

> Semiconductor tape-out refers to the final stage of chip design before manufacturing, when the completed design is literally "taped out" to the foundry for production. Industry standard practice involves multiple design iterations, extensive testing with "risk wafers" (small test runs), and cautious validation before committing to full production. Bitfury's decision to skip these safeguards and bet everything on their first design was either brilliantly confident or recklessly naive, but it worked, producing functional chips that established their technological credibility.

Though semi-retired from traditional VC and pursuing his love of kite surfing, Bill remained deeply engaged with innovation through his Extreme Tech Challenge (XTC), a global competition fostering startups focused on positive impact. Crucially, he had also become an early and vital supporter of the nascent Bitcoin ecosystem, particularly around Stanford University, mentoring young founders and bridging the gap between hackers and capital. He recognized Bitcoin's revolutionary potential long before most of the Valley.

Bill quickly became a key ally, joining our board and bringing his invaluable network. Through him, we connected with Dr. Jackson Hu, the former CEO of UMC, Taiwan's second-largest fab behind TSMC. His deep understanding of foundry operations and connections in Taiwan was critical for scaling our chip production. Bill also introduced us to Young Sohn, then President and Chief Strategy Officer at Samsung Electronics, a visionary leader with profound semiconductor expertise. We were also fortunate to meet Bob Dykes, a seasoned payments executive and former CFO of VeriFone and Juniper Networks, whose experience bridged traditional finance and emerging tech. Together, Bill, Jackson, Young, and Bob formed the nucleus of a powerful advisory board, lending Bitfury instant credibility.

The Sand Hill Road Shuffle

Despite these influential endorsements, fundraising proved unexpectedly challenging. The Bitcoin mining landscape in 2014 was a chaotic gold rush. Numerous companies loudly proclaimed mining prowess, but few possessed genuinely working, efficient hardware. Bitfury was among the handful with proven technology, yet differentiating ourselves amidst the hype and the lingering skepticism post-Mt. Gox was difficult.

Our meetings on Sand Hill Road, the epicenter of venture capital, followed a frustrating pattern. We'd present our technology, our operational success in Iceland and Finland, our dominant market share, and our clear roadmap. The VCs would nod and express admiration, but ultimately demur.

"I don't get it," Val vented after yet another polite rejection, the sleek glass doors of a VC firm closing behind us. "Working chips, profitable operations, market leadership—what more do they want? The price is down, yes, but the network is growing!"

"I think," I sighed, watching a Tesla glide silently past, "These guys aren't really 'venture' capitalists anymore. They've become followers, not risk-takers."

The capital requirements for mining were immense: tens of millions for a new chip tape-out, tens of millions more for data center construction. This scale of investment, especially in a volatile new industry still reeling from scandal, seemed too daunting for the Sand Hill Road consensus.

During our meetings, we also started noticing a recurring theme: the mention of a stealth startup called 21e6. Named after Bitcoin's fixed supply of 21 million Bitcoins (each divisible into 100 million smaller units called "satoshis" or "sats"), the company was helmed by Stanford duo Balaji Srinivasan and Matt Pauker and backed by an all-star roster of Silicon Valley's elite: Andreessen Horowitz, Peter Thiel's Founders Fund, RRE Ventures, and Khosla Ventures.

"Notice how every time we talk hardware, they bring up 21e6?" I observed to Val over coffee in Palo Alto.

Val nodded grimly. "It seems the Valley has already placed its big bet in mining hardware."

21e6 (later 21 Inc.) would raise over $120 million from top-tier VCs with a vision of embedding Bitcoin mining chips into everyday devices like routers and smartphones. The company's stellar founder credentials and Valley pedigree attracted massive investment, but the business model ultimately proved unworkable. The company pivoted multiple times before eventually being acquired by Coinbase. Their massive funding round essentially crowded out other mining hardware companies from accessing Silicon Valley capital.

While I admired Marc Andreessen for his historic launch of Netscape and his influential "Why Bitcoin Matters" essay arguing for Bitcoin's revolutionary potential, it appeared 21e6 had captured the attention and capital of the key players before we arrived on the scene. Silicon Valley was closed for business to us.

"We need Plan B, and we need it fast," I said. "Silicon Valley isn't the only money in the world."

"Where do we go?" Val asked.

"We go where our strengths are recognized. Where power is cheap. Where we have an edge." I tapped the table. "We pivot. We go East, not West."

The urgency was palpable. Bitfury was mining substantial amounts of Bitcoin, around 15,000 BTC per month, and this even before our new chip arrived. But without external capital, we were forced to sell a significant portion of this mined Bitcoin to cover capex and operational expenses. Every Bitcoin sold felt like a missed opportunity, a potential fortune relinquished. We needed funding not to expand necessarily, but to hold our Bitcoin and to build our treasury based on our conviction in its long-term value.

The Race Against Time: Gori Calling

Compounding the pressure was the imminent arrival of our next-generation chip: a cutting-edge 55-nanometer ASIC boasting record-breaking efficiency. This technological leap was crucial for maintaining our lead, but it presented a logistical nightmare. The chips were being manufactured in Taiwan, and we had mere weeks to build and commission a new twenty-megawatt data center to house them upon arrival.

"Four weeks? To build a twenty-megawatt facility?" Bob Dykes exclaimed on an emergency board call. "Guys, that's impossible! These projects take months, years!"

"We don't have months," Val stated flatly. "The chips are coming. They're useless without a home."

A frantic global search ensued. We explored expanding existing sites in Iceland and Finland, but the timelines were too tight. Our focus quickly shifted to my homeland, Georgia. The newly elected government was actively courting foreign investment, promoting reforms, and, crucially, offering access to abundant, cheap hydroelectric power, potentially as low as three cents per kilowatt-hour.

We initiated discussions with George Bachiashvili, the sharp, INSEAD-educated head of the Georgian Co-Investment Fund (GCF), a $6 billion sovereign wealth fund mandated to attract strategic investments into the country. George immediately grasped the potential.

"This won't be just a data center," he enthused during an early meeting. "This could be a technological anchor for Georgia, signalling our place in the digital future."

"And the power cost? Really, three cents?" Val pressed.

"Indeed," George confirmed.

Through George, we met Remi Urumashvili, a brilliant, well-connected lawyer who instantly understood Bitcoin's disruptive power.

"Bitcoin is the future," Remi declared with unwavering conviction at our first dinner, raising his glass. "And Georgia must be part of it."

Remi, a self-made professional hailing from the ancient town of Bolnisi, became our indispensable man on the ground, navigating local complexities and championing our cause. His signature toast, "Gaumarjos!" (to victory!) would soon become legendary among many Bitfury visitors.

But talk needed to translate into action and quickly. Spreading a map of Georgia across a table laden with the remnants of a traditional supra (feast), we scanned for locations near major power transmission lines. Our eyes landed on Gori, a town about sixty kilometers west of Tbilisi, infamous as the birthplace of Joseph Stalin.

"Gori?" Val raised an eyebrow, a smile playing on his lips. "Stalin's hometown?"

"The very same," I confirmed, savouring the historical irony. "Building a decentralized system in the birthplace of the ultimate centralizer. Poetic justice, perhaps?"

Gori's association with Stalin created a unique symbolic dimension to our Bitcoin mining operation. Joseph Stalin, born Ioseb Besarionis dze Jughashvili in Gori in 1878, became the embodiment of centralized, authoritarian control. Building a decentralized Bitcoin mining facility in his birthplace felt like a rejection of everything he represented—a technology designed to eliminate the need for trusted central authorities rising from the very place that produced history's most notorious centralizer.

After a typically lengthy Georgian lunch featuring tender lamb shanks, juicy khinkali dumplings, and copious toasts led by Remi, we rushed to scout the potential site. What we found was a derelict Soviet-era industrial park, dominated by an abandoned cannery building adjacent to a large electrical transformer. The place exuded neglect: rusted metal, crumbling concrete, weeds reclaiming the pavement, the air thick with the smell of decay.

"This is brilliant," Val said immediately, his eyes scanning the site with obvious excitement as a stray dog ambled past. "Look at that transformer capacity, the building structure—we can work with this. We just need to build it, and every day matters."

"Perfect location, perfect timing," Remi said, his confidence unwavering. "This is where we build something that matters."

From then on, the events moved with astonishing speed, characteristic of Bitfury's business culture. The local mayor, thrilled at the prospect of investment, located the site's owner. Within two hours, a deal was struck. We secured a ten-year lease on the entire cannery facility for a mere $5,000 per month. The owner, overjoyed, thanked us profusely.

"Five thousand a month? For a site capable of handling twenty megawatts?" Bill Tai sputtered when I called him with the news. "That's unbelievable!"

"Welcome to Bitfury, Bill," I laughed. "Where the impossible is nothing."

Building at Breakneck Speed

The moment the lease was signed, construction began. Akaki, a trusted associate whose construction firm had become captivated by Bitcoin, took charge. The site became a hive of activity, operating 24/7 in three shifts. Workers swarmed the old cannery, gutting interiors, reinforcing structures, installing cooling systems, and laying miles of high-voltage cable.

"How's it going, Akaki?" I'd ask during our regular check-ins.

"Like war!" he'd often reply, his voice hoarse. "But we are building, not destroying."

Parallel to the frantic construction, we finalized our crucial $20 million funding round. The round included strategic investments from the Georgian Co-Investment Fund, Harry Yeh's Binary Financial, Brock Pierce's Crypto Currency Partners, Queensbridge Venture Partners, and ZAD Investments.

ZAD's involvement came through an unexpected connection. My Wharton classmate Ali Syed, who was running a successful high-net-worth family office platform out of Singapore, brought in one of his clients, Prince Al Saud of Saudi Arabia, who had become increasingly curious about Bitcoin and its potential. Through a series of meetings, the Prince's interest deepened.

During one of our final meetings, we gathered for evening tea at the Four Seasons in Mayfair. The Prince was still deliberating on the investment, weighing the implications carefully. "Will this really change the way we conduct financial transactions?" he asked, his tone both skeptical and hopeful.

"Absolutely," Val answered with conviction.

As if responding to some cosmic cue, at that exact moment, all the lights in the Four Seasons lobby went dark. For five long seconds, we sat in stunned silence. When the lights flickered back on, the Prince's eyes were wide with amazement.

"This is a sign!" he declared. "I am in!"

We all burst into laughter, the tension breaking into relief and excitement. It was one of those moments that made the early Bitcoin days feel almost magical. Even the universe seemed to be conspiring to push this technology forward.

This funding, secured outside the traditional VC channels, was a vital validation of our eastward pivot.

> The funding sources for this round reflected the early Bitcoin ecosystem's unique composition. Binary Financial was one of the first institutional Bitcoin trading firms, Crypto Currency Partners represented entertainment industry money flowing into crypto, and Queensbridge was the investment arm of hip-hop producer Nas. This eclectic mix of investors showed how Bitcoin was attracting capital from non-traditional sources when mainstream VCs remained skeptical.

But the clock was ticking relentlessly. The new 55 nm chips were en route from the foundry in Taiwan to assembly partners in South Korea. From there, they would be loaded onto chartered Boeing 777 cargo planes and flown directly to Tbilisi. The logistics were terrifyingly complex. Any delay, whether caused by customs issues, flight problems, or construction snags, could render the brand-new, multi-million-dollar chips obsolete before they even generated a single hash.

Sleep became a luxury. My waking hours were consumed by calls, troubleshooting, and coordinating a dozen moving parts. The pressure was immense, the stakes existential. Failure wasn't an option.

Miraculously, defying all reasonable expectations, the Gori data center was ready in exactly twenty-eight days. Racks stood waiting, massive cooling fans whirred, and the upgraded electrical substation hummed with potential energy. As the cargo planes touched down in Tbilisi and trucks laden with state-of-the-art mining hardware rolled towards Gori, the final installations were still being completed.

"It's like conducting a symphony in a hurricane," Val remarked, watching the organized chaos as teams installed the newly arrived miners.

It remains one of the most audacious entrepreneurial feats I've witnessed—a testament to sheer will, relentless focus, and the Georgian capacity for rapid execution. A week later, Harry Yeh arrived on a private jet for an inspection.

We toured the facility, now filled with row upon row of Bitfury miners, their indicator lights blinking in unison, the air vibrating with the sound of computation and cooling. The sheer scale was breathtaking.

"This is bigger than anything I've seen," Harry admitted, clearly impressed by the speed and scale of the deployment.

Val, surveying the vast operation, allowed himself a small smile. "You hear that sound, Harry?" he asked, gesturing towards the overwhelming hum. "That is the sound of real money being made."

In that moment, the abstract concept of Bitcoin mining felt intensely real, tangible, and powerful.

That evening, we celebrated with another epic Georgian supra. The table overflowed with khachapuri (cheese bread), mtsvadi (kebabs), badrijani (eggplant rolls), and countless other delicacies. Remi led the toasts with his customary vigor, raising the traditional drinking horn.

"Gaumarjos! To Bitfury! To Georgia! To Bitcoin!"

Harry, grinning widely, suddenly asked us: "Do you know how Bitcoin sounds in Chinese?" Without waiting for an answer, he bellowed with theatrical enthusiasm: "Bitcoinaaaaaaa!"

The cry became his trademark at our gatherings, and we all joined in whenever the moment called for celebration.

Amidst the feasting, Harry pulled me aside, a look of mock seriousness on his face. "George, amazing food! But… where's the rice? We Chinese need rice!"

I chuckled. "Not really a staple here, Harry."

"Unacceptable!" he declared. "We must rectify this tomorrow."

"Why wait for tomorrow?" I replied, embracing the Bitfury spirit of immediate action.

I dispatched a driver. An hour later, to the bemusement of the restaurant staff, he returned triumphantly with a brand-new Korean rice cooker. We plugged it in at our table, much to Val's amusement.

"Investor relations, Val," I grinned. "If Harry wants rice with his Chakhokhbili stew, Harry gets rice."

As Harry's visit concluded, an unexpected call came from Bill Tai.

"George, Val, congratulations!" Bill's voice buzzed with excitement. News of the funding round and our rapidly climbing hashrate was making waves. "Listen, I have a couple of spots open for my Extreme Tech Challenge event on Necker Island next month. Richard Branson will be there, along with other key investors. You have to come pitch Bitfury."

Before he could finish, I jumped in. "Bill, we're in!"

"Getting there from Europe might be tricky on short notice, though—" Bill began.

"Bill," I interrupted, "we'll paddle a canoe from Georgia if we have to."

And just like that, another improbable, potentially game-changing chapter in the Bitfury saga was about to begin.

CHAPTER 4

NECKERED

Fun is one of the most important and underrated
ingredients in any successful venture.

—Richard Branson

Our journey to Necker Island began with an unexpected, rum-fueled layover on the island of Saint Martin. Maho Beach's famous Sunset Bar & Grill became our temporary headquarters as we waited for the connecting flight to the British Virgin Islands. There's a unique thrill to sipping potent rum punches while massive Boeings and Airbuses roar just feet above your head, landing at the adjacent Princess Juliana Airport. It felt surreal, a world away from the intense pressures of building data centers and navigating the volatile crypto markets.

Our connecting Air France flight from Paris arrived too late for the final hop to Necker that day, granting us an enforced pause. We checked into the Sonesta Beach Hotel, and the evening unfolded with exquisite Caribbean indulgence at La Terrasse: Chef Mathieu's tuna tataki and unforgettable lobster bisque, paired with a crisp Chablis, under a starlit sky.

As we wrapped up dinner, we noticed a commotion next door and discovered we were adjacent to the famous casino in St. Maarten. Feeling tipsy from the wine and caught up in the evening's magic, we wandered into the bustling halls where some fifty tables—from blackjack to roulette—were going strong. The atmosphere was electric, a perfect counterpoint to our elegant dinner.

Without thinking, Val approached one of the roulette tables. As the croupier's spin was about to wind down, he placed $100 on black 28. "That's it," the croupier announced, and in those heart-stopping ten seconds as the ball danced around the wheel, time seemed suspended. Then—impossibly—it landed exactly on black 28.

The table erupted. Val's spontaneous bet had hit 35-to-1 odds, turning $100 into $3,500 in a single, magical moment. It felt like the Caribbean itself was welcoming us, blessing this transition from the gritty reality of our Georgian build-out to the almost mythical paradise of Richard Branson's private island.

This brief interlude felt like stepping through a portal. Walking back to our hotel under the starlit Caribbean sky, still buzzing from the incredible roulette win, we couldn't help but laugh at the sheer audacity of it all.

"Unbelievable," Val said, shaking his head in amazement.

"It's a good omen. The universe is clearly on our side," I replied, feeling the weight of both exhaustion and exhilaration from our journey.

We acknowledged the sheer improbability of our trajectory—and this perfect, serendipitous night. Little did we know that the connections we were about to forge on Necker Island would soon propel Bitfury into an entirely different stratosphere.

Island Introductions and Jacuzzi Strategies

The welcome on Necker Island in June 2014 was as warm as the humid Caribbean air that enveloped us. Sir Richard Branson greeted us personally, and his famous laid-back charm instantly disarmed us. Dressed simply in shorts and a linen shirt, devoid of any entourage, he radiated genuine curiosity.

"Ah, the Bitcoin guys Bill Tai won't stop talking about!" he grinned, extending a hand.

"Sir Richard, it's a true honor," I managed.

"Just Richard, please," he insisted. "Now tell me, what exactly is this Bitcoin thing you chaps are building?"

Necker Island, Richard Branson's seventy-four-acre private island in the British Virgin Islands, has hosted world leaders, celebrities, and innovators since Branson purchased it in 1978. The island's informal atmosphere and stunning natural beauty created a unique environment for high-level discussions away from traditional corporate settings. Branson's philosophy of mixing business with adventure and his genuine curiosity about disruptive technologies made Necker an ideal laboratory for exploring Bitcoin's potential with influential minds.

For the next hour, we dove into our vision, consciously avoiding dense technical jargon. We spoke about financial inclusion, empowering the unbanked, and creating a more transparent, resilient global financial system, themes that resonated with Richard's own history of challenging established industries.

One afternoon, the playful spirit of Necker collided with Bitfury's cutting-edge tech. Niko and Bill Tai's tech-savvy sixteen-year-old son, Julien, set up a makeshift demonstration on a coffee table in one of the open-air villas: a simple Raspberry Pi connected to a cluster of bright red USB sticks, each containing Bitfury's powerful ASIC mining chips. As Richard and a group of intrigued investors and entrepreneurs gathered around—including Bryan Johnson, fresh off his $800 million sale of Braintree to PayPal, and Jamie Siminoff, the visionary founder of Ring—Niko powered it up. Within moments, lines of code scrolled across the small screen. The device was actively mining Bitcoin, right there in paradise.

Richard leaned in, fascinated. "You're telling me this little thing actually makes Bitcoins?" he asked, a mixture of amusement and wonder in his eyes.

"Indeed," Val confirmed, before launching into the Bitfury story for the assembled group. He spoke of how our operational scale was approaching forty megawatts across Iceland, Finland, and the newly operational Gori facility in Georgia, which was massive at that time. He recounted the near-impossible feat of building the Gori data center in just twenty-eight days. The audience, composed of seasoned tech veterans and investors, was audibly impressed.

"Wait, you really built a twenty-megawatt site in four weeks?" exclaimed Lars Rasmussen, his voice laced with admiration. "That's insane!"

Lars Rasmussen's presence on Necker illustrated the caliber of tech talent that gravitated to these gatherings. As co-founder of Google Maps and later Director of Engineering at Facebook, where he managed Graph Search and helped initiate Workplace, he understood the complexity of large-scale computing operations. His astonishment at Bitfury's rapid deployment highlighted just how exceptional our Georgian build-out had been. Even seasoned tech veterans who had built global infrastructure were impressed by our execution speed.

As the technical discussion continued, I noticed seven-year-old Cody Siminoff had wandered away from the group over to Richard's chess set near the terrace, studying the board with intense concentration.

"Fancy a game, young man?" Richard asked, following my gaze and stepping away from the Bitcoin demonstration.

Cody looked up with the serious expression only children possess when they're completely focused. "Sure!"

Richard chuckled, settling into the chair across from him. "Well, I've been playing for a few decades myself. Let's see what you've got."

What followed was a genuinely competitive match that stretched over an hour, running parallel to the ongoing tech discussions. Richard would make a move, then get pulled back into the Bitcoin conversation, only to return to find Cody had been patiently studying the position, chin resting on his hands.

"You're quite patient for a seven-year-old," Richard observed between technical discussions.

"Chess is fun," Cody replied simply, making his next move.

Bryan Johnson, who had been watching both the chess match and the mining demonstration with equal fascination, looked thoughtful. "I'll tell you what made Braintree work," he said, his gaze moving from the mining rig to the chess board to the horizon. "We obsessed over the developer experience. Not the banks. Not the suits. Just the damn *code*. Payments should disappear into the product."

I nodded, watching the mining chips blink in rhythm while Cody contemplated his next move. "That's exactly why Bitcoin caught my attention. It's *frictionless*. A global transaction layer that's invisible, inevitable."

Their chess games became a fixture of the afternoon—long, thoughtful battles that demonstrated Cody could genuinely give Richard a run for his money, trading wins and draws in marathon sessions. Jamie watched proudly from nearby as his son held his own against one of the world's most successful entrepreneurs.

"I love it!" Richard declared after tying a particularly hard-fought game. "Reminds me why I enjoy challenges so much."

Prophetically, Bryan's "next" would become Kernel—his bid to map and interface with the human brain—and eventually, Blueprint, his moonshot to reverse biological aging. Jamie would sell Ring to Amazon for over $1 billion. And little Cody? He'd grow up in a world where both chess mastery and cryptocurrency mining were just normal parts of childhood. But that week on Necker, we were sketching the early blueprint of financial decentralization, years before the mainstream would catch up.

This Necker trip proved incredibly fertile ground. We connected with several early Facebook employees and kite surfing enthusiasts who, along with Lars, would become crucial angel investors in our next funding round, aimed at financing the development of our even more ambitious 28-nanometer chip. Among them were Meagan Jones and her husband Conrad, as well as Peter Kravtsov, early Facebook employees who immediately grasped Bitcoin's potential and would become steadfast supporters, riding the wave with us through the ups and downs ahead.

Amidst the kite surfing lessons and beachfront brainstorming sessions, Bill Tai planted another crucial seed during an impromptu strategy discussion.

"You know, guys," Bill mused one evening as we watched the sunset paint the sky, "you shouldn't just be miners. With your position and your insights, you should be strategic investors in the ecosystem. Help build the companies that will use the infrastructure you're creating."

The idea struck a chord. Later that night, Val and I found ourselves continuing the conversation in the master suite's jacuzzi, the warm, bubbling water fostering creative thought.

"Bill's absolutely right, Val," I said. "We have a unique perspective. We see the gaps, the opportunities. We should be backing the next generation of Bitcoin entrepreneurs."

"The community needs it," Val agreed, his voice echoing slightly. "Especially now, with the market so uncertain and capital scarce after Gox. We can provide money, yes, but also technical guidance and partnerships."

And so, in a Necker jacuzzi, the concept of Bitfury Capital was born. Our investment thesis was straightforward: identify and support founders who possessed not only a deep understanding of Bitcoin's potential but also the grit and commitment required to navigate its volatile landscape.

The concept of strategic investing by infrastructure companies was relatively new in the Bitcoin space. Traditional venture capital firms often lacked the technical depth to evaluate early-stage Bitcoin companies, while mining companies typically focused solely on their core operations. Bitfury Capital represented a hybrid approach, combining deep technical knowledge with investment capital and operational expertise. This model would later be replicated by other infrastructure companies across the crypto ecosystem.

Returning to San Francisco, we moved quickly. Marat, who had relocated his family to the Bay Area, took the helm, formally launching Bitfury Capital in July 2014. The response was overwhelming. Proposals flooded in. We rapidly developed a screening process, focusing on teams building essential infrastructure and services for the ecosystem.

One of our first investments was in BitGo. The collapse of Mt. Gox had brutally highlighted the desperate need for robust security solutions. BitGo, founded by savvy tech entrepreneurs Mike Belshe and Ben Davenport and led by CEO Will O'Brien, was pioneering multi-signature wallet technology, offering institutional-grade security.

"Mt. Gox wasn't a Bitcoin failure; it was a catastrophic security failure," Will stated emphatically when we met. "A single point of compromise. Our multi-sig approach eliminates that. It's like needing multiple keys to open a bank vault."

His clarity and the obvious market need made the decision easy. We invested, and importantly, Bitfury also became a key enterprise customer, using BitGo's technology to secure our own rapidly growing Bitcoin treasury.

> Multi-signature technology was a crucial innovation that emerged from the Mt. Gox crisis. Traditional Bitcoin wallets used single private keys. If compromised, all funds were lost. Multi-sig requires multiple parties to sign off on transactions, dramatically reducing the risk of theft or loss. BitGo's implementation was particularly sophisticated, offering enterprise-grade security while maintaining usability. This technology became the standard for institutional Bitcoin custody and helped legitimize Bitcoin for serious investors.

We also deepened our relationship with Wences and his company, Xapo. Wences, who had so effectively articulated Bitcoin's value proposition to me months earlier, was now building the self-proclaimed "Fort Knox of Bitcoin," focusing on ultra-secure cold storage.

"Where do you actually keep the Bitcoin, Wences?" I asked during one meeting.

He smiled cryptically. "Think deeper. Much deeper."

"Underground? Military bunkers?" I guessed.

"Precisely. A decommissioned Swiss military bunker, deep inside a mountain. Physical barriers, Faraday cages, armed guards. Digital gold deserves a digital vault."

Again, the vision was compelling. We participated in Xapo's funding round alongside established players like Benchmark and Fortress, solidifying another crucial ecosystem partnership.

Our investment portfolio would expand by strategically investing in Abra. I had first met Abra's founder, Bill Barhydt, at a blockchain conference in San Francisco, where his pitch about financial inclusion immediately caught my attention.

"Workers sending money home pay up to eight percent in fees. That's robbery," Bill explained during our meeting in Palo Alto. "Bitcoin solves this by being the rails, but we hide the complexity. Users never know they're using Bitcoin—it's just digital cash on their phone."

Val nodded, impressed. "So the everyday user gets the benefits without the technical hurdles."

What resonated most was Abra's architecture: a non-custodial wallet with smart contracts that pegged value to local currency, giving users the stability of fiat with Bitcoin's borderless advantages.

Abra's approach addressed two of Bitcoin's key adoption challenges: volatility and complexity. By creating a layer that abstracted away Bitcoin's technical complexity while leveraging its global reach, Abra demonstrated how Bitcoin could serve as infrastructure for financial services without requiring users to understand or interact with it directly. This "Bitcoin as rails" concept would later become a dominant theme in cryptocurrency application development.

"Your investment isn't just capital," Bill told us after closing the deal. "It's validation from miners who understand Bitcoin's fundamentals."

Abra has since evolved into a comprehensive crypto wealth management platform, offering services such as trading, lending, and yield generation on digital assets, validating our early thesis about the critical infrastructure needed for mainstream adoption. And we are glad we joined Bill on that journey.

Bring Out the Horn: Forging Bonds in the Bear Market

As Bitfury Capital began deploying funds, the broader Bitcoin market remained sluggish through the second half of 2014. Prices continued their downward drift, eventually slipping below $300 by autumn. Yet, in a paradox of sorts, development activity beneath the surface was gaining momentum. It was against this backdrop that we headed to London in September for a major Bitcoin conference organized by Pamir Gelenbe, another industry OG.

Bitfury had a significant presence, showcasing our operational scale and hinting at the breakthrough 28 nm chip under development. The conference provided another opportunity to continue our tradition of Bitcoin Clubs, co-hosted with Matt and Brock.

> The 2014 to 2015 Bitcoin bear market was a crucial period that separated committed builders from speculators. While prices declined and media attention waned, serious entrepreneurs and technologists continued developing the infrastructure that would support Bitcoin's next growth phase. This period saw the launch of crucial services like BitGo, Xapo, and numerous other companies that would become pillars of the Bitcoin ecosystem. The bear market acted as a filter, concentrating resources and attention on projects with genuine utility rather than mere speculation.

These gatherings were deliberately informal, a counterpoint to stuffy corporate networking. We sought out unique venues, often vibrant ethnic restaurants, creating an atmosphere of camaraderie. A fixture at these events became the Georgian khantsi, or drinking horn. Filled with wine (or sometimes champagne, a favorite of Harry), it would be passed around for toasts to celebrate victories, share learning lessons from defeats, reaffirm friendships, and always, always to toast Bitcoin's future. Following tradition, each toast required drinking the horn's contents completely, then tipping it upside down over one's head to prove it empty.

In London, we convened at Marani, a superb Georgian restaurant in Mayfair. Around forty pioneers of the Bitcoin space gathered, including developers, entrepreneurs, investors, and thinkers. The air crackled with energy and debate.

"Gaumarjos! To the future!" I initiated the toasts, raising the horn high.

"To the future!" the room roared back.

Harry, by now a seasoned veteran of Georgian toasting, seized the horn next. "To all the bankers who called Bitcoin 'rat poison'! May they one day beg us for allocations!"

Arthur Hayes, the charismatic founder of BitMEX, grabbed the khantsi. "To volatility! Without it, where's the fun?"

> The Georgian toasting tradition, with its emphasis on honor, friendship, and shared values, proved remarkably suited to the Bitcoin community's culture. The ritual of passing the horn, making heartfelt toasts, and completely emptying the vessel created bonds that transcended mere business relationships. These gatherings became legendary in Bitcoin circles, with attendees often citing them as formative experiences that reinforced their commitment to the technology during challenging times.

Laughter and more toasts followed, each revealing the unique personalities and shared conviction of the group. These Supper Clubs, replicated in cities across the globe—Amsterdam, New York, Las Vegas, Miami, Hong Kong, Dubai—became more than just parties. They were vital bonding rituals, forging resilience during Bitcoin's first prolonged bear market. As the price languished, testing the faith of even ardent believers, and mainstream headlines gleefully penned Bitcoin's obituary, these gatherings reinforced our collective resolve. The horn, the toasts, the shared meals all became symbols of a community united by a belief in something revolutionary, even when the market screamed otherwise.

The attendee list read like a who's who of early Bitcoin: Erik Voorhees (ShapeShift), Jesse Powell (Kraken), Adam Back and Samson Mow (Blockstream), Bobby Lee (BTCChina), Charlie Lee (Litecoin), Elizabeth Rosiello (BitPesa), Vitalik Buterin (Ethereum), David Bailey (Bitcoin Magazine), Elizabeth Stark (Lightning Labs), Michael Terpin (BitAngels), Tuur Demeester (Adamant Capital), Max Keiser and Stacy Herbert (Keiser Report), Andreas Antonopolous (Let's Talk Bitcoin!), Jeff Garzik (Bloq), Vinny Lingham (Gyft), Perianne Boring (Chamber of Digital Commerce), Jez San (crypto investor), Bart and Brad Stephens (Blockchain Capital), Meltem Demirors (CoinShares), Dan Held (ZeroBlock), Dan Morehead and Steve Waterhouse (Pantera Capital), the late Toni Lane Casserly—a visionary thinker and radiant spirit whose presence is still deeply missed—and many more.

We shared war stories of regulatory battles, technical hurdles, and near-death corporate experiences. We debated scaling solutions, privacy enhancements, and adoption strategies, sometimes fiercely, but always with mutual respect. These were the crucibles where the future of Bitcoin was being forged, relationship by relationship, toast by toast.

By October 2014, amidst this challenging market, we successfully closed our second $20 million funding round. This capital was earmarked for the crucial tape-out of our next-generation 28 nm chip and further expansion of our mining footprint towards an ambitious 100 megawatts. The timing was critical. The bear market was acting as a brutal filter, shaking out weaker competitors. Butterfly Labs faced FTC shutdowns for fraud. Cointerra drowned in lawsuits. HashFast declared bankruptcy. Even Sweden's KNC Miner stumbled. It was a Darwinian struggle for survival, and Bitfury, fortified by fresh capital and superior technology, was determined to emerge as a dominant force.

The Bottom and the Book

The start of 2015 brought yet another shock. In January, the prominent exchange Bitstamp suffered a major hack, losing nearly 19,000 BTC. The news sent the already fragile market reeling, and Bitcoin's price plunged from $300 to its cycle low, briefly touching $170. The "Bitcoin is dead" chorus reached a fever pitch.

> The Bitstamp hack of January 2015 involved the theft of approximately 19,000 BTC (worth about $5 million at the time) from one of Europe's largest Bitcoin exchanges. The incident occurred when hackers compromised an employee's personal computer and used it to access the exchange's systems. While Bitstamp covered the losses and remained operational, the hack contributed to Bitcoin's price decline and reinforced concerns about exchange security. It highlighted the need for better security practices and helped drive adoption of more sophisticated custody solutions.

Yet, even as skeptics danced on Bitcoin's perceived grave, signs of maturation began to emerge. Just as the price bottomed, Wall Street Journal reporters Michael Casey and Paul Vigna published their landmark book, *The Age of Cryptocurrency*.[5] It was a seminal work articulating Bitcoin's significance far beyond mere price speculation. They framed it as a foundational technological breakthrough: a way to solve the age-old problem of trust in transactions, bypassing the need for fallible intermediaries. The book struck a chord, igniting serious conversations in boardrooms, regulatory circles, and global think tanks. Bitcoin was no longer just a fringe curiosity. It had become a topic of mainstream debate.

During that same moment of intellectual shift, I flew back to Necker Island for another XTC gathering in early 2015, a few fresh copies of the book in hand. Tennis had quietly become our unwritten tradition whenever I was on Necker—tennis and chess, of course. During one of our breaks between matches, Richard Branson asked me about the book. Presenting him a copy felt almost ceremonial.

"Sir Richard," I said with a wink, "if you're going to read one book on Bitcoin, make it this one."

He accepted it with genuine curiosity, flipping through the pages.

"Fascinating," he said. "So you truly believe this can upend the entire financial system?"

"Without a doubt," I replied. "The revolution is already under-way—even if most people don't see it yet."

The Age of Cryptocurrency by Michael Casey and Paul Vigna was published at a crucial moment when Bitcoin needed intellectual legitimacy. The authors, both experienced financial journalists, provided a serious analysis of cryptocurrency's potential beyond speculation. Their work helped shift the narrative from "digital money for criminals" to "foundational technology for financial innovation." The book's timing, coinciding with Bitcoin's price bottom, helped lay the groundwork for renewed institutional interest that would emerge in subsequent years.

Ever the disruptor, Sir Richard peppered us with questions, clearly intrigued by the parallels to other industries he had helped reimagine. The Bitcoin ecosystem was evolving at breakneck speed—a volatile, chaotic dance of innovation, idealism, and breakthrough thinking. And now, it was gaining serious traction with the kind of people who could move the world.

During a campfire gathering near Flamingo Beach, Bill Tai had another flash of inspiration.

"Hey," he began, the firelight flickering across his face, "what if we organized a dedicated Blockchain summit right here on Necker? Like a modern-day Homebrew Computer Club, bringing together the brightest minds to shape the future."

Val's eyes lit up. "I love it, Bill. This island feels like a natural incubator for big ideas."

The Homebrew Computer Club reference was particularly apt. Founded in 1975, this Silicon Valley gathering of computer enthusiasts included members like Steve Jobs, Steve Wozniak, and other pioneers who would create the personal computer revolution. Bill Tai's vision of recreating that collaborative spirit for Bitcoin reflected an understanding that revolutionary technologies often emerge from informal gatherings of passionate innovators rather than formal corporate settings.

And just like that, the concept for the first Necker Blockchain Summit was born. We immediately began planning, setting the dates sometime for late spring of that year. I reached out to Mike Casey and invited him to lead the event's discussions and introductions. He was in. So while Bitfury's engineers worked tirelessly to deploy the new 28 nm chips across our expanding data centers, further consolidating our positions, our leadership team focused on curating a guest list of global thought leaders.

The inaugural Blockchain Summit was held in May of the same year, bringing together an eclectic and influential mix of participants. Among them were Bitcoin OGs Matt Roszak, Brock Pierce, Harry Yeh, and Bobby Lee, as well as regulatory veterans former CFTC Chairman Dr. Jim Newsome and former Department of Justice Cybercrime Chief Jason Weinstein, both of whom had become key advisors to Bitfury. The guest list also included global development leaders like Peruvian economist Hernando de Soto; Laurent Lamothe, former Prime Minister of Haiti; Gabriel Abbed, Founder of BITT, the Caribbean's largest crypto exchange; Ted Rogers, CEO of XAPO; and Virgin Galactic astronaut Beth Moses.

Also in attendance were young UAE Sheikhs Zayed and Ali, along with their friends Waleed "Oktobud" and Tareq "Dealmaker," who was famous for cracking good jokes and always being in great spirits. We would become close friends with all four over the years, their forward-thinking approach to technology making them natural allies in our mission.

Early Bitcoin investor and founder of DCG, Barry Silbert, was also there, along with Nick Sullivan, Founder of Changetip, Elizabeth Rossiello, CEO of BitPesa—Africa's leading cross-border payments system—and investors: Marc van der Chijs (Pacific Capital), Danny Lee (Blue Pool Capital), and Terrence Philips (Citi Private Bank Asia). The summit was also attended by Brian Forde, director of Digital Currency at MIT Media Lab.

Brian brought a unique perspective to our discussions. Here was someone who had briefed President Obama and Prime Minister Cameron on Bitcoin's technological breakthrough, bringing a level of governmental insight that elevated our conversations beyond pure business strategy. His ability to translate complex blockchain concepts for world leaders made him an invaluable voice in our conversations about Bitcoin's institutional future.

The setting itself fostered collaboration. Formal sessions in open-air pavilions gave way to informal discussions during snorkeling trips, sailing excursions, or hikes around the island. Evening dinners under the stars dissolved hierarchies, encouraging candid exchange.

With lemurs overlooking us, sushi boats floating by, and flamingos and exotic animals all around, Richard Branson proved to be a gracious host as we contemplated where the world was headed. He always showed up with his black notebook, writing down ideas, asking questions. I'll never forget how every time I visited Necker—I've been to Necker nine times throughout the years—Sir Richard was always gracious with his advice, whether we were hitting tennis balls with him in the morning or playing chess. Being part of his company and pranks has left a lasting impression.

"You know what I've learned about innovation?" Branson told me during one memorable chess match, the ocean stretching out behind him. "It never comes from people who are protecting the status quo. The real breakthroughs come from outsiders who aren't invested in the old way of doing things."

He moved his bishop decisively. "Check and mate," he added with a grin.

As mentioned earlier, Necker also became famous for its jacuzzi sessions. We would soak there, drinking Angel's Envy (Jim's favorite) and hearing wild stories of Jason catching criminals while at the DOJ. So during the first summit, we incubated another important idea.

"You know what most people get wrong about Bitcoin and crime?" Jason told us one evening, the sunset painting the sky in spectacular colors behind him. "They think it's anonymous. It's actually the opposite. The blockchain is a permanent, immutable record of every transaction."

"So it's more like a criminal's nightmare," I responded, swirling the amber liquid in my glass.

"Exactly," Jason nodded emphatically. "Every move leaves a trace. And those traces never disappear."

Jim leaned forward, the water bubbling around him. "The problem is getting this message to legislators who still think Bitcoin is just for criminals and terrorists."

"What if we created a simple, direct channel between our industry and law enforcement and regulators?" Val suggested, his voice thoughtful. "So they'd know who to turn to when they have questions. So they don't make the wrong moves just because they didn't understand the tech. So they learn what this technology can and can't do—and we learn how to build with responsibility from day one."

He paused, looking around at the group. "Let's not repeat the same mistakes the early Internet companies made twenty years ago by ignoring the regulators. We can do better this time—together!"

> The perception of Bitcoin as primarily a tool for criminals was one of the biggest obstacles to mainstream adoption in the early years. This misconception stemmed from high-profile cases like Silk Road and was perpetuated by media coverage that focused on Bitcoin's pseudonymous nature. However, as law enforcement became more sophisticated in blockchain analysis, they discovered that Bitcoin's public ledger actually made it easier to track illicit transactions than traditional cash. This realization became a powerful argument for Bitcoin's legitimacy.

Jason, having overseen the DOJ's cybercrime unit, knew this firsthand. From this insight, we established the Blockchain Alliance— a task force that serves as a coordination mechanism with law enforcement agencies to quickly identify and pursue nefarious actors. This initiative bridged the critical gap between the blockchain industry and law enforcement. In October 2015, Jason sent an email to industry leaders announcing its formation.

As the final day of each summit approached, there was a palpable sense that something significant had occurred. This conference was the beginning of a community that would help shape the future of Bitcoin technology for years to come.

"We need to make this an annual tradition," Bill declared at our final dinner together during that first summit. "The Necker Blockchain Summit should be the place where the industry's biggest challenges get solved and its boldest visions get articulated."

Everyone raised their glasses in agreement, and Sir Richard, ever the perfect host, promised that Necker's doors would remain open to us and our growing community of blockchain pioneers.

On the final evening of that great memory, the Caribbean sun was setting behind us as Sheikh Zayed and I stood at the edge of Necker Island, watching the golden light dance across the water. The first Blockchain summit had been more successful than any of us had dared to hope.

"This view never gets old," I said, breathing in the salt air.

Sheikh Zayed nodded, but his mind was clearly racing elsewhere. He turned to me suddenly, eyes alight with possibility.

"George, I would be delighted to welcome the group in my homeland of the United Arab Emirates," he said, gesturing expansively. "It will be a great experience."

"And your group," he continued, "you can explain what Bitcoin truly is. Not the headlines or the speculation, but the foundation of what's coming."

I extended my hand. "Let's do it, then."

Right there, with the waves crashing below us, we agreed on the spot to embrace Sheikh Zayed's vision. Within weeks, plans were underway for the first inaugural UAE Blockchain Summit.

CHAPTER 5
BITCOIN OASIS

*The future belongs to those who believe
in the beauty of their dreams.*

—Eleanor Roosevelt

As we were finalizing plans for the Abu Dhabi gathering, we were simultaneously building the next phase of Bitfury. It was becoming increasingly clear that immersion cooling technology was essential for efficiently running our computers and chips. Bitfury was actively searching for such a company, and that year, we finally identified a promising candidate called Allied Control, based out of Hong Kong.

"Their immersion cooling technology is exactly what we need," Val explained during one of our late-night strategy calls. "It's not an incremental improvement, it's revolutionary."

After countless visits and delicate negotiations, we finally struck a deal to acquire Allied Control and its technology. This would prove pivotal as we pioneered the industry's transition toward immersion cooling.

"This technology will transform data centers as we know them," Val predicted as we signed the final papers. "This will drive the future of computing."

Immersion cooling technology involves submerging computer components directly in thermally conductive but electrically insulating liquids. This approach is far more efficient than traditional air cooling, allowing for higher computational density and significantly reduced energy consumption. Allied Control's technology used 3M's Novec engineered fluids, which could absorb vastly more heat than air while maintaining stable operating temperatures. This acquisition would prove prescient as the technology later became crucial for AI data centers and high-performance computing applications.

Allied Control would later be spun off as LiquidStack and become one of the key players driving the AI data center revolution. Val had been visionary in locating them early on.

We decided to apply this technology immediately, and an opportunity arose to deploy it in my native Georgia. Our new chips were coming, and the timing was perfect to build an immersion cooling data center there.

Georgia had an attractive law where you could acquire land for a symbolic $1, provided you invested significant capital and employed Georgian professionals. We seized the Ministry of Economy's proposal and identified an 18-hectare location right outside Tbilisi's suburbs, where a major interconnection of electricity lines made it ideal for our needs. In the end, we invested over $50 million and employed over a hundred individuals. The partnership with the Ministry of Economy would be a major success.

Georgia's "Invest in Georgia" program was part of the country's broader economic liberalization following the Rose Revolution. The government offered land grants and tax incentives to foreign investors who met minimum investment and employment thresholds. This program attracted significant international investment and helped establish Georgia as a regional technology hub. The availability of cheap hydroelectric power, combined with business-friendly policies, made Georgia particularly attractive for energy-intensive industries like cryptocurrency mining.

"This land is completely abandoned now," Akaki said as we surveyed the property, "but imagine what we can build here."

Remi looked across the barren landscape and nodded. "This data center will be a vision of the future."

Construction began immediately, with work continuing day and night. Akaki spearheaded the project, overseeing the development of a 100 MW facility, with 40 MW allocated to our immersion cooling technology.

"We're building something no one has attempted at this scale," Val told me one evening as we walked through the rapidly developing site. "In a decade, everyone will be doing this, but we'll have been the first." It was 2015, and we were clearly pioneers. This indeed would eventually trigger a wave of immersion cooling technologies being constructed across the United States a decade later.

Investment and Enlightenment

In July, as construction was progressing at full speed, we announced that we had closed another funding round, this time led by DRW, a diversified trading firm based in Chicago known for its active presence in global financial markets. DRW's subsidiary Cumberland Mining was one of the world's biggest Bitcoin traders, and its Bitcoin trading desks worked closely with Bitfury.

In a statement on the raise, DRW's visionary founder, Don Wilson, praised our efforts: "DRW's investment in Bitfury is an acknowledgment of the impressive work Val and the team have done to become a leader in the business of securing the blockchain."

The round was followed by investments from several angels as well as iTech Capital, a private equity and venture capital firm founded by shrewd investor Gleb Davidyuk, headquartered in Riga, Latvia. Gleb, serving as the managing partner, brought his vast experience in private equity to the table.

> DRW's investment represented a significant milestone as one of the first major traditional trading firms to invest directly in Bitcoin mining infrastructure. Founded by Don Wilson, DRW had built a reputation as a sophisticated quantitative trading operation across multiple markets. This investment demonstrated how traditional financial firms were beginning to recognize Bitcoin's legitimacy and potential.

While the construction progressed and funding closed, I spent the summer of 2015 immersed in *Mastering Bitcoin* by Andreas Antonopoulos.[6] It wasn't just a book. It was a gateway. Page after page, Andreas broke down the mechanics of Bitcoin with the precision of a cryptographer and the clarity of a teacher. But more than that, he made it *human*. Through his words, Bitcoin became a philosophy of freedom, decentralization, and financial sovereignty.

> Andreas Antonopoulos had emerged as Bitcoin's most articulate evangelist—a Greek-British computer scientist who had discovered Bitcoin in 2012 and immediately recognized its world-changing potential. Unlike many early adopters who focused on price speculation or technical minutiae, Andreas possessed a rare gift: he could explain Bitcoin's revolutionary implications to anyone, from computer scientists to grandmothers. His talks at conferences had become legendary, often moving audiences to tears with his passionate vision of how Bitcoin could bank the unbanked and restore financial dignity to billions. He spoke not of getting rich, but of empowering the poor, not of disrupting banks for profit, but of creating a more equitable financial system. His book, *Mastering Bitcoin*, had become the definitive technical guide to understanding not just how Bitcoin worked, but why it mattered.

At the time, Bitcoin was still licking its wounds from the Mt. Gox collapse. Public interest had faded. Headlines had quieted. The price was languishing under $250. But this book—the ideas inside it—felt like they were building toward something much bigger.

Lake Tahoe Summit

Fresh off our funding round and with my mind still buzzing from Andreas's insights, we took a short break in September for Dan Morehead's Bitcoin Pacifica event at Lake Tahoe. Nestled in a beautiful villa overlooking the lake, Dan would gather thirty to forty attendees for his annual event that spanned from crypto OGs to computer scientists to government officials. As an ex-Tiger Management alumnus, he had gotten into Bitcoin early and, alongside Pete Briger and Mike Novogratz of Fortress, was among the earliest group from traditional alternative asset management to embrace the promise of Bitcoin.

> Dan Morehead's transition from traditional hedge fund management to Bitcoin represented a broader trend of institutional finance beginning to take cryptocurrency seriously. Tiger Management, founded by Julian Robertson, was one of the most successful hedge funds of the 1980s and 1990s, and its alumni network included some of the most respected names in finance. Morehead's early embrace of Bitcoin through Pantera Capital provided crucial legitimacy and institutional expertise to the emerging cryptocurrency ecosystem.

Being neighbors with Dan at Spear Tower, we overlapped quite often while in San Francisco, sharing ideas and co-investing in some deals. The event in Tahoe didn't disappoint. Just like Necker, the setting was very informal and allowed for open exchange of ideas with many OGs. It felt like a continuation of our time at Necker just a couple of months earlier, with many of the same faces.

My only disappointment was that I was so jet-lagged that I missed the poker night where, with a total pot of 23 BTC, the final standings were impressive:

- 1st place – Gavin Andresen with 11.5 BTC
- 2nd place – Marco Santori with 5.75 BTC
- 3rd place – Erik Voorhees with 3.45 BTC
- 4th place – Jesse Powell with 2.3 BTC

This poker game, with its 23 BTC pot worth approximately $10,000 at 2015 prices, would be valued at over $2.3 million at Bitcoin's $100k per coin peak prices. The game featured some of Bitcoin's most influential figures: Gavin Andresen, Bitcoin's lead developer after Satoshi's departure; Marco Santori, a leading cryptocurrency lawyer; Erik Voorhees, founder of the leading exchange ShapeShift; and Jesse Powell, founder of the major trading platform Krake.

In the early morning, gearing up for my paddleboard outing, I looked back and saw Dan sipping on his coffee on the deck overlooking the water.

"Not as warm as on Necker," Dan smiled, watching the mist rise off the lake.

"Where we come from, this is warm," I joked. "You should come to the lakes in the Caucasus mountains, 10,000 feet elevation. That's where it's fun."

Dan laughed. "I'll take your word for it. You Bitfury guys are built differently."

As I paddled out onto the calm morning water, I reflected on how fortunate we were to be part of this small global community, gathering at these informal summits from Necker to Tahoe, from London to soon-to-be Abu Dhabi, all united by our belief in this revolutionary technology.

By early October, I had finally finished Andreas's book. The fog had lifted. All the technical scaffolding, ideological clarity, and global potential snapped into place. And in the early morning of October 4, 2015, I tweeted:

You connect all the dots and realize it will be simply huge...

I pinned that tweet—not for optics, not for engagement—but because it captured the moment my conviction in Bitcoin crystallized. It was quiet, but deeply personal. A timestamp of belief. A line in the sand. That tweet would eventually be viewed by millions.

Presciently, from that point forward, Bitcoin would slowly but surely begin its ascent out of the doldrums. While people still slept on it, the tide was quietly turning. The believers were building. The network was strengthening. The next chapter was already underway.

That tweet wasn't just a hunch. It was a call shot. And *Mastering Bitcoin* was the lens that brought the entire picture into focus.

The Majlis Sessions

With my conviction crystallized and our funding secured, the stage was set perfectly for our Abu Dhabi meetup. In early October 2015, we assembled an esteemed group of tech investors and former senior government officials to fly to Abu Dhabi, where Sheikh Zayed was waiting to welcome us.

His family's beautiful Jumeirah Hotel at Etihad Towers had been allocated for the event, and our delegation—myself, Val, Bill Tai, Matt, Brian Forde, Hernando De Soto, Dr. Jim Newsome, Jason Weinstein, and several others—descended on the beaches of the UAE for our first inaugural gathering with the royal family.

"Welcome to my home," Sheikh Zayed said warmly as he greeted us in the opulent lobby. "What you're doing with blockchain technology fascinates my family and friends, and we want to learn more."

The hospitality was simply amazing. Sheikh Zayed rolled out the red carpet for all attendees. We had evening sessions with leaders and royal family members, discussions in the majlis, and many lively conversations.

"Your technology," one prince asked during a particularly engaging session, "can it truly revolutionize trust in financial systems?"

Bill Tai leaned forward. "It already is. What we're discussing today will be standard practice in finance within a decade."

The UAE's early interest in blockchain technology was driven by the leadership's vision of economic diversification beyond oil. The royal family's willingness to engage directly with Bitcoin pioneers demonstrated their understanding that technological leadership would be crucial for the country's future prosperity. This forward-thinking approach would later position the UAE as one of the world's most crypto-friendly jurisdictions, with Dubai becoming a major blockchain hub.

On one memorable day, Sheikh Zayed organized a helicopter tour to take us to a beautiful property in the desert. As we flew over the golden dunes, I found myself seated next to Sheikh Ali, a thoughtful member of the royal family who would later become a dear friend.

"What do you see when you look at this desert, George?" Sheikh Ali asked, gesturing toward the endless sand below.

"Beauty, vastness, and possibility," I replied.

He nodded, smiling. "Most see emptiness. But my ancestors saw opportunity. They created trade routes where others saw nothing but obstacles. This is why I'm drawn to your Bitcoin vision. It creates highways of trust where before there were only barriers."

We landed at a stunning desert oasis where Sheikh Zayed waited to greet us.

"This is where my ancestors lived," he explained as we gathered around. "They survived by trusting one another completely. Your blockchain technology reminds me of that essential trust, but modernized for a global scale."

Sheikh Ali pulled me aside as the others explored the property. "You know, George, many advisors tell us to avoid this Bitcoin phenomenon. They say it's too speculative, a Western creation that might undermine our financial sovereignty."

"And what do you think?" I asked.

His eyes crinkled with amusement. "I think that anything this controversial deserves serious attention. The future rarely announces itself politely."

The UAE royal family's engagement with Bitcoin reflected a sophisticated understanding of technological disruption. Having built their wealth through strategic positioning in global trade and energy, they recognized that financial technology could be the next major wave of innovation. Their willingness to engage directly with Bitcoin pioneers, despite skepticism from traditional advisors, demonstrated the kind of forward-thinking leadership that would later make the UAE a global blockchain hub.

While in the desert, we experienced true Arabian hospitality, including falcony exhibitions, horseback riding, and even sand surfing. The conversations continued as Bitcoin hovered around $400.

As night fell across the desert, Sheikh Ali turned to me with curiosity in his eyes.

"What gives you such conviction about Bitcoin's future?" he asked, the firelight reflecting in his thoughtful gaze.

I gazed at the stars above before answering. "Throughout history, currency has fundamentally been about trust. And through centuries, governments have failed that trust test. Bitcoin simply transforms that trust into mathematical certainty—a system immune to human manipulation."

Sheikh Ali considered this, running his fingers through the sand beside him. "Trust. In our culture, one's word carries the weight of absolute honor. Our modern world has lost this simplicity. Perhaps what Bitcoin offers is a return to fundamental values, but through technology."

I was struck by the profound nature of his observation. "That perspective captures its essence better than most analysts I've met."

With a warm smile, he extended his hand. "Let us journey into this future as friends and allies."

Our connection endured through the years. During Bitcoin's volatile periods, his calls became familiar: "My advisors are alarmed by Western headlines declaring Bitcoin's demise. Should I waver?"

"Remain steadfast," I would counsel. "These fluctuations are merely waypoints in a longer expedition."

When we reconnected years later, his knowing smile said it all. "Your counsel proved wise, George. Our Bitcoin holdings have rewarded our patience handsomely."

The Abu Dhabi event had significant ramifications for global adoption because the UAE is such a visionary country. I like to think that we, in some small way, laid the foundation for the positive crypto regulations that came as a result of those meetings and engagements.

Under the patronage of young Sheikh Zayed—a brilliant computer scientist who had spent a summer internship with Bitfury in our San Francisco office—we established a friendship and relationship with the UAE royal families that would endure for years to come.

From Desert to Ocean: New Horizons

After the success in Abu Dhabi, we had to head back to San Francisco for a major tech conference organized by Credit Suisse, where Bitfury was presenting. On the flight, I saw The Economist's front cover featuring Bitcoin as "The Trust Machine."

"Look at this," I said to Val, showing him the magazine. "The establishment isn't ignoring us anymore. We're moving to the next stage."

> The Economist's October 2015 cover story, "The Trust Machine," marked a watershed moment for Bitcoin's mainstream acceptance. The prestigious publication's serious analysis of blockchain technology helped legitimize Bitcoin in the eyes of policymakers, academics, and business leaders worldwide. The article's focus on blockchain's potential to create trust without intermediaries resonated far beyond the crypto community, spurring interest from governments, corporations, and institutions globally.

But before moving to the next stage, we got an invitation to the Summit at Sea, and we were moving to the ocean. It was November, and Val and I were invited by Brock to join him for Summit at Sea where we would spend three days out in the sea with tech entrepreneurs. The cruise would run from November 9 through 12, departing from Miami to the Bahamas on a Norwegian ship filled with some of the most influential minds in technology and business.

"This lineup is incredible," I mentioned to Val as we reviewed the speakers. "Eric Schmidt, Travis Kalanick, and they're even hosting Harry Belafonte and John Legend."

"And don't forget Snowden via video link," Val added. "That should be interesting."

On our first evening aboard, we found ourselves at the outside bar on the upper deck, the warm Caribbean breeze providing perfect relief from the day's heat. And as I was looking around, I saw the Winklevoss twins, Cameron and Tyler, making their way over, drinks in hand.

"The Bitcoin boys of Bitfury," Tyler grinned, clinking his glass against mine. "Heard you guys had fun on Necker. Sorry we could not make it. Been tied up with ETF."

"That's what we hear," I smiled. "But hopefully, soon you guys will get it. We are rooting for you."

Cameron leaned against the railing, looking out at the darkening horizon where ocean met sky. "This industry isn't for the faint of heart," he observed. "Every day is a battle."

"To victory," I said, raising my glass.
"To victory," Brock joined in.

> The Winklevoss twins' Bitcoin ETF efforts represented one of the earliest and most persistent attempts to bring Bitcoin to traditional financial markets. Having won their lawsuit against Facebook and invested the proceeds in Bitcoin when it was still under $100, they were among the largest Bitcoin holders globally. Their ETF application, first filed in 2013, would face years of regulatory challenges before finally being approved in 2024, demonstrating the patience required for Bitcoin's institutional adoption.

The conversation flowed as easily as the drinks, punctuated by laughter and animated debates about governance, scaling, and the future of decentralization. As night fell and stars appeared above the vessel, the Summit at Sea proved to be exactly what we needed—a moment to connect with fellow visionaries away from the constant demands of our growing businesses. The ship sailed through calm waters, but we all knew the revolution we were part of was just beginning to make waves.

The 16-Nanometer Triumph

In December, we returned to Georgia for the grand opening of our data center. A futuristic building was rising in the suburbs of the capital, Tbilisi. Inside were forty data tanks, each with a one-megawatt capacity, boiling with 3M Novec solutions running chips and hashing Bitcoins. The team had produced another miracle, erecting a 40 MW, state-of-the-art, immersion cooling data center in under four months. The grand opening ceremony was attended by the Georgian Prime Minister, who had a ribbon-cutting ceremony and congratulated us all on our achievement.

"The entry of such a tech company like Bitfury in Georgia indicates that the investment climate in our country is even more improved than it was before," said the Prime Minister.

Just a few days after that triumphant opening, our R&D team delivered even more electrifying news: a major breakthrough with our next-generation 16-nanometer chip design. This wasn't some sort of hypothetical announcement but an actual test of a working chip, broadcast to the entire world by our chip designers. Our mailboxes and phones were flooded with messages from customers around the world wanting to place massive pre-orders.

The rest of the week, we hosted numerous investors to showcase our new data centers, and everyone was amazed by what was built in such a short time. The simulations and test results from our chip were phenomenal, a true home run. The chip parameters were, frankly, spaceship-level—far exceeding contemporary industry standards in terms of performance and, crucially, energy efficiency.

> The development of 16-nanometer Bitcoin mining chips represented a significant technological leap. Moving from 28 nm to 16 nm doubled transistor density while reducing power consumption per hash, dramatically improving mining economics. This advancement required partnerships with leading foundries and represented millions of dollars in R&D investment. The timing was crucial as Bitcoin mining was becoming increasingly competitive, and efficiency gains translated directly to profitability advantages.

We were showcasing an unprecedented peak efficiency of 0.06 Joules per Gigahash (J/GH), leveraging a design methodology focused on achieving the highest possible transistor density. This improvement promised to redefine the economics of Bitcoin mining and potentially usher in the "Exahash era," pushing the total network hash rate beyond one quintillion hashes per second.

We were ecstatic, celebrating what felt like a guaranteed victory. The year was ending on the highest possible note.

I was also getting the sense it was a crazy fast year, and I needed rest, so I flew with my family back to the UAE to celebrate the survival of a Bitcoin bear market. Bitcoin had stabilized at around $430, and it seemed like the bear market of 2014–2015 had come to an end.

During that holiday visit, I spent more quality time with our young sheikhs.

"Do you think Bitcoin will hit $1,000?" one of them asked.

I answered, "It's not a matter of if but a matter of when. Patience, my friends."

As the sunset painted the Arabian Gulf in hues of amber and gold, I opened my Bitfury email and saw a message from Val to the entire company.

Dear Team! The year 2015 was full of inspiring achievements! In the last year together, we have worked very hard to get the Bitfury to the next level. Today, we have more than 150 team members from 16 countries. By working together, we will succeed! Keep calm and keep making the impossible possible in the New Year 2016! I wish all the best to you and your family for a prosperous 2016! Happy New Year!!! V.

The note perfectly captured Val's leadership style—optimistic yet grounded, demanding yet appreciative. Reading his words as the last light faded over the water, I felt a surge of pride in what we'd accomplished and excitement for what lay ahead.

Indeed, we were finishing the year on a high note, but little did we know that 2016 would bring new challenges, and with those challenges, new opportunities.

PART II

THEN THEY LAUGH AT YOU

ნაწილი II: შემდეგ შენ დაგცინიან

CHAPTER 6

HOUSTON, WE HAVE A PROBLEM

A gem cannot be polished without friction,
nor a man perfected without trials.

—Seneca

The early days of 2016 carried the scent of optimism, but with it, an undercurrent of tension. After the crucible of the 2014–15 bear market, Bitcoin had stabilized around $430, and Bitfury stood strong. Our new immersion cooling facility in Georgia was operational, and our next-generation 16 nm chip design was ready to revolutionize the industry. The future stretched before us like an open road.

Just weeks earlier, I had stood on the shores of the UAE with my friends and family, watching 2015 conclude with spectacular fireworks illuminating the Arabian Gulf. The culmination of our year couldn't have been more triumphant—from our operational facilities in Georgia and Iceland to our expanding global presence, technological break-throughs, and growing treasury of Bitcoin.

Yet experience had taught me that, in both Bitcoin and business, calm waters often precede the fiercest storms. The lessons of my child-hood echoed in my mind: systems that appear stable can collapse with shocking speed, and resilience requires preparation for the unexpected.

As was customary for us by now, Val and I attended CES in Vegas in early January, where Bill and Young Sohn served as judges for the Extreme Tech Challenge's semi-finals. From there, we flew directly to the North American Bitcoin Conference in Miami. The crypto community was abuzz with discussion about Bitcoin Core developer Mike Hearn's controversial exit from the space just a week earlier.

Mike Hearn's resignation from Bitcoin development in January 2016 sent shockwaves through the cryptocurrency community. His blog post, titled "The Resolution of the Bitcoin Experiment," declared Bitcoin a failed experiment due to scaling disputes and governance paralysis. Hearn had been a prominent Bitcoin developer since 2009 and was known for his work on Bitcoin and advocacy for larger block sizes. His dramatic exit, combined with his decision to sell all his Bitcoins, created significant negative publicity just as Bitcoin was attempting to recover from its bear market.

"What do you think about Hearn's 'resolution of the Bitcoin experiment' piece?" Adam Back, Bitcoin OG, who was working closely with our Sysman on the "small block side" of the Block Wars, asked me during a reception, his tone entertained. "He's selling all his coins at $400 and calling it quits."

"I think it's very short-sighted. Honey badger don't care." I replied, sipping my gin and tonic. "The irony is, just a couple of months ago, he praised Bitfury's white paper on public versus private blockchains. This sudden reversal feels theatrical."

At the conference, we participated in another of our now-legendary Supper Clubs, as well as a gathering of Coin Center patrons. Jerry Brito, who ran the organization, had become one of the key voices lobbying for sensible Bitcoin policies on Capitol Hill, and Bitfury, together with many other Bitcoin companies, was a proud supporter of their work.

"When will we finally be getting tax clarity on Bitcoin?" I asked Jerry half-jokingly over drinks.

He winked, a conspiratorial gleam in his eye. "Working on it."

Coin Center, founded in 2014 by Jerry Brito, emerged as cryptocurrency's primary advocacy organization in Washington, DC. Operating as a non-profit focused on policy issues affecting open blockchain networks, Coin Center became crucial for legitimizing Bitcoin and other cryptocurrencies with policymakers. Their work involved educating regulators, testifying before Congress, and providing technical expertise to government agencies grappling with cryptocurrency regulation. For companies like Bitfury, supporting Coin Center was essential for creating a favorable regulatory environment.

The atmosphere reminded me of our early meetings with Val in Kyiv, when we'd dreamed of building Bitfury 2.0. We had come so far, yet I sensed we were still at the beginning of our journey. However, the coming year would test us in ways we hadn't yet imagined.

The Davos Detour

As the Miami conference was winding down at Brock's private yacht party, my phone buzzed with a message from Gena Gazin, an ex-McKinsey partner who managed investments for Viktor Pinchuk, one of Ukraine's wealthiest businessmen.

"George, are you heading to Davos next week?" Gena's message read.

I looked up from my phone at Val, who was deep in conversation with Adam and Sysman across the deck. "Val," I called out, "what would you think about a spontaneous trip to Davos after this?"

Val raised an eyebrow, intrigued. "The World Economic Forum? Isn't it too late to get in?"

"Probably, but when has that stopped us?" I grinned. I think we should go. Bitcoin needs representation in the mountains."

The World Economic Forum in Davos represents the annual gathering of global political and business leaders, held each January in the Swiss Alps. By 2016, blockchain technology was beginning to capture attention among traditional financial institutions and governments, but Bitcoin itself remained controversial. The forum's exclusive nature made it difficult to access without proper credentials or connections, but it also represented an opportunity to educate influential decision-makers about cryptocurrency's potential.

The impromptu decision reminded me of that moment in the Kyiv café years ago, when Val and I had first committed to building Bitfury together. We had been making these intuitive leaps from the very beginning. It was part of our DNA.

Twenty-four hours later, we were on a flight to Zürich, from where we drove to Davos. The timing was too late to secure accommodation in Davos itself, so we booked a hotel half an hour away and hired drivers. Despite the logistical challenges, the impromptu decision proved fruitful. We spent our days at the Sheraton Waldhuus, orange-pilling institutional fund managers and government officials who were curious about Bitcoin's future.

"So how do you like Davos?" I asked Val one evening as we navigated yet another exclusive reception, this time at the "Ukraine House," the Alpine night glittering with snow outside the windows.

"Not bad. But we need to do this properly next time."

"Indeed," I agreed, raising my glass. "This is just our reconnaissance mission. Next year, we'll bring the entire crypto cavalry."

In that moment, we realized we had established yet another tradition—a small beachhead for Bitcoin in the very heart of the traditional financial system. It felt like we were inserting a Trojan horse of sorts.

Return to Necker: The Partnership

As we wrapped up our Davos adventure with Val giving interviews for TechCrunch and Bloomberg, Necker Island was calling yet again. This marked our fifth visit for the XTC finals, where Bitfury and Zoom stood among the chief sponsors. Bill had been an early investor in Zoom, and we were early adopters and huge fans of what Eric Yuan was building.

Necker had become our unofficial think tank—a place where the usual constraints of business seemed to dissolve in the Caribbean breeze, allowing for a purer form of innovation. This felt like a continuation of our long collaboration with Sir Richard, beginning with our first visit chronicled in "Neckered," where we had further educated the Virgin Group founder on the revolutionary potential of Bitcoin.

Zoom's early development story illustrates the power of patient capital and strategic guidance. When Eric Yuan left Cisco's WebEx to start his own company in 2011, the video conferencing market appeared saturated with established players like Skype, GoToMeeting, and WebEx itself. However, Yuan recognized that existing solutions were built for the previous generation of Internet infrastructure and user expectations. His vision of seamless, reliable video communication would prove prescient as remote work became mainstream.

Bill, as humble as he is, doesn't like to advertise that he played a pivotal role in Zoom's early days, but the story had become something of a legend in our circles. Back in 2011, when Eric left Cisco's Webex to start his own venture—initially named Saasbee—Bill was among the initial investors who contributed to the $3 million seed funding round. This wasn't just about money; Bill's early commitment lent crucial credibility to Eric's vision in a market dominated by giants like Microsoft and Google.

"Eric's product was so clearly superior," Bill had told me during one of our flights together. "The problem was getting anyone to notice in such a crowded space."

Beyond financial backing, Bill also offered strategic guidance during critical moments in Zoom's development. During internal debates about their business model, Bill had cautioned against a pure freemium approach, suggesting it might devalue the product. Eric's commitment to accessibility eventually led to a brilliant compromise: unlimited one-on-one meetings for free, with a forty-minute limit on group calls—just enough to prove the value without giving everything away.

What always impressed me about Bill was his willingness to back founders when other VCs remained skeptical. His unwavering belief in Eric's vision, even when conventional wisdom suggested the video conferencing market was saturated, demonstrated the kind of contrarian thinking that had also drawn him to Bitcoin early on.

By this time, I had also improved my tennis game and relished my morning matches with Sir Richard at 7:30 a.m. These games provided exercise as well as precious moments to discuss Bitcoin and Ukraine. Richard had long supported Ukraine, and I made it a point to update him on developments between games.

What made each Necker visit special wasn't just the business conversations or Caribbean setting—it was the small rituals that developed. Richard's red golden retriever, Sumo, had somehow decided I was worth following to dinner each evening. I'd always save a choice piece of meat from my plate. "Good boy, Sumo," became my nightly tradition, and Richard would smile knowingly from across the table. It was these quiet moments of connection that made even the most intense business discussions feel more human.

One particularly competitive game ended with a decisive forehand winner down the line.

"Your forehand has more precision now," Richard observed with a smile, wiping his brow as we walked to the net.

"I wanted to make sure I gave you a good workout," I replied, shaking his hand.

Richard laughed heartily. "Mission accomplished."

The magic of Necker never ceased. On this visit, we grew closer to Terence Phillips, an ex-Marine turned private banker with CITI Asia, who had attended the original Necker summit a year before. Terence had become a big fan of our Bitfury ethos—what we called the "Marine Corps way" of conducting business: doing more with less. He was particularly impressed by our adoption of *The Marine Corps Way: Using Maneuver Warfare in Leading a Winning Organization*, a book penned by my Wharton classmate Jason Santamaria, which had become Bitfury's field manual for navigating the brutal landscape of ruthless competition.

The Marine Corps Way by Jason Santamaria applies military maneuver warfare principles to business strategy. The concept emphasizes speed, flexibility, and decisive action over resource-heavy approaches. For a company like Bitfury, operating in the fast-moving Bitcoin industry with limited resources compared to venture-backed competitors, these principles provided a framework for achieving maximum impact with minimal resources. The book's emphasis on adaptability and quick decision-making resonates particularly well with startup culture.

"Your approach reminds me of my days in the Corps," Terence had mentioned during one of our conversations. "Most startups burn cash; you guys maximize output with minimal resources. It's refreshing."

On this particular trip, Terence had rented a yacht that was docked outside with a group of Asian investors. He invited us to join them for a gathering that would prove unexpectedly consequential.

As we boarded the impeccable yacht for a champagne brunch, Terence greeted us in his signature Panama hat.

"George, Val, this is Phang," Terence said, gesturing towards a Singaporean businessman in swim trunks and a polo shirt. "Phang is the CEO of Credit China Fintech Holdings, listed in Hong Kong."

Phang's handshake was firm, his gaze assessing. "So you are the Bitcoin guys I've heard about. Your reputation precedes you."

As the yacht navigated the crystal waters around Necker, our conversation quickly moved beyond pleasantries. Phang, who had served in Singapore's military, displayed the precision of his training in his direct business approach.

Credit China Fintech Holdings represented the wave of Asian fintech (financial technology) companies emerging in the mid-2010s. These firms were often more aggressive in adopting new technologies like blockchain compared to their Western counterparts, driven by less regulatory constraint and greater market opportunity in underbanked Asian economies. Hong Kong's position as a financial hub made it an ideal base for companies looking to bridge traditional finance with emerging fintech innovations.

"Credit China is becoming a big player in mainland fintech," he explained, swirling his champagne thoughtfully. "We're looking to make a strategic entry into the blockchain space. What you're building, both the mining infrastructure and enterprise software, is precisely what the market needs."

The synergy felt immediate and authentic. We moved back to the island for dinner and later to our Master Suite for after-party drinks prepared by Necker's bartender, Ave.

"Let me be frank," Phang stated, sipping a perfectly mixed gin and tonic. "I really want to do something with you guys. I propose my technical team visits your operations. I believe we have the basis for a significant investment and joint venture."

Val raised his glass in a toast: "To the beginning of a beautiful partnership!"

From that point, we began developing the framework for a deal. We would host the Credit China team, and I would travel to Hong Kong to meet their team and lay the groundwork for our strategic partnership. Our strategic pivot eastward seemed to be yielding dividends, with substantial capital potentially within reach.

Looking back at our first conversation with Val about pivoting East after our rejections on Sand Hill Road, this relationship with Credit China felt like the perfect manifestation of that strategy. Where Silicon Valley had hesitated, Asian partners were eager to engage with the transformative potential of blockchain technology.

The First Signs of Trouble

In late February, I flew to Hong Kong for meetings with Credit China. Terence greeted me as I checked into the Upper House, a luxury boutique hotel designed by architect André Fu, offering panoramic views of Victoria Harbour.

"Welcome to Hong Kong," he said warmly, extending his hand. "How was your flight?"

"Long, but comfortable enough," I replied, shaking his hand.

"The city has been waiting for you," Terence said, gesturing toward the floor-to-ceiling windows framing the glittering skyline. "Hong Kong has a way of energizing even the most jet-lagged traveler."

He arranged dinner at Café Gray Deluxe on the forty-ninth floor. With stunning views and Cantonese-inspired cuisine, it felt like we'd never left Necker. The dinner and drinks lasted several hours, and as we were wrapping up, Val called.

His voice was calm but carried an unmistakable weight that immediately set off alarm bells. "Say hi to Terence," he began casually, "but we need to talk. The chip has issues."

I stepped away from the table, my pulse quickening. "What do you mean, it has issues?" I asked, the Hong Kong skyline suddenly seeming unreal behind the glass.

"There's an issue with the production wafers," he replied, his tone measured but grave. "A major issue."

"How can that be?" I stammered, my mind racing. "The MPW production was perfect. Bill said this is like one hundred percent guaranteed. Let's get everyone on Zoom ASAP."

Multi-Project Wafers (MPW) are test runs where multiple chip designs share space on a single wafer to reduce costs during the development phase. These small-scale productions typically show high yields because they use the best portions of the wafer and benefit from optimal manufacturing conditions. However, transitioning to full-scale production can reveal issues not apparent in MPW runs, including process variations, contamination, or design flaws that only emerge at scale.

The contrast couldn't have been starker—just moments earlier, I had been basking in the glow of our expanding Asian partnerships and growing partnership. Now a fundamental threat to our core business had emerged without warning. The moment reminded me vividly of that day in 1991 when my father had announced we needed to leave Georgia as the Soviet system collapsed. Just as then, the ground beneath my feet suddenly felt less solid.

We convened an emergency call, gathering key members of our engineering team, many of whom were in Hsinchu, Taiwan. A horrifying paradox emerged: our chip design was flawless, validated thoroughly on the initial MPW runs. But when it transitioned to full-scale production at TSMC, the world's leading semiconductor foundry, the yield, which should have been near one hundred percent based on the MPW results, had utterly collapsed.

"This doesn't make sense," Bill said, his voice filled with disbelief. "I've never seen anything like this in my career."

Our key advisor, Dr. Jackson Hu, was equally puzzled. "Something fundamental has changed between the test runs and mass production. We need to investigate immediately."

I stayed up all night assessing the situation and speaking with various parties. We decided that as soon as Jackson gathered more information from the design house, I would fly to Taiwan to evaluate the situation firsthand.

For Bitfury, this technical glitch was an existential crisis. We had bet everything on this 16 nm chip. We went all in. A non-functional chip, coupled with our existing customer commitments for the new hardware, had catastrophic implications. The survival of Bitfury hung by a thread.

> Taiwan Semiconductor Manufacturing Company (TSMC) is the world's largest contract chip manufacturer, producing processors for companies like Apple, NVIDIA, and AMD. Founded in 1987 by visionary Dr. Morris Chang, TSMC pioneered the foundry model where companies design chips but outsource manufacturing. By 2016, TSMC controlled over fifty percent of the global foundry market and was considered the gold standard for semiconductor manufacturing quality and reliability. A yield failure at TSMC was virtually unprecedented, making Bitfury's situation particularly shocking.

As I stared out at Hong Kong's glittering skyline, I couldn't help but reflect on the pattern that seemed to define my life. From the collapse of Soviet certainties to the wild swings of Bitcoin's value, to now this semiconductor crisis, prosperity and stability had always come with the shadow of sudden, unexpected challenges. The Georgian tea ceremony came to mind—the tradition of dipping sweet treats into bitter tea, a reminder that life always blends the sweet with the bitter.

The taste in my mouth now was decidedly bitter. But just as I had navigated the collapse of one world and helped build another, I knew we would find a way through this crisis too. The resilience forged in my childhood, strengthened through Bitcoin's early turbulence, would now be tested once more.

Taiwan: The Hunt for Answers

The flight to Taiwan felt interminable, my mind cycling through scenarios and contingencies. Upon landing, it became brutally clear that something unusual was happening. Jackson arranged dinner with Sysman and our top chip designer, Vlad, at a local restaurant.

"We just had a meeting with TSMC and GUC," Jackson said gravely as we took our seats. "The situation is worse than we initially thought. Out of the first batch, less than one percent of the chips are functional."

I slammed my fist on the table, causing nearby diners to glance our way. "That's impossible! We had ninety-nine percent yield on the MPW!"

Vlad, our chip design lead, looked exhausted, with dark circles under his eyes. "We've combed through every line of the design code. There are no errors. The design is identical to what we validated on the MPW."

"Then what happened between MPW and mass production?" I demanded, struggling to keep my voice level.

Jackson sighed deeply. "That's exactly what we're trying to figure out. The wafer test report shows the electrical properties of the chips are completely off from what we expected. TSMC suspects there might be manufacturing issues."

Global Unichip Corporation (GUC) is a TSMC affiliate company that provides chip design services and acts as an intermediary between TSMC's foundry operations and fabless chip companies. When companies like Bitfury design chips for TSMC manufacturing, GUC often handles the technical interface, ensuring designs meet manufacturing requirements and troubleshooting any issues that arise during production.

"I am as upset as you are about the new wafer results," Jackson continued, his voice measured but concerned. "My observation right now focuses mainly on the wafer execution. I suspect some process parameters affected the chip behavior that we didn't encounter in MPW."

"How is this possible?" I pressed, bewildered. "What are we talking about? Did they use different materials?"

Vlad shook his head, pushing aside his barely touched food. "It's more subtle than that. Our design operates at half the standard voltage for these processes. We're pushing the boundaries of what's possible."

My frustration boiled over. "We prepaid them tens of millions! It's like a thunderbolt in the middle of a clear day!"

"I know, I know," Jackson tried to calm me. "I've already reached out to senior leadership at TSMC. We need to be strategic here."

The sense of déjà vu was overwhelming. Once again, I found myself facing a seemingly insurmountable challenge where the rules of the game had suddenly changed. Just as in the post-Soviet chaos, when my parents watched their life savings evaporate overnight, we were now watching our massive investment vaporize due to factors beyond our control.

The next morning, we met at the GUC offices. The atmosphere was tense as we waited in their sleek conference room.

Jim Lai, CEO of GUC, entered with his team, his expression carefully neutral.

"Jim," I began without preamble, "How did we go from ninety-nine percent yield on the MPW to one percent in production? We followed every design parameter you gave us."

His response was measured. "We're investigating all possibilities. There could be variances in the manufacturing process that weren't apparent in the smaller MPW run."

"That's not good enough," I replied, my voice steady but firm. "We've staked our company's future on these chips. We have customers waiting."

Vlad jumped in, technical data in hand. "Our design was validated against your models. There were no red flags. Nothing that would indicate this level of failure."

Jim nodded sympathetically, but I could tell we weren't getting the full story. "We're committed to finding the root cause. TSMC is running tests on different wafers with various parameters."

After several more hours of technical discussions that went nowhere, we left with more questions than answers. Back at the hotel, I called Val.

"They're stonewalling us," I said, pacing in my room. "We need to escalate this directly to TSMC's leadership."

"I agree," Val replied. "This smells like a cover-up. Get Jackson to pull every string he has."

Jackson, who was beside me, nodded grimly. "I'll contact Lora Ho, TSMC's CFO. We need someone at the GUC board level to look into this."

In the days that followed, a flurry of emails revealed the gravity of our situation. Vlad's analysis showed that the process deviation was far more significant than GUC had admitted.

"Vlad suspects the transistor properties are the culprit," Jackson reported after another conference call. "According to TSMC's published specifications, all other wafers are in spec. So let's keep our fingers crossed."

But our hopes dimmed as each test wafer came back with similarly abysmal results. Jackson arranged an emergency meeting with TSMC's top brass, including Maria Marced, TSMC's president of Europe.

In that tense meeting at TSMC's European headquarters in Amsterdam, Maria began with diplomatic platitudes. We understand your concerns and are committed to finding a solution."

I cut straight to the chase. "Maria, we're bleeding hundreds of thousands of dollars every day this isn't resolved. Our customers are waiting. Our investors are anxious. We need to find a technical solution in order to survive."

And then Vlad presented compelling evidence, spreading technical diagrams across the polished conference table. "The engineering wafers missed the target by a huge margin. They were manufactured with completely different electrical properties than what we specified."

Maria's expression changed subtly. It was clear she hadn't been told the full extent of the problem.

"This, this is highly unusual," she responded, clearly concerned. "I need to look into this further."

Jackson, ever the diplomat, stepped in. "Maria, we need to move beyond blame. What matters is finding a path forward that works for both parties."

Over the next months, a pattern emerged in our exchanges with TSMC. Every potential solution was met with complications. Every promising test wafer showed only marginal improvement. The process of identifying the exact problem was painstakingly slow.

"This is absolutely mind-boggling," I wrote to Jackson after another disappointing update. "We achieved near-perfect yield on the MPW at the world's most advanced semiconductor fab, and now production gives us almost nothing? It's as though we've entered some alternate reality where the laws of physics have changed. This defies all logic and engineering principles!"

Jackson's reply was thoughtful. "They have so much experience debugging, and it shows. They're doing the obvious things—looking for 'variance' in the processing or product completion. The commonality across the shuttle and production was the mask set, so that's unlikely to be the cause. The packaging and possibly electrical connections are the obvious big changes to examine, and they're doing that."

By April, we were deep in negotiations with TSMC, with Jackson serving as our bridge. We pushed for compensation, priority on new wafer runs, and anything that would help us salvage our position.

"TSMC's standard operating procedure stated that if the Bitfury design worked in the models, it would work in silicon," Vlad insisted during one particularly heated call. "We were all blindsided by this failure."

During a rare moment of downtime, Val and I found ourselves at a small fish restaurant in Amsterdam, seeking refuge in the simple pleasure of fresh seafood and anonymity.

"You know what keeps me up at night?" Val said, picking at his herring. "Not just the chips failing. It's that while we're stuck here with TSMC, the Chinese competitors are expanding aggressively. Every day we're delayed is a day they gain market share."

I nodded grimly, watching boats go by in the canal, tourists waving as they glided past the centuries-old buildings. "The timing couldn't be worse. With the Bitcoin halving coming up, miners everywhere are upgrading their equipment. If we miss this window…"

> The Bitcoin halving event, which occurs approximately every four years, reduces the reward for mining new blocks by half. The 2016 halving, scheduled for July, would reduce mining rewards from 25 to 12.5 Bitcoins per block. This created urgency for miners to upgrade to more efficient hardware before the event, as less efficient equipment would become unprofitable after the reward reduction. For hardware manufacturers like Bitfury, the pre-halving period represented a crucial sales window.

Val didn't need me to finish the thought. We both knew the stakes.

After months of detective work, our engineers, alongside TSMC's team, finally isolated two critical issues: the gate length in the transistors was too small, and there were inconsistencies in the doping process that affected the electrical properties of the chips. These were parameters that neither we nor TSMC had properly accounted for with our ultra-low voltage design.

"The larger gate length has improved efficiency significantly compared to the original results," Jackson reported in a breakthrough email. "We now have a 'good enough solution' to mass produce our chips and ship them to waiting customers."

But the clock had been ticking relentlessly. By early summer, frustration mounted as negotiations continued to drag. Despite Jackson's tireless efforts and connections in Taiwan, Maria and her team seemed to be stalling.

"We need to change tactics," I told Val during one of our late-night strategy calls. "TSMC isn't moving fast enough, and we're bleeding cash every day."

"What do you have in mind?" Val asked, his voice weary but resolute.

"I think it's time to pull in some bigger diplomatic guns," I replied.

Through our numerous visits with regulators in Washington, DC, we were introduced to Thomas "Mack" McLarty, the founder of McLarty Associates and former White House Chief of Staff under President Bill Clinton. I had a gut feeling Mack would have a solution for us.

> Thomas "Mack" McLarty served as White House Chief of Staff from 1993 to 1994 and later founded McLarty Associates, a strategic advisory firm specializing in international business and government relations. The firm's ability to navigate complex international business disputes through diplomatic channels made it particularly valuable for companies facing challenges in global markets. McLarty's connections with senior officials worldwide provided unique leverage in resolving commercial disputes.

We flew to Washington, DC, for a private meeting with McLarty at his firm's offices. The place exuded quiet power—understated elegance and the subtle hum of influence. As we laid out our case in meticulous detail, Mack listened intently, occasionally taking notes.

"This is precisely the kind of situation where diplomatic back channels can help," he said, leaning back in his leather chair. "Dr. Morris Chang is highly respected in both business and diplomatic circles. I believe Ambassador Negroponte has a longstanding relationship with him."

Ambassador John Negroponte, who had served as the first Director of National Intelligence and the US Ambassador to the United Nations, was now affiliated with McLarty Associates.

Dr. Morris Chang founded TSMC in 1987 and served as its chairman and CEO until 2018. Often called the "father of the foundry industry," Chang revolutionized semiconductor manufacturing by creating the pure-play foundry model. His influence extended far beyond business into Taiwanese politics and international diplomacy. Direct appeals to Chang were rare and typically reserved for matters of significant strategic importance.

"Let me see what we can do through diplomatic channels," McLarty assured us. "Sometimes the most effective approach is the most discreet one."

The very next day, we received a message that contact had been made with Dr. Chang, and that "he listened intently and promised to help." Sure enough, within a day of that message, we received an urgent email from Maria saying she was ready to meet and finalize our agreement.

When we met with Maria shortly after, she couldn't help but ask, "Why did you feel it necessary to bother Dr. Chang with this matter?"

"The fate of our company is on the line," I replied simply. "We have some personal connections, and we felt it was important to ensure everyone understood the gravity of our situation."

From that moment on, things moved remarkably smoothly. The power of strategic thinking, creative problem-solving, and knowing which levers to pull had proven vital in navigating this crisis.

By late August, we had signed the settlement agreement. The terms: all of the already reproduced wafers for free, all money we paid to GUC would be used as credit to produce new wafers, and performance guarantees for future production.

Val sent an email to our team: "Today, a very important milestone has been achieved—we signed the settlement agreement with TSMC. I want to thank everyone for their hard work and contribution to this!"

The Bitter Victory: Last Man Standing

The victory was bittersweet. We had survived, but at tremendous cost. Those nine months proved instrumental, but not in the way we had hoped.

Would things have played out differently if our perfect chip had launched on time? Absolutely. The market dynamics, the competitive landscape, perhaps even Bitcoin's trajectory, might have shifted. But the crisis taught us, in the harshest way possible, that external factors beyond our control will intervene.

Success isn't about brilliance; it's about resilience. The way we rallied, pooled resources, navigated the complex relationship with TSMC, and ultimately survived—albeit with significant momentum lost—embodied our "impossible is nothing" spirit.

What made our survival all the more remarkable was that 2016 proved to be a graveyard for Bitcoin mining companies worldwide. While we were fighting our battle with TSMC, the industry landscape underwent a dramatic consolidation.

The 2016 Bitcoin mining industry consolidation was driven by several factors: the approaching halving event, increased competition from Chinese manufacturers, and the general difficulty of competing in the ASIC development arms race. Many companies that had raised significant funding in 2013-2014 found themselves unable to deliver competitive products by 2016. The combination of technical challenges, market timing, and capital requirements proved insurmountable for all but the most resilient companies.

One evening after closing the TSMC settlement, Val and I sat on the rooftop bar of our Amsterdam hotel, watching lightning illuminate the city.

"Did you see the news about KnCMiner?" Val asked, scrolling through his phone.

"They filed for bankruptcy?" I asked, though I already knew the answer.

Val nodded. "Once the golden child of European ASIC manufacturing, they took millions in pre-orders but couldn't deliver a competitive chip. They couldn't handle the combination of rising network difficulty, falling block rewards ahead of the halving."

"And they're not alone," I added, taking a sip of whiskey. "Spondoolies in Israel ceased operations earlier in May. Court-ordered liquidation. They ran out of capital before they could release their next-generation hardware. The price wars with Chinese manufacturers were too much."

"Even 21e6 is pivoting away from hardware," Val continued. "Despite their massive $120 million funding round, they've stopped selling their miners entirely, focusing on software instead."

We sat in silence for a moment, letting the implications sink in. Around us, Amsterdam's lights sparkled like a circuit board come to life.

"By the end of this year," I said finally, "we'll be the only non-Chinese player of significance left in the mining hardware business."

Val raised his glass. "To being the last man standing."

"To survival," I echoed.

The stakes felt even higher with my second son, David, on the way. During those dark months of uncertainty, I couldn't help but worry about how this business catastrophe might affect my growing family. The responsibility weighed heavily—not just to the company and our investors, but to the people who depended on me most.

If you ask me when I truly feared it was all over during the entire Bitfury journey, that summer of 2016 was undoubtedly it. The breaking point. I remember standing alone on the balcony of my Amsterdam hotel room one night, looking out at the city lights, thinking, "Here we are, this incredible startup with amazing momentum and one catastrophic problem, likely not even our fault, could wipe us out." I had invested my own capital, my friends' capital, everything. The thought of telling my family we were bankrupt, of starting again from scratch with no clear path forward, was terrifying.

Yet, even in those dark moments, a deeper conviction remained. Hesitation never truly took root. Somehow, I knew we would be okay. I can't explain the source of that certainty, but the vision of Bitfury succeeding, of contributing to an age of technological abundance, persisted. It provided strange but vital courage and comfort in the darkest hours.

The stress was immense. But when the dust settled, the core principle held: Impossible was nothing. We had faced the abyss and found a way through. We had done it. We had survived both our own crisis and the industry-wide extinction event that claimed so many of our peers.

As we prepared to leave Amsterdam, I received a text from Bill: "Most startups die from self-inflicted wounds. The truly exceptional ones survive the wounds inflicted by fate. You guys are in the second category now."

I smiled, typing back: "What doesn't kill you makes you stronger."

"No," came Bill's reply seconds later. "What doesn't kill you makes you Bitfury."

With the semiconductor crisis behind us, albeit at great cost, it was time to refocus on our broader vision. The silver lining of this ordeal was that it had forced us to accelerate our diversification beyond mining hardware. Now, with both mining and software initiatives advancing in parallel, we were poised to reshape Bitcoin mining and the very infrastructure of trust in the digital age.

CHAPTER 7

IN LAND TITLES WE TRUST

The future is already here—it's just not evenly distributed.

—William Gibson

Even as we battled our semiconductor crisis, Bitfury's vision was expanding beyond hardware. The 16 nm chip delay had taught us a crucial lesson: putting all your eggs in one basket was a recipe for disaster.

"We're miners at heart," Val said during a rainy San Francisco strategy session in early 2016. "But what if we could bridge the gap between Bitcoin and big business?"

The idea was simple yet revolutionary. While everyone else was building "private blockchains" (which, let's be honest, were just fancy databases), we'd create something different—a hybrid that gave enterprises privacy while anchoring their data to Bitcoin's unbreakable security.

This thinking led to Project Exonum, our answer to the enterprise blockchain dilemma. Think of it as having your cake and eating it too: private operations with public security.

"As miners, there's beautiful symmetry here," I pointed out. "These security timestamps generate Bitcoin transaction fees. We're creating a new revenue stream while strengthening the entire ecosystem."

"If we're going to do this," I told Val over khinkali and wine at the Georgian restaurant Shoti in Kyiv, "we need the best minds in the business."

Ukraine, with its abundance of mathematical geniuses and coding wizards, was the perfect hunting ground. We began recruiting like a tech-hungry dragon hoarding talent instead of gold.

Ukraine's emergence as a global tech talent hub was rooted in the Soviet Union's emphasis on mathematics and engineering education. Universities in Kyiv, Kharkiv, and Lviv produced world-class programmers who often worked remotely for Silicon Valley companies. The combination of exceptional technical education, relatively low costs, and strong English proficiency made Ukraine an attractive destination for tech companies seeking top-tier development teams.

Then Marat called with an idea that would change everything.

"Guys, I've been thinking," he said. "Remote work is fine, but magic happens when brilliant minds collide in person. I've found the perfect space—a 1,000-square-meter penthouse overlooking Kyiv's Olympic Stadium."

The twenty-eighth-floor penthouse quickly transformed into something between Google's campus and a mad scientist's laboratory. Walking in, you'd find Ping-Pong and chess battles raging next to intense coding sessions, a fully stocked kitchen, beds for those too engrossed to go home, and a library ranging from *Only the Paranoid Survive* by Andy Grove to *The Rust Programming Language* book (dog-eared and annotated by half the team). Anya, our office manager, kept the entire operation running smoothly.

What happened next exceeded our wildest dreams. The space became a magnet for Ukraine's brightest—national chess champions, physics prodigies, and mathematical savants, all drawn by the promise of building the future.

"This is exactly what I envisioned," Marat beamed, surveying his kingdom of controlled chaos. "Look at them—they're not just writing code, they're writing history."

The Property Rights Revolution

The software application breakthrough came in June during yet another Necker gathering where we'd been discussing Hernando de Soto's *The Mystery of Capital*—his groundbreaking work on how unclear property rights trap trillions in "dead capital" worldwide. Earlier that day, *Forbes* reporter Laura Shin, who was emceeing the event, had Hernando on a panel and was probing him on blockchain applications of his concepts. She also used the special occasion to launch her podcast *Unchained*.

Laura Shin's *Unchained* became one of crypto's most influential media platforms, featuring in-depth interviews with industry leaders, developers, and regulators. Launching in 2016, the podcast filled a crucial gap in crypto journalism by providing long-form, substantive conversations about blockchain technology and its implications. Shin's background as a senior editor at *Forbes* gave her the credibility and connections to attract high-profile guests, while her direct interviewing style and technical understanding helped demystify complex topics for mainstream audiences. The podcast's success helped establish crypto as a legitimate beat in financial journalism.

That evening, after the day's intense discussions and hearing Imogen Heap playing a beautiful solo version of "Let Go," Bill Tai and I soaked in the jacuzzi under a canopy of stars, when an idea struck me like lightning.

"Bill," I said, the wheels turning in my head, "Hernando's concept of dead capital has always haunted me. Growing up in Georgia, I watched relatives unable to prove they owned homes their families had lived in for generations."

This wasn't theoretical for me. After the Soviet collapse, property rights were a mess. My own family couldn't use their property as collateral or sell it fairly because ownership was unclear—a problem affecting millions across the former Soviet Union.

Post-Soviet property rights were particularly complex because the communist system had abolished private land ownership. When the Soviet Union collapsed, many properties lacked clear documentation of ownership, creating a legal limbo that persisted for decades. This uncertainty prevented property owners from accessing credit markets, selling their assets at fair value, or making improvements, effectively trapping wealth and hindering economic development across the region.

"What if blockchain could unlock all that trapped wealth?" I continued, sitting up so fast I nearly splashed Bill. "What if we could create an immutable record of land ownership that no corrupt official could tamper with?"

Bill's eyes widened. "You're talking about transforming property rights for billions of people."

The next morning, still buzzing with excitement, we had breakfast with Hernando.

"Your work has been revolutionary," I began, "but implementation has always been the challenge. We have the technology now—blockchain can provide the transparent, tamper-proof ledger you've always envisioned."

"I would love to explore this," Hernando replied, his academic reserve giving way to genuine excitement. That was all I needed to hear.

After getting the green light from Hernando, we moved at the speed of light. Within weeks, we were in Tbilisi pitching the idea to government officials.

"So you're telling us," said Papuna Ugrekhelidze, Chairman of Georgia's Public Registry, leaning forward intently, "we could have a land system that's transparent, tamper-proof, and recognized internationally?"

"Exactly," confirmed Remi, our advisor on the ground. "Imagine foreign investors knowing property rights are rock-solid. Think about citizens easily mortgaging their land to start businesses."

The National Agency of Public Registry of Georgia had already undergone significant modernization as part of the country's post-Rose Revolution reforms. The agency had digitized records and streamlined processes, but blockchain offered something unprecedented: a tamper-proof system that could guarantee property rights even if governments changed or corruption attempted to infiltrate the system. This was particularly significant for a country that had experienced multiple upheavals in its recent history.

For me, this moment was deeply personal. The country whose economic collapse had shaped my family's experience was now poised to pioneer technology that could prevent such catastrophes for future generations.

Georgian tea was served with traditional watermelon and cherry preserves as the minister consulted his team. Then, with surprising decisiveness, he stood and extended his hand.

"When can we begin?"

By April, at a ceremony at Georgia's Ministry of Justice, we announced the world's first blockchain-based land registry. The current system required physically visiting a registry, taking a full day, and paying anything from $50 to $200. Our solution would move this online and cost just pennies.

"The Republic of Georgia can lead the world in revolutionizing land titling," the Minister declared.

Hernando added, "Of 7.3 billion people globally, only 2 billion have effective legal title to their assets. Blockchain is the missing link."

Success in Georgia opened floodgates. In July, we publicly released Exonum as open-source software, with Val taking the stage at a packed London room at Rocco Forte Brown's hotel.

"This is blockchain's next evolution, bringing enterprise-grade capabilities to the technology," he declared.

Lawrence Wintermeyer, CEO of Innovate Finance, and Ben Brabyn from Level39, London's fintech accelerator, were in the audience. Lawrence leaned over to me. "This opens doors far beyond cryptocurrency. Governments skeptical of Bitcoin might embrace this."

The same month, we unveiled another initiative born on Necker. Together with my Johns Hopkins classmate Tomicah Tillemann, we launched the Blockchain Trust Accelerator with New America and the National Democratic Institute.

> The Blockchain Trust Accelerator represented one of the first organized efforts to apply blockchain technology to governance and social impact rather than purely financial applications. This marked a crucial shift in how blockchain was perceived. It went from a tool for financial speculation and cryptocurrency trading to a fundamental infrastructure that could address challenges like corruption, identity verification, and transparent governance in developing nations.

"While tremendous capital flows into financial blockchain applications," Tomicah explained at our D.C. launch, "we want to ensure this technology makes people's lives better, not just their bank accounts."

We even hosted former Secretary of State Madeleine Albright at San Francisco's exclusive Battery Club. "Blockchain can transform governance globally," I presented. It felt surreal explaining cryptocurrency to America's former top diplomat.

The Lightning Collaboration

Our Kyiv brain trust wasn't idle. Working with Lightning Labs founder Elizabeth Stark, they tackled Bitcoin's biggest challenge: transaction speed.

"Without solving scalability, mass adoption hits a wall," Elizabeth explained during one brainstorming session, her intensity filling the room.

> The Lightning Network was a proposed "Layer Two" solution to Bitcoin's scalability limitations. While Bitcoin could only process about seven transactions per second on its main blockchain, Lightning enabled near-instantaneous micropayments by creating payment channels between users. The challenge was routing payments efficiently through this network of channels without requiring each node to know the entire network topology—a problem that required sophisticated algorithmic solutions.

"Our team has been obsessing over this," Marat replied. "What if we reimagine how payments route through the network?"

This collaboration produced "Flare," an algorithm that sounds boring but was actually revolutionary—it made Bitcoin transactions faster and cheaper without compromising security. When French company ACINQ successfully tested it, Elizabeth sent congratulations: "This is exactly the innovation Bitcoin needs!"

During a celebration dinner with our Kyiv team, I raised a toast. Looking around the table at these brilliant twenty-somethings who were reshaping global finance, I couldn't help but smile. "To solving the unsolvable with mathematical elegance!"

Candles vs. Electricity

By 2017, our software initiatives were exploding. In a hotel overlooking Kyiv's Maidan Square, we signed what Val called "the biggest government blockchain deal ever" with Ukraine.

"This is personal," Val told officials after signing. "I've seen how corruption undermines trust here. This technology can rewrite that story."

We deployed Exonum for Ukraine's government auction platform, bringing transparency to a system historically riddled with corruption. Meanwhile, in Georgia, we'd successfully recorded three hundred thousand land titles on the blockchain, making them virtually unhackable.

The impact rippled globally. Harvard Business School published a case study titled "Bitfury: Blockchain for Government," authored by professors Mitchell Weiss and Elena Corsi.[7] The case examined how we were transforming government services and creating new standards for property rights protection. The case study started off with my quote comparing blockchain to electricity: "The world is changing fast. Blockchain is like electricity. Some are stuck making candles and refuse to change; only those that embrace change will prevail."

Academic validation felt good, but the real satisfaction came from knowing we were solving real problems for real people.

"This is a technological evolution," Hernando observed during a Tbilisi visit, "But it's also a governance revolution."

One evening, standing on a Tbilisi restaurant balcony as the sun painted the ancient city gold, Val turned to me thoughtfully.

"Remember when Bitcoin was just about digital money?"

I nodded, sipping Mukuzani, Georgian red wine. "Now we're transforming land registries, government auctions, voting systems…"

"This is just the beginning," Val said. "The real revolution is beyond finance—it's in how societies build trust."

Reflecting on our journey from mining Bitcoins to revolutionizing property rights, I felt we were fulfilling blockchain's true promise. Beyond hype and speculation, we were building systems that empowered people and created foundations for prosperity.

"To think," I laughed, raising my glass, "this all started with a conversation in a jacuzzi."

Val clinked his glass against mine. "The best ideas often do."

As darkness fell over Tbilisi, I felt profound purpose. The semiconductor crisis had nearly broken us, but pushed us to innovate. Now we were using blockchain to reshape the foundations of trust itself.

"Gaumarjos," I toasted in Georgian. "To victory."

"To trust," Val added, his glass catching the last light. "The most valuable asset of all."

CHAPTER 8

RISING SUN, RISING BITCOIN

Fall down seven times, Get up eight.

—Japanese Proverb

As we sorted out our chip situation with TSMC and finally launched our 16 nm chip, we closed the $30 million round with Credit China, coupled with a large order for chips. Given our firm's expansion into Asia, it was crucial to recruit a Head of Asia, and who better than my Wharton classmate Greg Li?

Greg, a Hawaiian of Chinese descent, had been a good friend since business school. I'd orange-pilled him on Bitcoin years earlier, and we'd kept in touch as cryptocurrency gained traction. Based in Singapore with his family, he was perfectly positioned to manage our Credit China relationship and expand into new Asian markets.

As we were closing the Credit China deal, I met Greg for dinner at Dragonfly in Hong Kong.

"Are you in, Greg?" I asked, leaning across the table. "This will be the ride of our lives."

Without hesitation, he replied, "I'm in."

From that moment, Greg became our Head of Asia, arriving just as the region was embracing cryptocurrency in unprecedented ways. In April 2017, Japan became the first major economy to officially recognize Bitcoin as legal tender for payments through an amendment to its Payment Services Act. While not classifying Bitcoin as currency per se, Japan treated it as having "asset-like value," usable for settlement, giving Bitcoin formal status and legitimacy in commerce.

Japan's decision to regulate rather than ban Bitcoin set a crucial precedent for other developed nations. The Payment Services Act amendment required cryptocurrency exchanges to register with the Financial Services Agency, implementing consumer protections while legitimizing the industry. This regulatory clarity attracted global crypto businesses to establish Japanese operations and gave institutional investors confidence to enter the market.

"This is a game-changer," I told Val during a late-night call. "Japan just legitimized what we've been building all these years."

"It creates a powerful precedent," Val agreed. "Other countries will be watching closely. If Japan succeeds, others will follow."

As soon as we heard this news, Bill, Greg, and I were literally on the next flight to Tokyo. We leveraged Bill's extensive network to arrange meetings with SoftBank, SBI Holdings, and Rakuten, as well as key regulatory officials. Greg proved invaluable, helping navigate cultural nuances during what became an incredibly productive trip with over forty meetings in a single week.

Through Bill, we connected with Morio Kurosaki, who became our key advisor in Japan, opening doors throughout the financial establishment. His influence in the Japanese tech ecosystem was legendary. Morio-san was one of the main backers and board members of Bill's co-founded IPInfusion—the company that invented "software defined networks." His semiconductor roots stretched back to Intel's early days in Japan, where he had served as an executive during the company's formative expansion into Asia.

Now running his own VC fund, Morio-san had co-invested with Bill in numerous successful ventures, including Zoom, Treasure Data, Voxer, and Tango. He had established himself as the essential bridge between Japanese capital and American innovation, understanding both cultures with a depth few others could match.

"Relationships are everything in Japan," Morio-san told us during our first dinner together at a traditional ryotei. "Technology matters, of course, but without the right introductions, even the best technology won't get a hearing."

"That's precisely why we value your guidance," I replied, raising my sake cup in appreciation. "We need someone who understands both the technology landscape and the cultural nuances."

Beyond his business acumen, Morio-san was also a renowned oenophile and one of Japan's most notable exclusive wine importers. He particularly appreciated the unique character of Georgian wines, with their eight-thousand-year viticultural tradition that predates European winemaking. From time to time, I would send him shipments of rare Georgian vintages from small family vineyards that still used the traditional qvevri clay vessels for fermentation.

> Georgian winemaking represents one of humanity's oldest continuous traditions, with archaeological evidence of wine production dating back 8,000 years. The traditional qvevri method involves fermenting and aging wine in large clay vessels buried underground, creating unique flavors and textures that have attracted wine connoisseurs worldwide.

"What a lovely wine," he would invariably comment after receiving these packages. "I must come visit Georgia one day to see these ancient vineyards myself."

"My door is always open," I would answer, recognizing how these cultural exchanges strengthened our business relationships.

The timing was perfect. There was a palpable feeling of optimism in Tokyo about Bitcoin's future. Exchanges were gearing up for more users, retail outlets were beginning to accept Bitcoin, and financial institutions were strategizing their approach to cryptocurrency. Three of the top seven exchanges worldwide were Japanese companies, with Bitflyer trading some seventy percent of Japan's volumes.

Building Alliances in Tokyo

While we met with all of the top Japanese financial institutions, one of our most promising connections was with Daiwa Securities Group, Japan's second-largest securities firm with approximately $185 billion in assets. Their Financial Innovation Committee had recently been established to explore practical applications of fintech with blockchain technology as a key focus area.

"What impresses me most about Bitfury," said Mr. Takashi, head of Daiwa's innovation team, during our meeting at their headquarters, "is how you've evolved from a mining company to a full-stack blockchain technology provider. That kind of versatility is exactly what we're looking for in strategic partners."

"We believe mining is just the foundation," I explained. "The real opportunity lies in building the infrastructure for the next generation of the Internet—a more secure, transparent, and efficient system."

This initial meeting would prove extraordinarily fruitful. Daiwa would not only become an investor in Bitfury but also establish a substantial commercial relationship, ordering our mining servers to offer to their institutional clients seeking exposure to Bitcoin mining. This win-win relationship would continue for many years, with Daiwa acting as both investor and distribution channel for our technology in the Japanese market.

In fact, through our early exploits with Daiwa, we would eventually register Japan's first regulated Bitcoin Mining Fund, creating a structure that allowed Japanese institutional investors to gain exposure to Bitcoin mining within their existing regulatory framework. This pioneering vehicle would onboard numerous Japanese clients who otherwise might have remained on the sidelines of the crypto revolution.

Our time in Japan was a whirlwind of high-level meetings with the country's most influential financial and technology players. We met with founders and senior leadership from Softbank, SBI, DMM, and GMO, all exploring potential partnerships in different aspects of our business.

Bill's network proved invaluable once again when he connected us with Harvard alumnus Hiroshi Mikitani, the founder and CEO of Rakuten, often called "Japan's Amazon." Mikitani-san hosted us in his stunning office overlooking Tokyo.

Rakuten is Japan's largest e-commerce platform, with over 100 million registered users and annual gross merchandise sales exceeding $14 billion. The company's ecosystem includes banking, securities, mobile services, and digital content, making it one of Japan's most comprehensive Internet conglomerates.

"E-commerce is ripe for blockchain integration," Mikitani-san observed after we explained Bitfury's technology stack. "The friction in payments remains too high, especially across borders."

"That's exactly our thinking," Val responded enthusiastically. "Imagine a future where micropayments flow as easily as information does today."

Mikitani-san nodded thoughtfully. "Rakuten has always embraced disruptive technology. We were early to mobile commerce when others hesitated. Perhaps we should be equally bold with blockchain."

As our meeting concluded, Mikitani-san stood and walked to his bookshelf. "Here is something I want you to have," he said, presenting me with a signed copy of his book, *The Power to Compete*.[8] The personal inscription reflected our shared vision for technological innovation and Japan's role in the global digital economy.

This meeting laid the groundwork for future collaboration, as Rakuten would go on to become one of Japan's most crypto-forward companies.

Another pivotal connection came through our meeting with Dentsu, Japan's largest advertising and public relations firm. With annual revenue exceeding ¥1 trillion and operations in over 140 countries following their acquisition of the UK-based Aegis Group, Dentsu represented a potential partner of tremendous influence.

The meeting took place in Dentsu's imposing Tokyo headquarters, where we were greeted by Mr. Yamamoto, their Chief Innovation Officer, and his team.

"We've been following blockchain technology for some time," Mr. Yamamoto began, after the customary exchange of business cards and pleasantries. "But we've struggled to find practical applications beyond cryptocurrency speculation."

Val leaned forward, immediately recognizing the opportunity. "That's precisely where our Exonum framework comes in. It brings blockchain's trust and transparency to enterprise applications without the volatility of cryptocurrencies."

"Can you give us a concrete example?" asked one of Dentsu's senior technologists.

"Imagine applying it to digital advertising," I explained. "The industry loses billions to fraud each year. A blockchain solution could verify ad delivery, ensure viewability, and create an immutable record of the entire process—eliminating the trust gaps that enable fraud."

Mr. Yamamoto's eyes lit up. "This aligns perfectly with the challenges our clients face. The lack of transparency in digital advertising has been a persistent problem."

We spent the next two hours exploring potential applications, with Dentsu's team growing increasingly animated as they grasped the transformative potential of Exonum for their business.

"We should formalize a partnership," Mr. Yamamoto concluded decisively. "Dentsu can bring these solutions to our clients across Japan and globally."

"We'd welcome that," Val replied. "Our technology combined with your reach and relationships could accelerate adoption dramatically."

As we prepared to leave, Mr. Yamamoto surprised us with an unexpected question. "We're also interested in exploring a strategic investment in Bitfury. Would that possibility be open for discussion?"

Val and I exchanged glances. "We would certainly be open to that conversation," I replied.

This meeting would bear fruit in multiple ways: Dentsu not only partnered with us to explore blockchain applications across their vast network but also ultimately became an equity investor in Bitfury, further cementing our foothold in the Japanese market.

During these meetings, I couldn't help but share a vision that had been forming in my mind since Japan legalized Bitcoin.

One of our most promising connections was with bitFlyer, Japan's largest exchange and the second-largest worldwide by volume in Q1 2017. We had three separate meetings with founder Yuzo Kano in a single week—a formal meeting at bitFlyer, a Japan Blockchain Association meeting (where Yuzo served as President), and evening drinks with Bill Tai and several others from the Bitcoin industry.

During our evening gathering at a hidden whiskey bar in Ginza, Yuzo-san shared his vision for bitFlyer's future. "We're creating the financial infrastructure for a new digital economy," he explained, pouring another round of 18-year-old Yamazaki.

"That aligns perfectly with our vision at Bitfury," I responded. "The technology needs to move beyond speculation and into practical applications that deliver real value."

Following the regulatory clarity, Bitcoin was seeing remarkable adoption among Japanese retailers. The next day, Bill and I decided to experience this firsthand with a shopping expedition to Bic Camera, one of Japan's largest electronics retailers, which had begun accepting Bitcoin through its partnership with bitFlyer.

Bic Camera's adoption of Bitcoin payments represented a significant milestone for cryptocurrency acceptance in Japan. As one of the country's largest electronics retailers with over forty stores nationwide, their decision to accept Bitcoin demonstrated how quickly mainstream businesses embraced the technology following regulatory clarity.

"Let's put this to the test," Bill suggested with his characteristic enthusiasm. "Let's buy something using Bitcoin!"

Inside the massive store, we selected a bottle of premium Japanese whiskey. At checkout, I pulled out my Xapo card, which was linked to my Bitcoin wallet.

"Bitcoin payment, please," I told the cashier in rudimentary Japanese.

Without missing a beat, she processed the transaction through a special terminal. Within seconds, the payment was complete.

"That was smoother than most credit card transactions in the States," Bill remarked as we left with our purchase.

"This is what mass adoption looks like," I replied. "Everyday utility."

As we walked out of the store, I glanced at my phone to check the Bitcoin price—around 135,000 yen per coin.

"You know," I said to Bill with a slightly rueful smile, "that whiskey we just bought will probably end up being the most expensive bottle in history. That amount of Bitcoin might be worth a hundred times more someday," I added ominously, my voice dropping to a near whisper as if sharing a prophecy.

Bill laughed. "The price of progress! Consider it a historical artifact—your contribution to cryptocurrency adoption in Japan."

"Well, when you put it that way," I grinned, "it's worth every satoshi. Let's just be sure to enjoy it properly."

Establishing a Foothold in Japan

The Park Hyatt Tokyo became our temporary headquarters—a fitting base for our ambitions in a city that had always embraced technological innovation. From our rooms high above the sprawling metropolis, we could feel the momentum building for blockchain adoption in Japan.

"There's something poetic about discussing Bitcoin's future with this view," Greg remarked one evening as we watched the sunset paint the city in hues of orange and gold, with Mount Fuji visible in the distance. "This is where the future happens first."

While there was some interest in deploying our servers in Japan, electricity costs north of ten cents per kWh posed a challenge compared to our operations in Canada, Iceland and Georgia. Still, some potential partners believed Japanese investors might accept lower returns to keep assets in-country.

As Daniel Saito, an entrepreneur who had been in Japan for twenty years, explained to us, "For Japanese investors, there's significant value in having physical assets on Japanese soil, even if the returns are somewhat lower. It's about control and proximity."

With this foundation established, we quickly opened an office in Tokyo, led by a former Deutsche Bank executive, Katsunori Aouma. Our days were filled with regulatory discussions, working groups, and building relationships with major financial institutions.

We also partnered the Global Blockchain Business Council (GBBC) with Japan Blockchain Association, which arranged numerous introductions to Japanese top regulators. GBBC, which we had co-founded during one of our Necker Island summits alongside Dr. Wang Wei and other industry pioneers, had evolved under the dynamic leadership of CEO Sandra Ro. It had become the blockchain industry's largest and most influential advocacy organization—a perfect partner for facilitating these crucial regulatory discussions in Japan.

One memorable moment came when we had a senior GBBC delegation headed by Dr. Jim Newsome visiting Tokyo, and JBA arranged a meeting in the offices of Parliament member Takeshi Fujimaki. A former banker and member of the House of Councillors, Takeshi Fujimaki was a vocal advocate for Bitcoin and blockchain technology. He emphasized the potential of cryptocurrencies to revolutionize the financial system and reduce reliance on traditional banking structures.

"Japan's approach is to regulate and legitimize rather than restrict," explained So Saito, legal counsel to JBA, during our preparatory briefing. "The government sees Bitcoin and blockchain as potential competitive advantages for Japan's financial sector, not threats to be contained."

The meeting with Fujimaki-san went extremely well. He asked penetrating questions about mining economics, network security, and the potential for blockchain to transform government services. Dr. Newsome's experience as former CFTC Chairman provided a valuable perspective on how balanced regulation could foster innovation while protecting consumers.

As we were wrapping up, Fujimaki-san shook my hand warmly, and with a playful wink and smile, leaned in and whispered, "I am Satoshi Nakamoto."

I laughed. We all laughed. There was a sense in that moment that we were all, in some way, Satoshi Nakamoto—all contributors to this revolutionary technology that was reshaping the world's understanding of trust, value, and exchange.

On our final evening in Tokyo, while Val had returned to Europe to attend to urgent business matters, our Japanese advisor, Ikuo Yasuda, invited me to dinner at Nobu. Yasuda-san, the former Country Head of Lehman Brothers Japan who had led its Investment Banking Division before founding Pinnacle, Inc.—a boutique advisory firm where he served as Chairman, President, and CEO—had become an invaluable guide through Japan's complex business landscape.

At the restaurant, we were seated at a premium spot near the sushi counter. Midway through our meal, Yasuda-san excused himself momentarily and returned with a distinguished gentleman in a chef's coat.

"George-san, please allow me to introduce my friend, Chef Nobuyuki Matsuhisa," Yasuda-san said with evident pride.

I stood immediately, bowing slightly as we exchanged business cards. "Nobu-san, it's an honor. I've been a patron of your restaurants for many years."

The legendary chef smiled warmly. "Yasuda-san tells me you are doing interesting things with this Bitcoin."

"We're working to build its infrastructure," I explained. "Making it more accessible and useful worldwide."

Nobu-san nodded thoughtfully before asking with genuine curiosity, "George-san, how far do you think this Bitcoin will go?"

Without hesitation, I replied, "To a million, Nobu-san."

His eyebrows raised slightly. "Million yen?"

"No," I smiled, "Million dollars."

There was a moment of stunned silence before Nobu-san broke into appreciative laughter. "You think big! I like that. In my business, too, you must think big."

As we departed Japan the next day, that conversation stayed with me. Here was one of the world's most successful culinary entrepreneurs, a man who had built a global empire through disciplined innovation, asking about Bitcoin's future. The questions were no longer whether cryptocurrency would survive, but how far it would go.

Our time in Japan had exceeded all expectations. We had secured investments, established partnerships, and laid the groundwork for long-term growth in one of the world's most important financial markets. As my plane lifted off from Narita Airport, I found myself already planning our return.

CHAPTER 9
MIDNIGHT IN HONG KONG

Beginning is half the task.

—Korean Proverb

South Korea was next. The country's tech-savvy population and forward-thinking regulators made it a natural target for expansion. Bill Tai's network once again proved invaluable. An Olympic champion sharpshooter turned executive, Eun Chul Lee, became our CEO there.

During our first meeting in Seoul, Eun Chul's passion for both technology and his country was evident. "Koreans adopt new technology faster than anyone," he explained as we toured the bustling Gangnam district. "Smartphones, social media, gaming—when Koreans embrace something, they do it wholeheartedly. Crypto will be no different."

South Korea's rapid technology adoption stems from several factors: high Internet penetration rates (over ninety-five percent), advanced mobile infrastructure, and a culture that embraces digital innovation. The country leads globally in mobile payment adoption and online gaming, creating an ideal environment for cryptocurrency acceptance.

This prediction proved accurate. Within months, South Korea would become one of the most active cryptocurrency markets globally, with trading volumes that belied the country's relatively small population.

Our Seoul office quickly became a hub for blockchain activity, hosting GBBC events and advancing Exonum projects. The Korean appetite for Bitcoin mining investment was particularly remarkable. Family offices and high-net-worth individuals from the country's chaebol conglomerates eagerly participated in our Bitcoin mining ventures, often making multi-million dollar commitments with remarkable speed and decisiveness.

I was in the middle of a crucial fundraising dinner in Seoul's Gangnam district when my phone exploded with an urgent call from Sysman. The Korean investors around the table politely paused their conversation as I glanced at the screen.

"Excuse me for just a moment," I said, stepping away from the table.

"George! Iceland has been hacked!" Sysman's voice crackled through the international connection, his usual calm replaced by barely controlled urgency.

My blood ran cold. "How bad is it?"

"They got into our hot wallet. I'm tracking the breach now, but they've taken 1,100 coins before I could stop them completely."

I excused myself from the dinner entirely, stepping onto the restaurant's terrace overlooking Seoul's glittering skyline. For twenty agonizing minutes, I paced while Sysman worked to contain the damage.

"I stopped the main breach," Sysman reported when he called back. "But this isn't over. I'm going to track every single satoshi."

I returned to apologize to the Korean investors for the interruption, offering only a brief explanation about an urgent operational matter that required immediate attention. The dinner continued, but my mind was clearly elsewhere.

What followed revealed why Sysman was so valuable to our operations. Using advanced blockchain forensics and his decades of cybersecurity experience, he began methodically tracking the stolen bitcoins across multiple exchanges and wallets. The hackers had used sophisticated mixing services and multiple transaction hops to obscure their trail.

"The attack signatures match techniques I've seen before," he reported a week later. "This wasn't random—they specifically targeted our infrastructure as part of a larger operation."

That's when we brought in Mr. Wolf—not his real name, but the moniker we used for a retired senior operative from one of the world's major intelligence organizations. Wolf had become our saving grace, someone we could call when situations required skills beyond normal business operations.

"Your man Sysman has done excellent forensic work," Wolf said during our encrypted video call. "I can help with the human intelligence side."

The investigation unfolded over the following month like a sophisticated thriller. Wolf's network of contacts helped trace the hackers through various jurisdictions, while Sysman's technical analysis mapped every transaction. The trail revealed a small but technically sophisticated group based in Eastern Europe that had been systematically targeting cryptocurrency operations across the continent.

"We've identified the primary actors," Sysman reported during one of our calls. "We know exactly where the bitcoins moved, what other cryptocurrencies they've been converted to, and which addresses they control."

While we couldn't physically recover the stolen bitcoins, Sysman had achieved something perhaps more valuable—complete visibility into the hackers' operations. "Every address they control is now under constant surveillance," he explained. "Those coins are effectively frozen. The moment they try to move them through any legitimate exchange or service, we'll know immediately."

The investigation led to the disruption of the entire hacking ring's operations, preventing future attacks on other cryptocurrency companies. The incident reinforced the importance of having world-class security expertise in-house and building relationships with people who could help in extreme situations. Wolf would indeed prove to be our saving grace on several future occasions.

Meanwhile, our Korean expansion continued to gain traction. "Korean investors understand high-risk, high-reward propositions," Eun Chul explained during one particularly successful fundraising session. "They've seen how technology can transform economies overnight. When they believe in something, they move decisively."

This decisiveness manifested in substantial capital flows through equipment purchases and mining fund participation. Several major Korean high-net-worth individuals became customers for our BlockBox solutions and partners in our mining ventures. Their capacity to deploy capital quickly for equipment purchases stood in stark contrast to the lengthy procurement processes we'd encountered with Western clients.

While we were building these Asian partnerships, Bitcoin's civil war was reaching its climax.

The Bitcoin scaling debate of 2015 to 2017, known as the "Block Size Wars," represented the cryptocurrency's first major governance crisis. The community split between those advocating for larger blocks (Bitcoin Classic, Bitcoin Unlimited) to increase transaction capacity immediately, and Bitcoin Core developers who favored maintaining smaller blocks while developing second-layer solutions like Lightning Network. This technical disagreement was fundamentally a philosophical battle over Bitcoin's future: should it prioritize being a payment network with higher throughput, or a decentralized store of value resistant to centralization? The deadlock had frozen development for nearly two years, and the uncertainty was suppressing Bitcoin's price and institutional adoption.

By May, Barry Silbert of DCG had gathered key stakeholders in New York—we sent Sysman to represent Bitfury's position—to orchestrate what became known as the New York Agreement, a last-ditch attempt to find middle ground in the scaling debate. My messages to Barry reflected the urgency we all felt: "Barry, we good to go? We need to move." I spent hours rallying last-minute support, calling CEOs and CTOs across time zones to get them to sign on before the window closed.

The Agreement was finally in place. A month later, Sysman called me with a proud announcement: "We just made history by being the first to signal support for SegWit activation." When CoinTelegraph asked about our position, Val was clear: "Politics aside, SegWit is just an elegant engineering solution. It's a good solution that will lead to capacity increase through Lightning Network."

SegWit (Segregated Witness) was a crucial Bitcoin protocol upgrade that separated transaction signatures from transaction data, effectively increasing block capacity without changing the block size limit. This allowed more transactions per block while maintaining backward compatibility and enabled second-layer solutions like the Lightning Network. The upgrade sparked heated debates in the Bitcoin community between 2015 and 2017, but ultimately activated in August 2017 and paved the way for Bitcoin's explosive growth that followed.

Some miners opposed us, but I remained pragmatic: "Miners should look at the price of Bitcoin. We think SegWit will increase the value of Bitcoin." History would prove us right—the resolution of the scaling debate cleared the path for Bitcoin's explosive growth that followed.

The Mongolian Detour

Our Asian tour even included a detour to Ulaanbaatar, Mongolia, at the invitation of GBBC ambassador Saruul Ganbaatar, who was CEO of an innovative BOGD bank. Landing at Chinggis Khaan International Airport, we were immediately struck by the contrast between the vast, open steppes and the rapidly modernizing capital city.

"Mongolia has some of the world's last truly unspoiled wilderness," our host explained as we drove from the airport, gesturing to the rolling hills beyond the city. "But we're also determined to be part of the digital future."

We explored potential mining facilities and were impressed by the Mongolian hospitality—traditional nomadic gers (yurts) had been set up for us to experience authentic Mongolian cuisine and culture, complete with fermented mare's milk (airag) and throat singing performances.

Despite the warm welcome and entrepreneurial spirit we encountered, we ultimately decided against establishing mining operations there—the power wasn't as affordable as we had hoped, and logistics presented significant challenges. It was a reminder that in the mining business, economics and practicality had to trump sentiment and adventure.

But we stayed friends with Saruul and check in every time Bitcoin passes a major milestone. I am certain he has orange-pilled many prominent Mongolians, and in my textbook, my mission was accomplished. Actually, that was one of my main motivations for going to as many countries and meeting as many decision-makers as possible—even if we didn't strike a partnership or do a deal, I would seed the value of Bitcoin into their minds and orange-pill them.

Throughout the years, one of the best feelings I've had is people reaching out to me, thanking me for introducing them to Bitcoin. I can't explain how great that feeling is! Whether it was a banker in Tokyo, an entrepreneur in Seoul, or a government official in Ulaanbaatar, these conversations planted seeds that would grow in ways I couldn't predict. Some would become investors, others advocates, and still others would simply understand that a different financial future was possible.

This evangelism aspect of our work was never in the business plan, but it became one of the most rewarding parts of the journey. Every new Bitcoin convert represented another voice in the growing chorus calling for financial sovereignty and technological transformation. In this way, our Asian tour accomplished something far more valuable than any single deal or partnership—it expanded the horizon of what was possible in diverse cultures and contexts around the globe.

The Georgia Facility Deal

Despite the signing of the New York Agreement, tensions in the Bitcoin community remained high throughout the summer of 2017. And then on August 1, the renegades Roger Ver and Bitmain co-founder Jihan Wu, supported by developers Amaury Séchet and Peter Rizun, decided to proceed with their own hard fork anyway. They rejected the compromise and pushed ahead with creating Bitcoin Cash, which would have 8MB blocks and no SegWit.

The Bitcoin Cash hard fork occurred at block #478,558. While Bitcoin (BTC) continued on the original chain with SegWit activated and a 1MB base block size, Bitcoin Cash (BCH) forked off with an 8MB block size limit and rejected SegWit entirely. The mechanism was simple: Bitcoin ABC nodes would only accept blocks conforming to the new 8MB rule, creating a permanent split.

The immediate aftermath was chaotic but revealing. Bitcoin initially dropped from $2,875 to $2,300 as uncertainty gripped the market, while Bitcoin Cash briefly surged to $700. But within days, the verdict was clear: Bitcoin rebounded strongly above $3,200 while BCH crashed below $300. The market had chosen.

Our early support for SegWit was vindicated. The market had spoken decisively—it valued Bitcoin's conservative approach and SegWit activation over Bitcoin Cash's bigger blocks. Through August, Bitcoin continued its relentless climb, reaching $4,600 by month's end while BCH struggled to find its footing.

What we didn't know at the time was the extent of Bitmain's commitment to Bitcoin Cash. Their 2018 IPO prospectus would later reveal they had liquidated over ninety percent of their Bitcoin treasury to support BCH. With Bitcoin Cash down 95 percent relative to Bitcoin to this day, it still ranks as one of the worst strategic blunders in the crypto industry.

As the price surged past these milestones, global attention intensified—and so did Credit China's interest in our operations. They were particularly impressed by our immersion cooling facility in Georgia during their due diligence visits. The technology's efficiency and innovation aligned perfectly with their vision for large-scale mining operations.

Sometime in August, I received an unexpected message from Phang in the middle of the night. "We are really interested in acquiring your Georgia facility," he wrote. "What's the price?"

This caught me by surprise during one of our celebratory outings at the newly opened 1OAK club in Tokyo. We hadn't considered selling the facility, as it was one of our crown jewels. However, as our focus shifted toward capitalizing on the business in Western markets, we decided to explore the opportunity.

I stepped away from our group into a quieter corner of the club, the pulsing music still audible as I called Val. "Phang wants to buy the Georgia facility," I said without preamble. "This could be a significant strategic pivot for us."

"What are you thinking?" Val asked after a moment's pause.

"If the price is right, it allows us to focus on software and our next-generation chips without the overhead of managing the facility. Plus, it strengthens our partnership with Credit China."

After extensive internal discussions, we proposed a price that reflected the facility's strategic value and our reluctance to part with it. Credit China countered, and negotiations began in earnest. I flew to Hong Kong with Greg Li at my side to close the deal.

The final forty-eight hours of negotiations took place in my suite at the Conrad Hotel in Hong Kong. Teams from both sides worked around the clock, hammering out details of what had become a complex deal.

"The key sticking points are still the timeline for transition and the ongoing maintenance agreement," our CFO noted during a late-night session, coffee cups and takeout containers littering the conference table in my suite.

"Tell them we can accelerate the timeline, but we need guarantees on the chip orders," I replied, scanning the latest draft of the agreement.

By morning, we had reached a consensus on the major points. Credit China would acquire the Georgia facility at a substantial premium price, and we would secure both cash and additional orders for our chips.

Finally, we reached an agreement. The documents were signed with little ceremony—just the quiet scratching of pens on paper, followed by handshakes and nods of satisfaction.

After the signing, Phang insisted on taking our team to celebrate at one of Hong Kong's most exclusive restaurants, a swanky establishment with panoramic views of the harbor. As champagne flowed and elaborate dishes arrived, a palpable sense of achievement filled the air around the table. Both sides had negotiated hard but fairly, and the result was a deal that genuinely benefited everyone involved.

"To a long and prosperous partnership," Phang toasted, raising his glass.

"And to the future of blockchain in Asia," I responded, clinking glasses with him and the assembled executives.

By the time I returned to my suite at the Conrad, I was completely spent. Arthur Hayes, founder of BitMEX, texted me: "Let's go out and celebrate with the boys!"

But exhaustion had finally caught up with me. After weeks of intense negotiations and travel across Asia, I simply crashed on my hotel bed, content in the knowledge that we had not only weathered the storm but emerged stronger than ever.

Tomorrow would bring a flight to Kyiv for meetings with our growing software team. But for tonight, I allowed myself a moment of satisfaction, gazing out at the glittering Hong Kong skyline—a fitting symbol of the heights to which Bitfury had risen.

CHAPTER 10

CANADA O CANADA

Luck is what happens when preparation meets opportunity.

—Seneca

The Lufthansa first-class cabin hummed with quiet efficiency as we cruised over the majestic Himalayas. Outside my window, the morning sun painted the snow-capped peaks in hues of gold and rose. After the whirlwind of meetings in Hong Kong, culminating in the completion of a major deal for Bitfury, the tranquility of the cabin was a welcome respite.

I particularly loved Lufthansa's complimentary email service. Unlike other airlines that made you jump through endless hoops for connectivity, the German carrier's system just worked. A testament to their famed efficiency.

Sipping a perfectly chilled glass of Krug, I scrolled through my emails, halfheartedly clearing the backlog that had accumulated overnight. A financial news headline caught my eye: "HIVE Blockchain Technologies Planning to Complete First Ever Crypto Mining RTO on Toronto Stock Exchange."

I nearly spilled my champagne, sitting bolt upright in my leather seat. Marco Streng, who was one of many resellers of our equipment, was planning to capitalize on his mining through a reverse takeover. The implications hit me immediately.

A reverse takeover (RTO) allows a private company to become publicly traded by acquiring a publicly listed shell company, bypassing the lengthy IPO process. For crypto companies in 2017, this represented a fast track to accessing public capital markets when traditional IPO routes remained largely closed to cryptocurrency businesses.

"If our reseller can do this…" I muttered to myself, already calculating possibilities. Bitfury was much larger, with its own technology and a diversified business model.

The flight attendant approached, noticing my sudden animation. "Is everything alright, sir? Can I get you anything?"

"Sehr gut. Just had a moment of clarity," I replied with a smile. "And perhaps another glass of champagne to celebrate it."

As if the universe was orchestrating events, as it typically does, an email from Marc van der Chijs popped into my inbox the moment my connectivity resumed. Marc, the Dutch entrepreneur whom I'd met at our first Necker Blockchain Summit, had become a good friend. He'd built Tudou.com, the "YouTube of China," and after selling to Alibaba, had pivoted into blockchain ventures, establishing First Block Capital in Vancouver—Canada's first registered cryptocurrency investment fund manager.

"George, have you seen the HIVE news?" his message read. "I'm in Canada, and we have all the right banking relationships. We could do this with Bitfury. Thoughts?"

My fingers flew across the keyboard, excitement building: "I was thinking the same! We already have Canadian operations and growing fast! This could work perfectly. When can we meet?"

His response came minutes later: "ASAP. This window won't stay open forever. The Toronto Exchange has opened up to crypto. Time is of the essence."

I immediately messaged Val, knowing he'd be awake despite the time difference: "Cancel everything. We need to be in the US tomorrow. Potentially company-changing opportunity."

"That serious?" he replied instantly.

"Yes," I wrote back. "It changes everything."

Chasing Stranded Energy

Before the Toronto opportunity even materialized, we had already been developing what would become one of Bitfury's most innovative solutions—the BlockBox. The concept emerged during one of our strategy sessions in Cyprus.

"We're looking to take Bitcoin mining global," Val said, pacing in front of our whiteboard, which was covered with calculations and diagrams. "But the challenge is always the same: finding cheap, reliable power."

"But what if we could go straight to the source?" he continued. "Instead of building permanent facilities, what if we created containerized Bitcoin mining solutions that could go wherever stranded energy exists?"

The idea grew and evolved over days of intense discussion. Energy that couldn't be efficiently transported to population centers, excess capacity during certain seasons, and renewable sources in remote locations—Bitcoin mining could monetize all of these scenarios.

> Stranded energy refers to power generation capacity that cannot be economically transmitted to consumers due to geographic isolation or infrastructure limitations. Examples include remote hydroelectric plants, seasonal excess from renewable sources, or industrial facilities with surplus capacity. Bitcoin mining's location flexibility makes it ideal for monetizing such energy resources.

"Think about it," our global energy lead explained enthusiastically. "There are countless situations where power plants are built ahead of transmission line infrastructure, or where there's excess renewable capacity that can't be stored. Bitcoin is the perfect solution to capture this stranded energy."

This approach to mining represented a profound shift in our thinking—one that built upon lessons I had carried from my childhood. Growing up during Georgia's energy crises in the post-Soviet era, when blackouts were daily occurrences, I had witnessed firsthand the consequences of inefficient energy distribution. Now, decades later, we were developing a technology that could transform energy inefficiency into value—turning a problem into an opportunity, just as my family had been forced to do during those challenging times.

Our global energy team began hunting for locations worldwide. Canada emerged as particularly viable—vast renewable resources, supportive regulations, and a cooperative utility infrastructure.

Throughout 2016, while we were wrestling with our semiconductor crisis, our team was simultaneously designing the BlockBox project. By fall, we had already identified our first location in Alberta, Western Canada, where energy capacity was begging for use.

"It's like the universe is aligning," I remarked to Marc during one of our messages. "We're already operating in Canada. We have these modular BlockBox units ready to deploy. And now this Toronto listing opportunity presents itself. We can raise the capital and accelerate the growth!"

Café Milano

Forty-eight hours later, exhausted but running on adrenaline, Val and I were seated at my favourite corner table at Café Milano in Georgetown, a haunt from my Johns Hopkins days. When Marc suggested meeting, I realized I couldn't get a Canadian visa in such a short time, so we decided to meet in DC instead. This worked perfectly, as we had some outstanding meetings with regulators already planned with our advisor, Jim Newsome. The restaurant hummed with the quiet conversations of Washington power brokers, the air perfumed with truffle oil and money.

"So this Canada listing," Val asked, glancing at his watch, "you're sure this is real?"

"Absolutely," I assured him. "It's all about the regulatory clarity," I explained. "The US is still figuring out how to classify crypto companies. Canada's already decided."

The restaurant door opened, and Marc entered with his partner Sean Clarke and two bankers.

"George, Val, meet Harris Fricker, CEO of GMP Securities," he said, gesturing to a sharp-eyed man with the poised confidence of someone accustomed to making nine-figure deals before breakfast. "And this is Andrew, his top lieutenant."

Harris, I quickly learned, was something of a legend in Canadian finance—he had worked with Elon Musk on PayPal and had a reputation for spotting transformative opportunities early.

> Harris Fricker's career spanned the evolution of financial technology from early Internet payments to cryptocurrency. His experience with PayPal during its formative years gave him unique insight into how digital payment systems could disrupt traditional finance, making him an ideal banker for crypto companies seeking public market access.

After ordering the round of antipasti and a fine bottle of Gavi di Gavi, Harris got straight to business, his voice low and measured.

"The Toronto exchange has opened the door to crypto mining listings," he explained, leaning forward slightly. "The regulatory path is clear, and investor appetite is enormous. We've never seen anything like it. Family offices, institutional investors—they're all looking for exposure to this sector."

"What's the timeline on something like this?" Val asked, ever practical, swirling his glass thoughtfully.

Harris looked to Andrew, who pulled out a slim leather portfolio.

"Aggressive? Sixty days from structure to listing," Harris replied, a glint of excitement breaking through his professional demeanor. "But we'd need to start due diligence immediately. Your data centers, your technology—our team would need unrestricted access."

I glanced at Val, who gave a slight nod, the gesture subtle but communicating volumes between us after years of partnership.

"Let's do it," I said, extending my hand across the table. "But understand—we move fast. Bitfury fast."

Harris's grip was firm as he shook my hand. "We wouldn't have it any other way."

From Banya to Bletchley Park

The next weeks were a blur of Zoom calls, legal documents, corporate structuring, and planning. Two weeks after our DC meeting, the Canadian team flew to Ukraine and Georgia to inspect our operations on the ground. The due diligence process would be thorough, examining every aspect of our business.

We met them at Kyiv's Boryspil Airport, the VIP arrivals hall buzzing with activity despite the late hour. All four of them looked a bit dazed from the long journey.

"Welcome to Ukraine, gentlemen," I greeted them as they emerged through customs. "Ready to see some serious operations?"

Harris raised an eyebrow. "Looking forward to it."

"All in good time," I smiled. "First, let's get you settled."

The evening they arrived was crisp and clear, the golden domes of Kyiv's churches catching the last light of day. After settling them at the Hyatt, we took them to a traditional Ukrainian feast at Tsarske Selo, where platters of vareniki, borscht, and tender meat appeared in endless succession.

As we toasted with ice-cold horilka, I surveyed our Canadian visitors, already looking more relaxed and open.

"Tomorrow," I suggested, raising my glass, "let's do business the Ukrainian way."

"What exactly does that mean?" Andrew asked, curiosity overcoming his initial reserve.

Val grinned. "You shall see."

The next day found us in a traditional banya on the outskirts of Kyiv—"Chumanski Shlyah," the intense heat and occasional birch branches creating an atmosphere that was simultaneously punishing and rejuvenating.

"This," I explained as the Canadian team adjusted to the scorching temperature, "is where the real deals happen. Here—the banya is our boardroom."

The banya tradition in Slavic cultures serves as both a physical and social ritual, where the shared experience of extreme heat and cold creates bonds of trust and openness essential for business relationships. Many significant deals in Eastern Europe are concluded in banya settings, where the physical challenge strips away pretenses and creates authentic dialogue.

Between rounds of sauna and plunges into cold water, the conversation flowed more freely. The physical challenge of the banya had stripped away pretenses, leaving a raw honesty that served our discussions well.

Harris, his face flushed from the heat, called out after a particularly intense steam session: "We need a name for this entity—something that captures what we're doing."

"It needs to be distinctive," Val added, passing around ice-cold kvass and shots of horilka. "Not another blockchain-something."

"And it should have meaning," I contributed. "A story behind it."

Harris, red-faced but suddenly animated, sat up on the wooden bench. "I've thought about it. Hut 8. Alan Turing's unit at Bletchley Park, where they broke the Enigma code."

Hut 8 was the section at Bletchley Park responsible for breaking German naval Enigma ciphers during World War II. Led by Alan Turing, the team's cryptographic work was crucial to Allied victory. The name symbolized the intersection of advanced mathematics, code-breaking, and transformative technology—perfect parallels to Bitcoin mining's cryptographic proof-of-work system.

The silence lasted only seconds before we all enthusiastically agreed. A name with history, intelligence, and cryptographic relevance—perfect for a company built on Bitcoin mining.

"To Hut 8," I toasted, raising another glass of horilka. "To making history."

And just like that, Hut 8 was born. We nominated Bill Tai to be its Chairman of the Board, a position he holds to this day.

The following days took us to Georgia, where our immersion cooling facility, as well as a few operational BlockBoxes left the visitors visibly impressed.

"I've toured a few mining operations," Andrew confessed as we walked between the humming data tanks. "Nothing comes close to this level of sophistication."

Harris nodded in agreement. "This is exactly what the market is looking for—real technology, real innovation, not just marketing hype."

Meanwhile, the GMP team was conducting extensive due diligence on our Canadian operations, checking everything thoroughly. The reports coming back to Harris were equally impressive, confirming the strength of our North American presence.

On their final evening, over a traditional Georgian supra with flowing wine and endless toasts from Tamada Remi, Harris raised his glass.

"I've seen enough," he declared. "We're going to make this happen. The Canadian capital markets are ready for a company like Bitfury. To our success!"

The Bull Run Roadshow

Our roadshow in December exceeded all expectations. Led by Sean and Bill Tai, with Bitfury lending the technology and industry credibility, the GMP Bank team ran a tight process, but even they were surprised by the response. Institutional investors who had never considered cryptocurrency investments were suddenly clamoring for allocation.

"It's unlike anything I've ever seen," Harris confided to me between meetings in Toronto. We were huddled in the back of black Suburbans, racing between presentations. "These are blue-chip investors—pension funds, family offices, institutions that normally wouldn't touch something this new. But they're afraid of missing out."

The experience of pitching alongside Bill Tai—the veteran of semiconductors and numerous tech waves—was invaluable. His deep understanding of technology cycles and ability to contextualize Bitcoin within the broader arc of computing history gave our presentations gravitas that money couldn't buy. When Bill spoke about blockchain's potential, drawing parallels to the early days of the Internet and semiconductor revolution, even the most skeptical investors leaned in.

After one particularly successful day of pitching, Sean came up to Bill. "Bill, your understanding of tech is inspiring. Everyone is learning so much from you!"

The timing couldn't have been better. Bitcoin was embarking on a historic bull run, with prices climbing daily. The market was electrified with possibility.

This bull run was no accident. It was the direct result of Bitcoin successfully navigating its greatest internal crisis. The activation of SegWit in August, following months of scaling debate resolution in which Bitfury had been a strong advocate for SegWit adoption, had removed the uncertainty that had been suppressing Bitcoin's price.

During one of the final presentations to a room full of Canadian pension fund managers at the Fairmont Royal York Hotel, I was midway through my slides when a murmur spread through the room. Attendees were glancing at their phones, whispering to colleagues.

I paused, sensing the distraction. "Is there something I should know?"

A silver-haired portfolio manager in the front row looked up from his screen. "Bitcoin just broke $20,000 in Korean markets."

The room fell silent, the implications sinking in. I set aside my prepared remarks and closed my presentation file.

"Gentlemen," I said, stepping away from the podium to address them directly, "we're witnessing history in real-time. The question isn't whether Bitcoin is legitimate—the market has answered that. The question is whether you want to be part of this technology of the future."

The room erupted in questions, the formal presentation format abandoned in favor of raw, engaged discussion that lasted well past our allotted time.

In the elevator afterward, Harris shook his head in amazement. "I've never seen the investor crowd that animated. Not even during the dot-com boom."

"This is bigger than the dot-com boom," I replied, checking messages on my phone. "The Internet changed information. Bitcoin is changing money itself."

The cryptocurrency craze was reaching a fever pitch. During one of our dinners at Alo, Toronto's swanky French restaurant, I noticed Marc constantly checking his phone.

"Everything okay?" I asked as he put his phone down for perhaps the fifth time.

He grinned sheepishly. "CryptoKitties. I'm trading them between meetings."

"CryptoKitties?" Val asked, his confusion evident.

Marc launched into an explanation of the digital collectibles built on Ethereum, his enthusiasm infectious. "It's the first mainstream application of blockchain beyond currency. People are paying thousands for these digital cats. I already got a few. It's fascinating."

CryptoKitties was one of the first popular blockchain-based games, allowing users to breed, collect, and trade unique digital cats on the Ethereum network. The game's popularity in late 2017 caused significant network congestion, demonstrating both the potential and limitations of blockchain applications. Individual CryptoKitties sold for hundreds of thousands of dollars, showcasing the market's appetite for digital collectibles.

The roadshow wound its way through Montreal, New York, and then back to Toronto. On the way from New York, we hitched a ride on a private plane with our investor and Bitcoin OG Michael Novogratz. In addition to running fundraising for Hut 8, GMP was running it for Mike's entity, Galaxy Digital—a leading crypto asset manager. And needless to say, his roadshow was running great as well.

As we toasted with champagne, Mike said, "We've come a long way since our first meeting in 2014."

"That's for sure," I agreed. "Remember when you were advising us to get into Ethereum at $2 at your kitchen in your SoHo place?"

"Should have, would have," Mike chuckled.

"We all have done well, no worries," I laughed. "You can't win 'em all."

By the time the plane touched down in Toronto, we learned from our teams on the ground that both fundraisings were over ten times oversubscribed—a staggering level of demand that surprised even the veteran bankers at GMP. The fundraising was a resounding success. Now with both official listings earmarked for early next year, we could relax and enjoy the final fortnight of the year with our families.

The Yacht Party

As I was wrapping up the final days in Toronto, Sheikh Zayed texted me: "Hey George, where are you gonna be for the New Year?"

I looked at my calendar, surprisingly empty after weeks of non-stop meetings. "I have no plans," I replied.

"Perfect! Why don't you come to the UAE? I'll have some tech entrepreneurs as guests, and I want to invite you for a small gathering."

I found myself packing bags with my wife and family, bound for Abu Dhabi, wondering what exactly Sheikh Zayed meant by a "small gathering."

True to Abu Dhabi style, the celebration was anything but small. Sheikh Zayed had organized a magnificent gathering of tech entrepreneurs and regional innovators, showcasing the same hospitality that had impressed us years earlier.

The weekend unfolded like something from the Arabian Nights. Sheikh Zayed's father, His Excellency Sheikh Suroor, graciously hosted us, arranging for a private tour of the newly opened Louvre Abu Dhabi and helicopter tours over the Kingdom into the desert. We settled into the brand-new Bulgari hotel in Dubai, its luxury so new that staff were still removing protective coverings from furniture.

On New Year's Eve, Sheikh Zayed invited us all to his yacht for fireworks viewing. As the vessel anchored in position with a perfect view of the Atlantis hotel, the guest list began to crystallize. Among the entrepreneurs was someone I hadn't expected to meet in such an intimate setting—Sergey Brin.

"This is a pleasant surprise," I said, extending my hand to the Google co-founder as we stood on the yacht's deck, the lights of Dubai shimmering before us. I had met Sergey before at the Sir Richard Ocean Gala, where Bitfury was one of the sponsors of the conservation. On one memorable night, Val had bid the project to "save the BVI turtles" to 350 bitcoins (some $35 million in today's terms).

"The pleasure is mine," Sergey replied. "Good to see you again."

As the evening progressed, we found ourselves switching to Russian, our shared language creating an instant bond despite our different backgrounds.

"You know," Sergey confided as we watched the preparations for the fireworks display, "my son Benjie is getting into Ethereum. He keeps trying to explain it to me, but I'm still trying to understand Bitcoin first."

I laughed, remembering my own early days of blockchain discovery. "The beauty of Bitcoin is its simplicity. Everything else builds from that foundation."

Our conversation meandered through topics—from the evolution of search algorithms to the lessons of scaling Google to the political systems that had shaped our early lives. The private setting allowed for a candid exchange impossible in formal business contexts.

"What do you make of all this?" Sergey asked, gesturing toward Dubai's skyline. "The intersection of oil wealth with new technology?"

"It's fascinating," I replied. "The region is embracing blockchain while parts of the West are still skeptical. Geography might matter less than vision in this revolution."

As midnight approached and the fireworks began to illuminate the sky above Atlantis, I found myself taking a mental snapshot of Bitfury's journey. We had weathered the TSMC crisis, innovated with BlockBox, and now stood on the brink of taking one of our subsidiary companies public.

"To 2018," Sheikh Zayed announced, raising his glass as explosions of color painted the night sky.

"To the future," I echoed, thinking of the numbers I had reviewed just hours before: over $200 million in cash and bitcoins on our balance sheet, operations grown to one thousand people across twenty countries, a massive pipeline of customers, expanding partnerships in software, and just finalizing the listing of one of our entities on the Toronto Stock Exchange.

As the fireworks continued, I pulled out my phone to capture a photo of the spectacular display when an email notification caught my eye. A message from Val, sent to the entire Bitfury team:

Dear Team, Thank you for your hard work, creativity, and dedication! The team has grown to almost 1000, and your commitment makes these achievements possible. Do good, make impossible possible, be a team player, and be a Gamechanger! Happy New Year to all!

I smiled, recognizing Val's characteristic optimism in this concise summary of our incredible year. But what caught my eye even more was a flash on my favourite ZeroBlock app. It reported the current Bitcoin price at $13,880—a stunning 14x increase in just one year.

"Look at this," I said to Sheikh Zayed and Sheikh Ali, showing them the screen. "Remember when people called us crazy for betting on Bitcoin?"

Sheikh Zayed, understanding the magnitude of what we were witnessing, said with a smile, "Habibi, and who is laughing now?"

PHOTO GALLERY

In the midst of construction. With Val and Akaki.

Chilling with Brock
and his dog in Malibu.

The Early Days. With Val,
Bill, Niko, and Marat

Bill visiting our data center in Iceland.

Bitcoin Supper Club. Brock toasting with a Georgian khantsi.

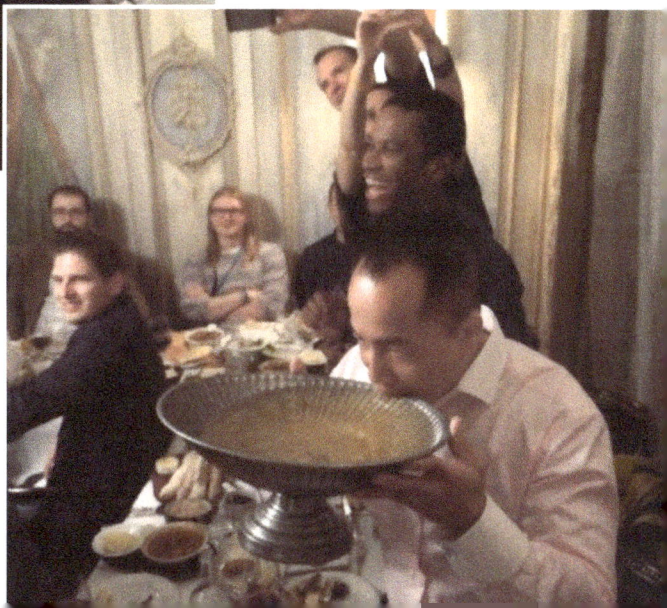
Bitcoin Supper Club. Harry toasting with a champagne chalice.

SQUAWK BOX

|||SQUAWK BOX|||
GEORGE KIKVADZE
BITFURY BOARD MEMBER & ADVISOR

S&P FUTURES
-8.50   -0.46%
1,851.50

CNBC

Our debut on *SquawkBox*.
"This Thing Mines Bitcoin?"

Our first orange-pilling trip
to Davos.

With Jack, Val, Bill, and Sir
Richard holding a Georgian
sword on Necker Island.

Necker Blockchain Summit. Pool divings guaranteed.

The infamous Necker Jacuzzi, where so many ideas were incubated.

Conceiving Blockchain Land Title Project with Hernando de Soto and Bill.

Arabian Nights, Desert Smiles. With Sheikh Zayed, Sheikh Ali, and Bill in the UAE.

Hernando De Soto presenting Blockchain and Bitcoin to the UAE Royal Family.

Incubating Hut 8 with Harris, Andrew, Marc, and Sean with Georgian Swords and Hats.

Hut 8 Public Listing on Toronto Stock Exchange.

Global Blockchain Business Council Meetup in Beijing.

Orange-pilling Madame Wu Xiaoling, China's Central Bank Legend.

From Kentucky to Tokyo, paid in Bitcoin. With Jim at the BIC Store.

With legendary Nobu Founder Nobuyuki Matsuhisa at Nobu Tokyo.

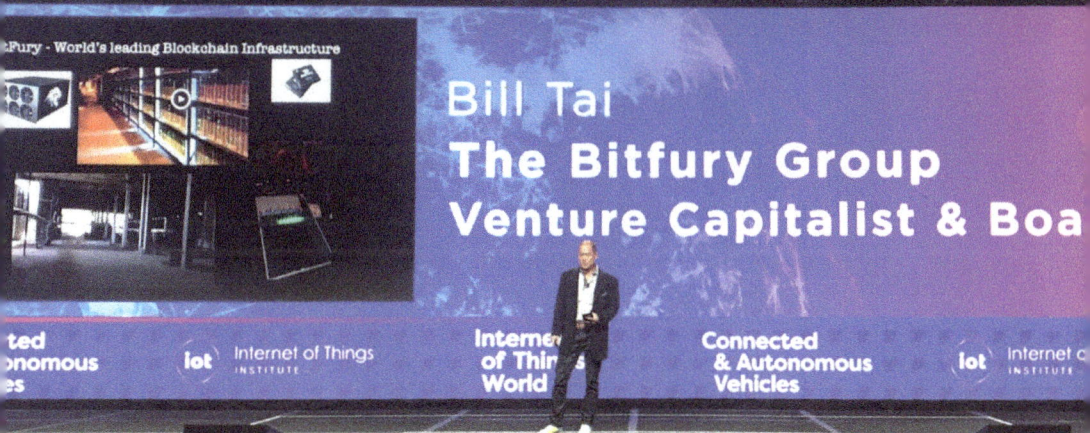

Bill presenting Bitfury to a packed investor audience in San Francisco.

Flying high the Bitcoin HODL flag at Burning Man and getting lots of thumbs up.

Lunch with the Dragon and his team somewhere in Bordeaux.

Sir Richard having fun at our Morocco Blockchain Summit.

Lars and Elo's wedding at beautiful Patmos, Greece.

Neha shares a fun moment in Morocco with Katie, Elizabeth, Sergey, and Brian.

My birthday at Namos Dubai
with Matt, Val, Harry, Michael,
Vivi, CZ, and David.

Hosting CZ in Georgia.
Georgian khantsi at work.

CZ's birthday at Cipriani
Dubai with Val, Guillaume,
and H.E. Gabriel.

Due Diligence Visits in Montana with Nazar, Rick, and Val. We did work hard.

With Paris before the reception. She knew a lot about Bitcoin.

Orange-pilling investors at the Milken Conference.

One of many tennis games with Sir Richard. So far, we are tied in score.

Downtime with family. Somewhere in Tuscany, Italy.

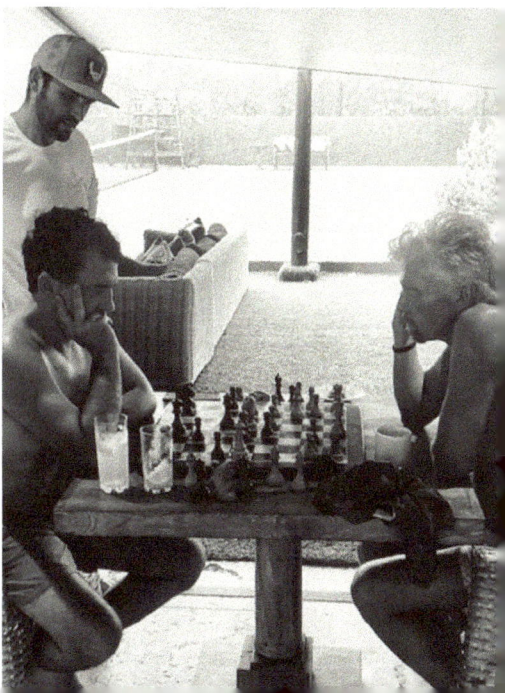

One of many chess games with Sir Richard, with Jack watching on in awe.

PART III
THEN THEY FIGHT YOU

ნაწილი III: შემდეგ შენ გებრძვიან

CHAPTER 11

ROCKET SHIP

Fortuna audaces iuvat.

—Latin Proverb

The private room at the high-stakes poker tables at the Wynn Casino buzzed with electric tension during CES week in January 2018. To my right sat Phil Hellmuth, the legendary "Poker Brat" himself, alongside Daniel Negreanu and several other high rollers. While trying not to lose my shirt, I found myself simultaneously orange-pilling them about the revolution happening right under everyone's noses. I figured the least I could do in this case was that.

Phil had become fascinated with Bitcoin through our mutual friend Vinny Lingham, also an avid poker player. As I studied my cards—two pair on the flop—Phil adjusted his signature sunglasses with theatrical precision. "So George, Bitcoin's up what—ten times from last year? And now it's stabilized around thirteen, fourteen thousand?"

"Stabilized is generous, Phil. But the animal spirits are definitely present," I replied, glancing at my hand. The intensity in Phil's calculating stare reminded me of early investor meetings—the same mix of showmanship and deadly serious calculation beneath the surface.

"What do you think—call?" Phil asked.

I looked at my hand, feeling confident. "I'd call, Phil. Sometimes you have to bet on what you believe in."

He smiled and folded. "That was wise. I was bluffing."

> Phil Hellmuth, known as the "Poker Brat," holds the all-time record with seventeen World Series of Poker bracelets and represents the theatrical side of professional poker. His fascination with Bitcoin through our mutual connections demonstrated how cryptocurrency was penetrating even traditional gambling circles. It was a perfect metaphor for the risks and rewards we were all navigating.

The very next hand, luck smiled on me. A straight from the flop, and I decided to get aggressive. Phil called on the turn, waiting for his flush, but the river didn't deliver. I won the pot. The gratification of beating a world champion was immense, but intoxicated by victory—a feeling I recognized from our early Bitcoin wins—I pressed my luck.

A few hands later, I found myself all-in, waiting for three of a kind to become a full house. "All in," I announced, feeling invincible.

Phil grinned knowingly. "Call."

The river card came: queen of hearts. No full house for me, but Phil was beaming. "Flush," he said proudly, flipping his cards. "Got it on the river."

I lost all my winnings in that moment, but walked away with something more valuable—a vivid reminder that in poker, as in Bitcoin, timing is everything. The lesson would prove more prophetic than I realized.

The Samurai and Satoshi

The next morning, Val and I headed to the Extreme Tech Challenge semifinals, but first decided to check out the "Samurai Exhibition: Armor from the Ann and Gabriel Barbier-Mueller Collection" at the Bellagio Gallery of Fine Art. As a teenager, I practiced martial arts and took Japanese language courses at my undergraduate school, so I was always fascinated by the Samurai and their way of life—Bushido.

The exhibition was extraordinary—over fifty pieces of authentic samurai armor, helmets, masks, and weaponry, some dating back to the fourteenth century. The centerpiece was breathtaking: a life-sized display of a samurai warrior mounted on a fully armored horse, providing visitors with an immersive glimpse into feudal Japan.

Standing among these artifacts with Val, I couldn't help but think about the connection. "You know," I told him as we examined an intricate katana, "there's something poetic about this. The samurai code, the precision, the commitment to a cause greater than oneself—it's not unlike what we're building with Bitcoin."

Val nodded thoughtfully. "Slicing with a katana through the existing inefficient systems."

"That's for sure," I replied, studying the sword's perfect balance. "The samurai lived by a Bushido code that transcended personal gain. We need to always remember that."

The parallel struck me deeply. Like the samurai, we were warriors in service of something larger than ourselves—not just a technology, but a fundamental shift in how humanity could organize trust and value. The bushido code emphasized honor, discipline, and loyalty to one's mission above personal gain—principles that would prove essential as we navigated the challenges ahead.

Later that evening, over dinner at Mizuya with Young Sohn and Bill Tai, our impromptu board meeting took on new urgency. Young observed the rapid consolidation in the semiconductor industry, noting that surviving companies would need the best technology and deepest pockets.

"That's exactly why our diversification strategy is crucial," Val replied, his expression darkening slightly as he recalled our recent challenges. "We need to start working with Samsung as well, especially after what we experienced with TSMC. We can't afford to be dependent on a single supplier again."

In Bitcoin mining, success depends entirely on having the most efficient chips. Each new generation of semiconductors—measured in nanometers—offers better performance per watt. Companies like Bitfury, Bitmain, and others were locked in constant competition to develop smaller, faster, more efficient processors. Missing a generation could mean extinction.

Later on that evening, I met up with an old friend of mine, Zhijun Yang, a fascinating character who served as the main deal architect for one of China's largest holdings. His company had successfully acquired Smithfield Foods in the biggest Chinese-US acquisition of all time, and his English had improved dramatically since becoming a senior fellow at Harvard.

"George!" he greeted me warmly at the Wynn bar. "How have you been. I have to thank you again. Remember that dinner in Beijing when you convinced me and my friends to buy Bitcoin when it was under a thousand? We're very, very grateful. Let's do something together in China."

These moments—seeing early Bitcoin adopters profit from their conviction—provided deep satisfaction. It wasn't just about proving our technology worked; it was about vindication for everyone who'd taken the leap of faith.

Miami Madness

After Vegas, we headed to Miami for the North American Bitcoin Conference, and the scene was unlike anything I'd ever witnessed. The event was five times bigger than previous years, absolutely overflowing with new faces, yacht parties, and nightclub celebrations.

At one memorable boat party, I watched Patrick Byrne, CEO of Overstock, literally dancing on tables while launching his tZERO platform, with Flo Rida performing live in the background. This was classic Byrne: blockchain meets bottle service, disrupting Wall Street while partying on South Beach.

Patrick Byrne embodied the libertarian spirit of early Bitcoin. A PhD economist turned retail CEO, he'd made Overstock the first major retailer to accept Bitcoin. His tZERO platform aimed to revolutionize securities trading through blockchain, mixing serious innovation with theatrical flair.

As the party reached its peak, Byrne turned to me with that mischievous grin and shouted over the music, "We having fun yet, George?"

I couldn't help but laugh at the surreal scene. "This is a bit louder than when we met in Utah!" I yelled back, referring to our earlier meetings in his home state to discuss cooperation and seeing if we could source the right energy for Bitcoin mining.

My buddy Gabriel from Barbados had joined the festivities. "This is insane!" he shouted over the music, rum in hand. "This is a bit louder than Necker!"

"It sure is!" I yelled back. "It feels like we are at the top of the cycle," I joked.

The euphoria of that era attracted characters that seemed lifted from a Hollywood screenplay. None was more memorable than Kostas, a larger-than-life Pontic Greek crypto trader I encountered that very weekend at LIV Nightclub inside the Fontainebleau. The legendary Miami Beach hotspot pulsed with energy, its massive LED screens casting brilliant colors across the packed dance floor while international DJs commanded the crowd.

That's when I spotted him at a VIP table, champagne flowing, his booming voice somehow cutting through the thunderous music. "George!" he roared, crushing my hand in a grip that suggested he'd hauled fishing nets through Black Sea storms. "The famous Bitfury man! Tonight we celebrate Bitcoin's conquest of the old world!"

What made our connection instant was discovering his roots. "My cousins still live in Poti!" he declared proudly over the music. "We Pontians, we never forget our mountains and our sea. Georgia is in my blood, just like Bitcoin is now!"

"You know what my secret is?" he asked, leaning close as the bass dropped around us. "I don't just trade Bitcoin. I *feel* Bitcoin. It's the Pontian way—we feel the sea, we feel the mountains, we feel the money!"

His methodology was pure instinct mixed with Greek mythology. "The market is like Odysseus," he explained, gesturing toward the spectacular light show above the dance floor. "Sometimes it wanders for years, lost at sea. But it always finds its way home. Bitcoin's home is the moon!"

We were joined by a crypto OG and Ether believer named Greg, known as "Jesus." With long dark hair and an intense look, his preaching style was remarkably similar to a messiah. He chimed in: "I do agree. I see Bitcoin doing OK and Ether going parabolic, and I believe ninety-nine percent of shitcoins will go down the toilet."

Kostas claimed thirty thousand coins by early 2018. "When Bitcoin hits one million, I buy a huge island in Greece and will turn it into a Bitcoin paradise."

"Kostas," I cautioned over the pounding music, "markets don't only go up. Maybe consider taking some profits?"

His expression turned serious, even as LIV's world-class production continued around us. "George, we Pontians know about tragedy. We know about hubris. But we also know about glory. Bitcoin is my glory. I ride it to Valhalla or die trying!"

When the 2018 crash came, Kostas disappeared from the scene. But his words stayed with me: "We Pontians, we know about tragedy." Indeed, the crypto space was about to learn hard lessons about hubris and gravity's return.

But it was right after that infamous party that something profound happened. While everyone else was caught up in the party atmosphere, I found myself restless with downtime. As I walked along the Miami beach, ideas started crystallizing.

I'm a big fan of reading biographies of great people, and at that time, I was reading a biography of Gandhi. His quote, "First they ignore you, then they laugh at you, then they fight you, then you win," had been sticking with me.

Walking along that Miami beach, watching the stars sparkle in brilliant colours, I realized we as an industry had clearly entered the "fight" stage. As the price of Bitcoin grew to noticeable levels, the establishment was now actively fighting against Bitcoin, and myths were percolating everywhere. People said it was criminal money, it was used for money laundering, the energy usage "boiled oceans," and they likened it to tulip mania. Understandably, these myths were being disseminated by the very intermediaries who had everything to lose from Bitcoin's success.

And right there on the beach, I decided to write what would become my first major Bitcoin manifesto: "Seven Myths of Bitcoin." The timing felt perfect. We were in the thick of the fight, and these misconceptions needed to be addressed head-on.

Blockchain Central Davos

After Miami and my reflective time there, we flew to Davos for what would become one of our most memorable World Economic Forum experiences. We'd rented out "Blockchain Central," a major space on the promenade at The Pavilion, as well as a massive villa overlooking the Swiss Alps, where we opened our doors to friends, board members, and advisors.

> The World Economic Forum brings together global political and business leaders each January in the Swiss Alpine resort of Davos. For crypto entrepreneurs, having a presence at Davos signaled legitimacy—moving from the fringes to the center of global economic discussion.

We transformed a traditional Swiss chalet into our Bitcoin head-quarters, housing close to fifty team members and partners. Our fleet of drivers shuttled us through the snow-covered streets between sessions, events, and late-night gatherings. The entire week became a blur of non-stop meetings, impromptu partnerships, and breakthrough conversations that would have been impossible anywhere else.

At Blockchain Central, we orchestrated a four-day program that became the talk of Davos. Each morning began with intimate breakfast sessions where ministers shared coffee with coders, followed by power lunches where billion-dollar ideas took shape over fondue.

Our favorite luncheon spot became the Schatzalp Panorama Restaurant, a magical venue perched high above Davos. To get there, we'd board the historic Schatzalp-Bahn funicular from Davos Platz and watch through frost-covered windows as it climbed to 1,860 meters over a scenic route. The restaurant offered sweeping panoramas of Davos, Lake Davos, and the surrounding alpine peaks through its large windows, with a cozy interior and sun-drenched terrace where toasts and discussions would flow as freely as the wine.

One memorable day, as we celebrated the cementing of yet another partnership, my dear Brazilian friend Paula Guedes nudged me for a toast. "Toast, Georgie. We want toast," she said in her captivating Brazilian accent.

I was all too eager to comply. Rising with my glass of wine, over-looking the mountain peaks that stretched endlessly before us, I said, "To always staying curious, my friends. To always asking, 'Why?'"

The venue pulsed with energy as hundreds of visitors flowed through, creating unlikely collisions of worlds. Prime ministers debated blockchain governance with Buddhist monks, Silicon Valley VCs compared notes with African entrepreneurs, and Nobel laureates learned about mining from twenty-something developers.

The real magic crystallized during our evening cocktail sessions. Wednesday night's panel on "How Should Governments Use & Regulate Blockchain" became a defining moment, with Val commanding the stage alongside EU Parliament member Eva Kaili, former Estonian Prime Minister Taavi Roivas, and former Haitian Prime Minister Laurent Lamothe. As snow fell outside and the Alpine lights twinkled below, the conversation inside was reshaping how nations would approach this revolutionary technology.

"The question isn't whether blockchain will transform governance," Val stated confidently during the panel. "The question is whether governments will lead that transformation or be left behind by it."

These Davos evenings would culminate in lavish invite-only dinners for one hundred carefully selected guests, where we'd continue the conversations over fine wine and alpine cuisine. These intimate gatherings featured keynote presentations that delved deeper into the transformative power of the technology, away from the crowds and cameras of the main conference halls. The combination of exclusivity, excellent food, and passionate discourse about blockchain's potential created an atmosphere where real connections were forged and meaningful partnerships began to take shape.

One of the new members of our extended group was Matt Sorum from Guns N' Roses. During one particularly memorable after-party, Matt was blasting "November Rain" and "Sweet Child O' Mine" through the crisp mountain air—a surreal experience I'll remember forever.

The Cuban Detour

After the big meetup in Bermuda for the annual crypto conference organised under the patronage of good friend Prime Minister David Burt and Canadian investor meetings before Hut 8's listing, Bob Dhillon—a good friend of ours and prominent Canadian real estate entrepreneur—made an unexpected suggestion during our downtime.

"Hey, guys, seems like you have a little break before the company's official listing. Why don't we take a trip to Cuba? I have connections there, and I can host us properly."

In our typical fashion, we said, "Why not?" From Toronto, we flew into Havana.

Bob had rented a huge villa in the Ambassador District with a beautiful swimming pool nestled inside palm trees. When we arrived at the villa, we were greeted by a large package of superb Cuban cigars. From the very first morning, Bob would start each day with his signature call: "You boys ready to puff?" and hand out fresh ones to all of us. Throughout the day, "Let's puff" became one of his favorite rallying cries, and smoking four or five cigars per day became a natural and pleasant rhythm to our Cuban adventure.

We spent time smoking incredible cigars and eating at great restaurants with amazing music flowing through the streets. During the days, we would rent old American convertibles and drive through Havana with the wind in our hair, classic cars everywhere, and faded colonial architecture creating a cinematic backdrop.

One afternoon at the legendary National Hotel, drinking Cuban coffee and watching waves crash against the Malecón while discussing Bitcoin's potential in emerging markets, the irony wasn't lost on me. Here we were, in a country representing the ultimate centralized economy, talking about decentralized digital money.

No trip to Havana would have been complete without visiting the massive Plaza de la Revolución, where Fidel had given his record-breaking speeches to massive crowds. Standing in the shadow of the José Martí Memorial, I reflected on revolution itself.

"You know," I said to Val, "every revolution starts with people who believe in something different."

One night, Bob said mysteriously, "Hey, guys, I want you to meet someone." The door opened, and in walked Alejandro Castro, Fidel's son. He was apparently fascinated by Bitcoin and wanted to meet with us.

"I understand you're the Bitcoin pioneers," he said in accented English, settling into a chair with a premium Cuban cigar. "I am a big fan myself. Tell me more about what you do."

And there we were, discussing the ultimate decentralized currency with the son of history's most famous centralized revolutionary. Over drinks and cigars, we explained our business model. After a few rounds of rum, Alejandro spoke to me in Russian, which was part of his upbringing, and I responded in kind. "Let's go check out some locations," he suggested.

What happened next was unforgettable. Coming out of a restaurant, Alejandro said, "You guys come with me," and picked us up in a 1970s

Soviet military jeep. By this time, we were all pretty intoxicated, and he proceeded to show us his Havana while jetting down the streets at 70 mph in the middle of the night. Traffic cops everywhere would look at us, recognize who it was, and salute while he blasted old revolutionary songs.

The most memorable moment came while we were jetting around Havana when Alejandro put on his music and on came the Russian revolutionary song "Katyusha," that iconic ballad from World War II. Without skipping a beat, Alejandro started singing along in perfect Russian as he drove, his voice carrying the familiar lyrics about a girl sending her love to a soldier on the distant borderland. Here we were, racing through the streets of Cuba in a Soviet military jeep with Fidel Castro's son belting out a Soviet wartime song. It felt like stepping into some impossible intersection of history and cryptocurrency revolution.

I looked at Val. He looked at me. The experience was absolutely surreal.

The next day, Alejandro discussed with us a potential mining location, but when we ran the numbers, electricity would be prohibitively expensive—prohibitively high to make things work over a long time. Cuba had energy deficits and mostly ran on diesel, making it nowhere near the competitiveness of global hydro or renewables that were driving the most efficient mining operations worldwide. As a parting gift, he brought out Ziploc bags filled with fifty unmarked cigars each.

"This is my gift to you," he said graciously.

I brought those cigars back to Georgia and gave them to Remi, who's a cigar aficionado. According to him, they were by far the best cigars he'd ever tried. And the last we heard, Alejandro did end up setting up a small mining operation with someone else outside of Havana.

The Listing

We left Cuba and flew back to Canada for the final touches on our historic listing. And on Monday, March 26, 2018, we rang the opening bell at the Toronto Stock Exchange. Hut 8 was officially born.

I have that famous snapshot with Bill, Val, and me at the Toronto Stock Exchange before the bell rang, taken at 08:08:08. It was our way of infusing Hut 8 with luck, which for sure worked. We had everyone there—Marc, Sean, Harris, Andrew, all the other bankers that worked on the deal, the entire executive team. It was a massive event marking the birth of a company that would embark on an amazing journey with Bill at its helm.

That evening, we celebrated with a fantastic dinner at one of Toronto's top restaurants. The energy was infectious. We had just made history as one of the first major Bitcoin mining companies to go public. But when I returned to my suite at the Mandarin Oriental, I found myself restless, unable to sleep.

There was so much happening in the industry, and adrenaline from the day's events was still coursing through my veins. I opened Twitter and saw massive reposting of my "Seven Myths of Bitcoin" Medium article that I published weeks earlier. The response had been incredible.

Energized by recent events and inspired by the continued buzz around my first article, I sat down at my laptop in that Toronto hotel suite and started writing. Ideas flowed freely—thoughts about Bitcoin's resilience, the virtuous cycle we were witnessing, significant resources now backing the ecosystem, and the protection it offered against future financial crises.

By early morning, I had completed what would become my second major Medium article: "Bitcoin & The Point of No Return." The timing felt perfect. We had just listed our Canadian assets, Bitcoin was gaining mainstream acceptance, and I wanted to articulate why this technology had reached a tipping point where there was no going back.

The article opened with a quote from T. E. Lawrence:

All men dream, but not equally. Those who dream by night in the dusty recesses of their minds, wake in the day to find that it was vanity: but the dreamers of the day are dangerous men, for they may act on their dreams with open eyes, to make them possible.

It felt fitting. Satoshi had been one of those dangerous dreamers of the day, and here we were, acting on those dreams with open eyes. Writing that piece just hours after ringing the opening bell for Hut 8 felt like a perfect capstone to an extraordinary day.

CHAPTER 12

EUPHORIA

A rolling stone gathers no moss.

—Latin Proverb

By early 2018, Bitfury had grown into something I could barely recognize from our early days. As we approached what felt like unstoppable success, we held our annual strategy meeting in Barcelona.

Anna, our head of HR, had organized our yearly gathering with characteristic precision, renting out all meeting rooms at the W Hotel. The entire core team descended on Barcelona. There were close to 130 employees from over twenty countries, representing hardware, software, legal, finance, and an expanding portfolio of new projects. Walking through the bustling corridors, hearing conversations in Ukrainian, Russian, English, and Spanish, I felt a profound sense of accomplishment.

During one session, I looked at Val as we surveyed the huge meeting rooms filled with our troops. "Wow," I said, "we've really grown big."

Val nodded, but his expression was thoughtful rather than purely celebratory. "Sometimes I wonder if we still have the same agility we had when it was just twenty of us making decisions around a kitchen table."

Over the next four days, we had presentation after presentation on company plans, growth trajectories, and ambitious expansion schemes. But perhaps the most significant development was our introduction of Objectives and Key Results (OKRs), a goal-setting methodology that would transform how we operated.

The idea for implementing OKRs had come from an unexpected source. During that magical New Year's Eve celebration on Sheikh Zayed's yacht in Dubai, as fireworks exploded over the Atlantis hotel, I found myself in deep conversation with Sergey Brin about Google's remarkable scaling journey.

"Sergey," I had asked, as we stood on the yacht's deck watching the Dubai skyline, "how did Google manage to maintain its innovation culture while growing from a Stanford project to a global powerhouse? We're facing similar challenges at Bitfury."

Sergey had paused thoughtfully, swirling his champagne. "One of the most important things we implemented early was OKRs—Objectives and Key Results. John Doerr introduced the system to us, and it became our North Star for maintaining focus and alignment as we scaled."

"How does it work in practice?" I had pressed, genuinely curious.

"It's about transparency and measurable outcomes," he explained. "Every team, every individual, has clear objectives tied to measurable key results. Everyone knows what everyone else is working on and how success is defined. It prevents the chaos that kills most growing companies."

A few months later, as if the universe was orchestrating events perfectly, John Doerr published his influential book *Measure What Matters*, distilling decades of OKR experience into a practical guide. The timing couldn't have been better for our Barcelona strategy sessions.

Upon finishing the book, I instantly sent it to Val and our Head of Operations, Vadym, with a note: "We MUST install this at Bitfury."

Vadym, a guru of operational excellence and efficiency tracking, embraced the concept immediately. "This is exactly what we need," he said during one of our preparation calls. "We've grown so fast that some teams don't even know what other teams are building. OKRs will create the transparency and focus we need."

OKRs (Objectives and Key Results) were pioneered at Intel by Andy Grove and later championed by venture capitalist John Doerr, who introduced them to Google, where they became central to the company's management philosophy. The system combines ambitious, qualitative objectives with measurable, time-bound key results, creating transparency and alignment across organizations.

The four-day meetup culminated in presentations from our sales and marketing teams, where our CMO George Givishvili unveiled a revolutionary new chip campaign. George, a veteran of marketing at companies like Philip Morris, had grown frustrated with our technical naming conventions.

"We're transforming the industry," he declared during his presentation, "but we're marketing our chips like industrial components. Bitfury 55, Bitfury 16… these names say nothing about the revolution we're creating."

His solution was inspired: naming our chips after science fiction writers, recognizing that we were, in essence, writing the science fiction of our time. The first chip would be named "Clarke," after Arthur C. Clarke, as a tribute to the visionary who had imagined satellites and space exploration decades before they became reality.

"Clarke will make serious noise in the market," George predicted, and he was right. The rebranding transformed how customers and media perceived our technology, shifting from mundane hardware to revolutionary innovation.

After marketing, our sales team took the stage with projections that left everyone stunned. They presented a potential pipeline exceeding $2 billion, with customers around the world clamoring for our next-generation mining hardware. The demand was so overwhelming that they pleaded with operations to accelerate chip production to satisfy even a portion of the orders.

However, as the meetings wound down, I felt compelled to inject a note of caution into our collective euphoria.

"You know," I said, standing before the assembled team, "while we should absolutely celebrate how far we've come, let's also be cognizant that a significant part of our financial success has been tied to the massive appreciation of Bitcoin's price. We need to be conscious of that reality and think about what might happen if there's a correction."

Val immediately supported this perspective. "We should always make projections for multiple scenarios, including a bear market," he agreed. "Success in this industry requires preparing for volatility."

This approach had become our insurance policy—a preparation for downside scenarios that both Val and I considered essential. We both remembered that barely eighteen months earlier, we had been on the brink of complete wipeout during the TSMC crisis. That near-death experience had left a lasting impression, teaching us to remain optimistic while always maintaining downside protection.

In many ways, the 16 nm chip crisis had primed Bitfury's adaptive immune system for challenges to come. We had learned that external factors beyond our control could threaten even the most well-executed plans, and that survival required both preparation and resilience.

Right after Barcelona, Val and I flew to New York for investor meetings. While there, we met up with our Block Wars veterans for what felt like a long-overdue victory celebration. At Cipriani SoHo with Adam Back, Samson Mow, and our own Sysman, we reminisced about the scaling battles over perfectly aged steaks and Barolo. The vindication was palpable.

"We were right from the very beginning," Adam commented, swirling his wine with the satisfaction of someone whose technical vision had been completely validated.

"Indeed," I replied, pulling up my ZeroBlock app. Bitcoin was around $8,000 while BCH languished at $1,000. "And the price shows it."

Samson leaned back, a rare smile crossing his face. "The irony is beautiful. Bitcoin is stronger than ever, while BCH is already irrelevant. Technical merit always wins in the end."

"The code doesn't lie," Sysman added with his characteristic technical precision. "SegWit was always the superior engineering solution. The market just needed time to figure that out."

We raised our glasses in a toast to technical excellence over political expedience. The Block Wars were over, and we had emerged as architects of Bitcoin's future.

Institutional Round

From New York, Val and I flew to London for follow-up meetings with institutional investors. We were closing a strategic funding round that had begun six months earlier with Bryan Garnier, a boutique French investment bank introduced by François Garcin, one of our Monaco-based investors.

François was a jolly character from the asset management world—a big Bitcoin fan whose fund owned several villas in the South of France. He regularly organized Bitcoin orange-pilling events for wealthy Europeans, spreading cryptocurrency awareness through his affluent network.

I'll never forget one of François's gatherings where Steve Waterhouse from Pantera Capital and I became so passionate about Bitcoin's potential that an elderly Italian princess, overwhelmed by our presentation, went home and immediately ordered her wealth manager to purchase thousands of bitcoins. The price at the time was hovering around $350.

Rumor has it that her butler, overhearing the conversation about the lady's investment, decided to put a significant portion of his life savings into Bitcoin as well. He's now happily retired in his new villa somewhere in Provence—a perfect example of how Bitcoin's wealth creation extended far beyond traditional investment circles.

The idea behind our funding round was institutionalization—evolving from super angel investors to a proper Series C with institutional capital. We particularly liked Korelya Capital, our lead investor, whose limited partners included Naver Group, one of Korea's biggest companies. The strategic angle was compelling since we had numerous projects in Korea and were looking to expand further throughout Asia.

A Series C funding round typically occurs when a company has proven its business model and is ready for major scaling. At this stage, institutional investors like pension funds and sovereign wealth funds enter, bringing not just capital but credibility and strategic partnerships that can transform a company's trajectory.

We decided to set the valuation at a modest $1 billion and raise $50 million. Given that we already had $200 million in cash reserves, we clearly didn't need the capital for operations. Instead, we wanted validation and an institutional pre-IPO round before a major public listing, which, given the success of Hut 8 and the opening of Western capital markets to Bitcoin-related companies, we felt was twelve to eighteen months away.

While in London for the meetings, we also had dinner with Saifedean Ammous, who was in the process of publishing *The Bitcoin Standard*.[9] Friends had introduced us, recognizing the alignment between his academic rigor and our practical experience building Bitcoin infrastructure.

"You know what's fascinating about Bitcoin?" Saif said over dinner at a quiet restaurant in Mayfair, leaning forward with characteristic intensity. "We're approaching a moment in history where Bitcoin will become scarcer than gold—mathematically, verifiably scarcer. And the world hasn't grasped this yet. They still think of it as Internet money, not understanding that we're witnessing the birth of the hardest money ever created."

The conversation meandered through Bitcoin's monetary properties, the importance of scarcity, and the time value of sound money. Saif's ability to distill complex economic concepts into clear, compelling arguments was remarkable.

"The establishment is finally beginning to understand what we've been building," I observed. "But they still don't grasp the full implications of programmable scarcity."

We ended up ordering a large batch of books and pledged to support Saif by translating *The Bitcoin Standard* into several languages. We kept our promise, helping spread Bitcoin's intellectual foundation across linguistic and cultural boundaries.

While in London, I also reconnected with Ciro Orsini, a fascinating character who embodied the glamorous intersection of entertainment and emerging technology. Ciro was the founder of Ciro Pomodoro, a promotional entertainment company plugged into both Hollywood and Bollywood circles. His client list read like a who's who of action stars. Stallone, Van Damme, Bruce Willis, and Jackie Chan—all the superstars attended his events.

We'd first met in Ukraine when he opened a restaurant there, and I'd told him about Bitcoin when it was trading at $200. Every time we reconnected, the conversation followed a familiar pattern.

"George," he said in his thick Neapolitan accent over dinner at his Knightsbridge restaurant, "Every time we meet, I wish I had bought more Bitcoin, you know?"

This time, however, Ciro had more than regrets to share. "Actually, I know someone—Sammie from Guangzhou—who really wants to go big in Bitcoin mining. Why don't you meet him? I have a good feeling about this."

Since I was flying to Hong Kong anyway, I agreed to the introduction. Ciro's network had always surprised me with its reach and quality, so I trusted his judgment.

Sammie turned out to be a fascinating character who embodied the flamboyant excess of China's new wealth. Young and well-connected through his highly-placed father, he drove Lamborghinis and Mercedes G-Wagons with equal flair, ran beauty pageants, and possessed an infectious enthusiasm for Bitcoin's potential.

Sammie represented the new generation of Chinese entrepreneurs. He was young, wealthy, globally minded, and eager to deploy serious capital in emerging opportunities. His approach to business was refreshingly direct: identify the best opportunities, move fast, and bring overwhelming resources to bear.

Greg and I ended up spending considerable time with Sammie between Guangzhou, Hong Kong, and Macau, exploring potential partnerships and deployment strategies. Through Sammie's network, we learned about someone in Tajikistan who claimed to have a massive opportunity for Bitcoin mining in connection with underutilized hydroelectric capacity.

After perhaps too many whiskeys during one of our Macau dinners, we found ourselves saying, "OK, we'll go check it out."

True to our word, we chartered a private jet with Sammie's group. Zhijun, who had become part of our expanding Asian operations, joined the expedition. Our itinerary was ambitious: first to Ukraine to show Sammie our software operations, then to Georgia to showcase our immersion cooling data center, and finally to Tajikistan to investigate this mysterious mining opportunity.

The flight to Dushanbe was spectacular, crossing the Hindu Kush mountains as dawn broke over Central Asia. As we descended into Tajikistan, the landscape unfolded like something from an ancient Silk Road tale. Rugged mountains, deep valleys, and rivers carved through terrain that had witnessed centuries of history.

In Tajikistan, we were greeted by Java, Sammie's contact and head of the investment committee to the president. Java was impressive—intelligent, multilingual, and clearly well-connected within the government hierarchy. He immediately took us on what he promised would be an unforgettable journey into the mountains.

As our convoy wound through increasingly dramatic terrain, Java served as our guide and storyteller, explaining Tajikistan's complex history and its ambitious plans for economic development.

"The Soviet Union built incredible infrastructure here," he explained as we climbed higher into the mountains. "Much of it remains underutilized, particularly our hydroelectric capacity."

When we rounded a final bend and emerged into a vast valley, I gasped audibly. Before us lay one of the most impressive engineering achievements I'd ever witnessed. The Nurek Dam rose from the valley floor like a concrete mountain, its massive walls stretching 300 meters into the sky.

Completed in 1980, the Nurek Dam stands as one of the world's tallest dams, generating approximately 11,200 Terawatt-hours annually, which is three times the size of Hoover Dam and enough to power some million US households. During the Soviet era, it represented a triumph of engineering ambition, though much of its capacity remained underutilized due to Tajikistan's limited industrial base and remote location.

"What's the cost of electricity here?" I asked, still trying to process the scale of what I was seeing.

Java smiled knowingly. "It's practically zero because everything's been amortized decades ago. The challenge isn't generating power—it's finding productive uses for it."

As we stood on the observation deck, listening to the thunderous roar of water cascading through the spillways, I felt like I was in a paradise of renewable energy. The potential for deploying thousands of megawatts of Bitcoin mining capacity was immediately apparent.

We spent hours sketching plans and calculating possibilities, but it quickly became clear that realizing this vision would require more than just technical deployment. In Tajikistan, we would first need Bitcoin approved as a legal virtual currency—a process requiring extensive government engagement and regulatory development.

The bureaucratic timeline was daunting. While the opportunity was massive, the Bitcoin industry moved at the speed of light, and waiting for Tajikistan's legislative process to unfold could mean missing crucial market windows.

As our plane lifted off from Dushanbe, carrying us back to more immediate opportunities, I told Sammie, "The potential here is absolutely massive, but they need to establish the right legal framework first. In the Bitcoin world, where speed is everything, we simply can't afford to wait while the country's leadership works through the regulatory process."

The vision of that cascading water and the potential for deploying industrial-scale mining operations stayed with me, a reminder of both the global opportunities and the practical challenges inherent in our industry's expansion.

As we wrapped up our Central Asian adventures and finalized substantial equipment orders with Sammie for his deployment operations in China, I flew to Japan for a major Rakuten conference where I was scheduled as a keynote speaker.

The venue was packed with over a thousand attendees filling the auditorium, and I spoke passionately about Bitcoin's revolutionary potential and the power of decentralization. The response was fantastic, with animated Q&A sessions that ran well past the scheduled time.

"That was an excellent presentation, George-san," Mikitani-san commented during the cocktail reception afterward, his enthusiasm genuine.

"Domo arigato gozaimasu," I replied with a smile. "I couldn't do any less in the land of Satoshi Nakamoto."

Japan's embrace of Bitcoin regulation created a uniquely receptive environment for cryptocurrency education and adoption. Speaking in the country that had given birth to Bitcoin's pseudonymous creator felt symbolically significant, representing the technology's journey from cypherpunk experiment to mainstream acceptance.

Later that week, I visited our senior contacts at Daiwa Securities and Dentsu to update them on Bitfury's progress. The meetings were encouraging, with both organizations expressing continued interest in deepening their partnerships with us.

"We are ready to participate in your next funding round," Shindo-san from Daiwa commented during our meeting at their Tokyo headquarters.

"Excellent. Our bankers will send the documentation soon," I replied, appreciating their consistent support.

From Japan, I made one final trip to Hong Kong, where I met with Macquarie Capital. Jack Yee, who would become a good friend and valuable partner, headed their equities division and was considering joining our funding round with a strategic angle that extended far beyond pure investment.

Macquarie was a powerhouse in global energy infrastructure, and their interest lay in identifying energy locations worldwide where they could fund infrastructure development while we deployed mining operations. This partnership model promised to be extraordinarily fruitful for Bitfury's global expansion.

We closed the Series C round during the summer of 2018, and when all formalities were complete, Bitfury officially became a unicorn—the first Bitcoin unicorn from the European Union. The milestone felt surreal, considering our humble beginnings in Ukrainian offices and Georgian data centers.

Val and I flew to Amsterdam, where we brought all the investors together for a celebratory dinner at an elegant Dutch restaurant overlooking the historic canals. As glasses clinked and toasts echoed through the private dining room, there was a palpable sense of having reached a crucial inflection point.

"To victory! To our journey!" I toasted, raising my glass high.

"To the IPO!" Grégoire, our banker, followed up enthusiastically.

The mood was exuberant, electric with possibility. Everyone was eagerly anticipating the next chapter, confident that an IPO was the logical next step in our trajectory.

Right there, amidst the celebration and flowing wine, we made the decision to begin searching for investment bank underwriters and start preparing the company for a listing on either European or American stock exchanges.

The rocket ship was reaching escape velocity. What could possibly go wrong?

Atlas Mountains

Nothing, it seemed, could stop our momentum. We were gaining strength daily, acquiring customers globally, and approaching what felt like the summit of our entrepreneurial journey. With summer approaching, we decided to continue our annual tradition of meetups with Sir Richard Branson, but this time we chose one of his other spectacular global locations.

Morocco beckoned—specifically, Marrakesh. During one of our Necker retreats, Sir Richard's nephew Jack and his wife Alexandra, who had become dear friends, suggested we vary our scenery.

"George, I think Richard would appreciate hosting you in Morocco," Jack had said. "The property is absolutely amazing. We could do Morocco and then perhaps Ulusaba in South Africa."

Val and I loved the idea immediately and committed on the spot.

So in July, we organized our Fourth Annual Blockchain Summit at Sir Richard's Moroccan oasis, Kasbah Tamadot, nestled majestically in the Atlas Mountains. The beautiful and serene backdrop provided the perfect setting for what our invitation described as "a unique opportunity to counsel with an intimate selection of the world's leading thinkers and innovators on the transformative power of blockchain technology."

The four-day event in early July brought together an incredible roster of forty luminaries from across the global blockchain ecosystem. Our program featured panels on "Opportunities Beyond the West," with speakers including Roya Mahboob from Digital Citizen Fund, Sheila Warren from the World Economic Forum, Kenya's Telecom Minister Joe Mucheru, and our friend Sheikh Zayed Al Nahyan from the UAE.

We had powerhouse sessions on blockchain innovation featuring Sandra Ro, CEO of the Global Blockchain Business Council, Elizabeth Rossiello, CEO of BitPesa, and Young Sohn from Samsung. The regulatory panel was equally impressive, bringing together Eva Kaili from the European Parliament, Jim Newsome, Jason Weinstein, and government leaders, including Guy Verhofstadt, former Prime Minister of Belgium.

Perhaps the most forward-thinking panel was "Satoshi is Female"—focusing on building diversity into blockchain—featuring Katie Haun, former DOJ attorney and the first female partner at Andreessen

Horowitz; Nicole Shanahan, founder of ClearAccessIP who later would run on the VP ballot with Bobby Kennedy; Neha Narula, Director of the Digital Currency Initiative at MIT; and Elizabeth Stark, founder of Lightning Labs.

One particularly memorable moment came during Bill Tai's panel on "Encouraging the Green Revolution," where discussions of sustainable mining practices and renewable energy integration dominated the conversation. Another highlight occurred when Sergey Brin joined our panel on "The New Social Networks—Protecting Data, Returning Ownership to Creators."

Watching the Google co-founder discuss the future of data ownership alongside Matt Sorum from Guns N' Roses and Grammy-winning artist Imogen Heap was beautifully surreal—a perfect example of how our summits brought together unexpected but powerful combinations of minds from technology, entertainment, and creative industries.

That evening, as traditional Moroccan musicians filled the gardens with hypnotic rhythms, guests spilled out into the courtyards under lantern-lit olive trees. Peacocks from the nearby groves, stirred by the sounds and movement, began chirping into the warm night. Gigi Brisson, the ever-spirited founder of Ocean Elders, smiled as if greeting old friends. "Ka! Ka! Ka Ka!" she called out in her familiar rhythm—an echo from her California farm where she raised peacocks of her own. To everyone's delight, the birds answered back, their calls playful and sharp, echoing off the kasbah walls. It was a moment of pure joy, bridging continents and causes in the most unexpected way.

One memorable day, Sir Richard's mother, Eve Branson, organized a side trip deeper into the Atlas Mountains to visit a charity she had been working with for years. We spent a wonderful day exploring the rugged mountain terrain and witnessing the incredible work her foundation was accomplishing in local communities.

Eve Branson had founded the Eve Branson Foundation to support communities in Morocco's High Atlas Mountains, focusing on vocational training, preserving traditional crafts, and improving education and healthcare in the region. During our visit, we toured artisanal training centers teaching skills like weaving, embroidery, and woodworking, helping individuals generate sustainable income while preserving cultural heritage.

Over the years, Bitfury has been actively engaged in several Virgin Foundation initiatives—whether contributing to turtle conservation efforts in the British Virgin Islands or supporting Ocean Elders' environmental conservation work around the globe. Val was always an enthusiastic contributor to the Virgin Foundation's important work, a partnership we've maintained to this day.

The summit generated significant media attention and produced concrete initiatives that would shape the industry's development. We announced three major projects: the CryptoKitties for Conservation initiative (featuring the Honu Kitty supporting ocean conservation), Project Barking Dog with Hernando de Soto exploring blockchain applications for "smart capitalism," and Bitfury's BE BIG global blockchain education initiative aimed at democratizing access to blockchain knowledge.

BE BIG (Bitfury Educational Blockchain Initiative for Good) represented our most ambitious educational undertaking. As our first major project under this umbrella, we committed to translating Satoshi Nakamoto's original Bitcoin whitepaper into all major languages, working alongside project partner Coin Center.

The initiative would foster blockchain awareness across five key areas: governments, communities, schools and educational institutions, healthcare systems, and conservation organizations. As Val explained to the media, "We founded Bitfury in 2011 after the Satoshi whitepaper convinced me of the power of Bitcoin and blockchain. We want to make sure every person, no matter their country of birth or language, has the same educational opportunities so they can adopt blockchain for the causes they care about and in the communities they live in."

Michael del Castillo from *Forbes* attended the full summit and wrote extensively about our discussions, including Richard's passionate stance against single-use plastics and Sergey Brin's refreshingly candid admission that "Google is behind" on blockchain technology—a statement that would prove prescient as traditional tech giants scrambled to develop blockchain strategies.

As the summit concluded with our gala dinner on the final night, traditional Moroccan musicians filled the air with hypnotic rhythms while guests mingled under a canopy of stars. I felt a tremendous sense of achievement. Sir Richard found me on the terrace, overlooking the Atlas Mountains silhouetted against the starlit sky.

"George, this has been absolutely extraordinary," he said, placing a hand on my shoulder. "The caliber of minds you've brought together, the conversations happening."

"Thank you, Sir Richard. Your support has been instrumental in making these gatherings possible," I replied. "From that first meeting on Necker to now—we've come such a long way."

Previous summits had fostered partnerships and projects, including the Global Blockchain Business Council, Blockchain Trust Accelerator, and Blockchain Alliance. This year's gathering promised to catalyze equally powerful initiatives that would shape the industry's future.

The event was a fantastic success, reinforcing our position as conveners and thought leaders in the global blockchain community. But as it concluded, I had to tear myself away from the magical Atlas Mountains setting to focus on my next destination: China, where new opportunities awaited.

Enter the Dragon

This was when Sammie introduced me to one of the most intriguing characters in Chinese high finance—a flamboyant billionaire known simply as "Dragon." A member of Jack Ma's trusted inner circle and worth a few billion dollars himself, Dragon embodied the audacious spirit of China's tech boom. He moved through the world in private jets and Bentleys, wearing his success like a perfectly tailored suit.

But beneath the flash lay serious business acumen. Dragon had helped architect some of China's most successful tech ventures, understanding opportunities others missed. His wife, Vicki Zhao, one of China's most celebrated actresses, had parlayed her fame into becoming a major force in Bordeaux's wine industry, giving the power couple influence that spanned entertainment, technology, and luxury goods.

Our first meeting unfolded in Hong Kong's most exclusive cigar club, tucked away in the Central district, where the city's dealmakers gathered to shape Asia's future over Cuban tobacco and rare whiskeys. Crystal decanters caught the amber light as billions of dollars in deals took shape in hushed conversations around us.

"Sammie speaks highly of Bitfury," Dragon said, settling into his leather chair as smoke from a Cohiba Behike curled toward the coffered ceiling. "Tell me how you conquered Bitcoin mining."

As I walked him through our technology stack between sips of 18-year-old Yamazaki, I watched his eyes sharpen with interest. This wasn't just social courtesy—he was calculating possibilities, seeing angles.

"Blockchain could transform Jack's entire ecosystem," he mused, leaning forward. "E-commerce, logistics, payments—we could revolutionize how Alibaba operates. This technology is bigger than people realize. In addition, I like your AI chip project and data center cooling technology. Alibaba has a massive data center footprint, and this could be a great value-add."

Before I knew it, we were boarding his Gulfstream G650, bound for our mining facilities. Dragon wanted to see our operations firsthand—a good sign that meant serious interest, not just talk. As we toured our data centers, I watched his expression shift from curiosity to genuine respect. The sheer scale of our operations, the precision cooling systems, the symphony of thousands of machines mining Bitcoin—it was one thing to discuss it over cigars, quite another to feel the electric hum of computational power that had taken us years to perfect.

From there, we flew directly to London, touching down at Farnborough as the city lights sparkled below. Dragon had suggested continuing our discussions at George, the ultra-exclusive Mayfair club where membership was harder to obtain than a knighthood.

In a private dining room adorned with Basquiat paintings and overlooking Mount Street, we settled into leather banquettes as perfectly aged Burgundy was poured. The quiet confidence of old money surrounded us—this was where London's establishment mingled with international wealth, where discretion was absolute.

Dragon studied the wine's color against the candlelight before speaking. "We're prepared to move forward with $200 million," he said, with the same ease most people would mention lending twenty dollars. "Valuation remains to be determined pending full due diligence, but consider this our statement of intent."

The number hung in the air between us, transforming from possibility to probability. In that rarified atmosphere, surrounded by centuries of accumulated wealth, Bitcoin's future was being written one deal at a time.

That sounds reasonable," I replied, maintaining eye contact as I swirled the Burgundy in my glass. "But you need to understand—crypto moves at light speed. While traditional deals take months, our industry's windows of opportunity can close in weeks."

Dragon smiled, appreciating the directness. "Then we move fast too."

Right there, in that hushed Mayfair sanctuary where fortunes had been made for centuries, we shook hands on beginning immediate due diligence. The crystal glasses clinked with a resonance that seemed to echo beyond that private room—East meeting West, old money embracing new technology, tradition merging with revolution.

As our cars pulled away into the London night, I couldn't shake the feeling that we'd just crossed a threshold. The Dragon partnership represented China's tech elite betting big on blockchain's future. For Bitfury, it promised to be one of the most transformational alliances in our history, opening doors across Asia that no amount of money alone could unlock.

The game was changing, and we were writing the new rules.

As we launched the due diligence process with Dragon's team, I realized I was committed to attending a weekend gathering at Lake Como, hosted by Alan Howard at his spectacular lakeside estate. Alan, a prominent hedge fund manager who had embraced Bitcoin early and enthusiastically, was organizing an intimate weekend with thirty Bitcoin and crypto OGs to assess where the industry was heading.

In addition to the prospect of reconnecting with old friends and industry legends, I was particularly excited because my friend Marco had casually mentioned that I could use his McLaren 720S whenever I was in Milan—an offer I was definitely intent on accepting.

So there I was, behind the wheel of a beautiful McLaren, pushing through the Italian autostrada with Al Bano and Romina Power's "Felicità" blasting in the background. The drive to Lake Como was exhilarating, the car responding to every input with precision as the Italian countryside blurred past. I made excellent time and soon found myself sipping Bellinis with Alan and his distinguished guests.

Lake Como has long been a gathering place for Europe's financial elite, its dramatic Alpine backdrop and Italian elegance providing the perfect setting for high-level discussions away from the constraints of formal business environments. The combination of natural beauty and privacy made it ideal for the kind of candid conversations that shape industry direction.

At one memorable lunch, I found myself seated between Kevin Warsh, former head of the New York Federal Reserve, and our investor Don Wilson from DRW. The seating arrangement felt like destiny— here was a former Fed official who needed to understand Bitcoin's true nature, flanked by true believers.

"Kevin," I began, seizing the moment, "every time central banks expand the money supply, they're inadvertently making the case for Bitcoin. You can't print more Bitcoin—it's mathematically capped at 21 million coins. That's the elegance of programmed scarcity versus unlimited fiat creation."

Don leaned in, his trader's instincts sharp as ever. "That's exactly why DRW got into the Bitcoin story early. When you've spent decades trading markets, you recognize a paradigm shift."

Kevin listened intently, his Fed training evident in his measured responses. The conversation deepened when another Bitcoin OG— Danny Masters of CoinShares—joined our circle.

"Think of it this way," Danny offered, gesturing with his wine glass. "Gold worked brilliantly as analog money for millennia. But we're not analog anymore—we're digital beings living digital lives. Bitcoin is simply evolution catching up with revolution."

The former Fed official nodded slowly, processing this paradigm shift.

Later, we all took sleek Riva boats across Lake Como's mirror-like waters, arriving at La Punta in Bellagio just as the afternoon sun painted the mountains gold. The conversation continued on the terrace over fresh lake fish and chilled Franciacorta, with the Alps standing witness to our discussion of digital finance's future. For hours, we debated everything from monetary theory to practical portfolio allocation strategies.

The next day, I gave a presentation to the assembled group on "The State of Mining and Bitfury's Technology Leadership." I walked them through our journey from Ukrainian startup to global infrastructure provider, showcasing our state-of-the-art immersion cooling data centers and next-generation chip development.

The audience was genuinely impressed, particularly by our immersion cooling technology, which many hadn't seen implemented at such scale. The efficiency gains and environmental benefits resonated strongly with this sophisticated group of investors.

After my presentation, one of Alan's managing directors pulled me aside. "Listen, we want to look at investing in Bitfury directly. Is there an opportunity for us to participate in your next funding round?" he asked.

Almost immediately after, another large fund manager approached with the same question. I thought to myself: When it rains, it pours. Keeping track of all the potential investors was becoming a genuinely challenging problem—a good problem to have, but a problem nonetheless.

The Switch That Stayed On

In September, while we were riding high on investor interest and technological achievements, our main competitor, Bitmain, decided to hold their World Digital Mining Summit in Tbilisi, right in our backyard. From September 21-23, the Chinese miner gathered the crypto mining world in the very city where we had built our massive data centers and established deep roots with the Georgian government.

The choice of location felt deliberately provocative. Here was our competitor, hosting their major conference in the city we had helped transform into a blockchain hub. But we weren't going to let them have the stage unchallenged.

We prepared meticulously. In the days leading up to the summit, we plastered the entire city with Bitfury chip advertisements. Every major billboard, every prominent corner—wherever summit attendees would look, they'd see our technology on display. If Bitmain wanted to play in our backyard, they'd do so surrounded by reminders of who built this ecosystem.

During the conference, we organized lavish lunches and data center tours, keeping our sales team busy showcasing our technology to interested attendees. We also hosted elaborate dinners at my favorite restaurants for those considering switching sides. The Georgian hospitality we offered stood in stark contrast to the formal conference atmosphere, reminding everyone of our deep connections to this land. The strategy worked brilliantly—while Bitmain held its conference, we were closing deals on the sidelines.

The climax came at the Tbilisi Opera House, where Bitmain had rented the grand venue for their flagship announcement. Jihan Wu, their co-CEO, was set to unveil their new 7 nm ASIC mining chip that promised remarkable efficiency. This was to be their moment of triumph, broadcast live to audiences worldwide.

Georgia is a small country where everyone knows everyone. As fate would have it, the head of opera security was the uncle of a good friend. Minutes before Jihan's big reveal, my phone buzzed with a text:

"Mr. George, we have a green light?"

He was standing ready at the main electrical switch. One flip, and the entire opera house would plunge into darkness just as Jihan stepped forward to unveil their chip. The global livestream would cut to black. Their carefully orchestrated moment would become a disaster.

I stared at the message, my thumb hovering over the keyboard. The temptation was overwhelming. Here was our competitor, in our city, trying to steal our thunder. One push of the button, and their big announcement would be ruined.

But as I sat there, something held me back. We had built Bitfury on innovation, hard work, and integrity. We competed fiercely, but fairly. Sabotaging their event, however satisfying it might feel in the moment, wasn't who we were. We didn't need cheap shots to win.

"No, all good," I typed back. "Stand down."

Bordeaux Wineries

A few days after the Bitmain conference concluded, I was back in the air, this time bound for Bordeaux. Dragon had invited us to meet with Jack Ma's top team at one of the region's most prestigious wine estates.

"Get ready for some wine tasting," he texted me over WeChat.

"I always am," I replied.

We were expecting Jack himself to attend, which would have represented a culmination of months of strategic discussions. Dragon's wife, Vickie, had arranged for us to meet at one of the most prestigious wine estates in the region—a setting that perfectly embodied the intersection of Chinese capital and European luxury.

Chinese investment in Bordeaux wine estates had accelerated dramatically since 2010, with wealthy Chinese individuals and companies acquiring prestigious vineyards as both investments and symbols of cultural sophistication. The trend reflected China's growing appetite for luxury goods and alternative investments beyond traditional financial markets.

Dragon and Vickie had systematically built their Bordeaux portfolio, starting in 2011 with their acquisition of Château Monlot, a Saint-Émilion Grand Cru vineyard. Their success had helped guide Jack Ma's own wine investments, including his purchase of Château de Sours in 2016.

Jack's estate, located in Saint-Quentin-de-Baron within the Entre-Deux-Mers area, was undergoing an ambitious transformation under his ownership. Local residents had dubbed the renovations "mini Versailles" due to the extensive landscaping and architectural enhancements Jack was implementing.

The setting was perfect for our high-level discussions—surrounded by rolling vineyards, talking about the future of digital currency and technology partnerships. The symbolism wasn't lost on me: just as our Chinese friends were transforming the French estate with Chinese vision and capital, we were discussing how to transform the global financial landscape through blockchain technology.

We spent hours in detailed discussions about potential partnerships and the value that Alibaba Group could bring to Bitfury's global expansion. The synergies were compelling: Alibaba's massive e-commerce platform could benefit from blockchain-based supply chain transparency, while its financial services arm could leverage our infrastructure for digital currency integration.

After a lavish dinner featuring many of Jack's top lieutenants—men who had made fortunes in Alibaba's orbit and were now exploring blockchain opportunities—we descended into an underground karaoke bar where the real celebration began.

The scene was beautifully surreal: I found myself singing Chinese pop songs with Alibaba executives, then switching to ABBA classics, then Bruce Springsteen anthems. Premium Bordeaux wines—Pétrus,

Lafite—flowed freely, and the atmosphere was electric with possibility and mutual respect.

Looking back, that night represented the absolute peak of our confidence and ambition. Here we were, singing karaoke with some of China's most powerful business leaders, discussing hundred-million-dollar investments as if they were routine transactions. The hubris was intoxicating and, as we would later learn, potentially dangerous.

The next morning, Dragon emerged from his suite with characteristic panache, producing an ornate box from his luggage. "I always travel with this," he announced, revealing exclusive Chinese Oolong tea from his private collection. "It's the only cure for a proper Bordeaux hangover."

While we gathered in the château's dining room, Dragon's personal Spanish chef, Pellaio, commandeered the kitchen, whipping up an elaborate breakfast spread—perfectly poached eggs, Iberian ham, exotic fruits, and delicacies I couldn't even identify.

Amid the clatter of porcelain and the scent of truffle oil, I stumbled in, predictably hungover and staring down an existential espresso—only to find Nirvana Chaudhary already seated, perfectly composed, sipping tea like the night before had never happened.

Nirvana, heir to Nepal's most prominent business dynasty, carried a quiet gravitas. The Chaudhary Group—his family's sprawling empire—spans banking, real estate, consumer goods, and hospitality across South Asia. But Nirvana offered more than generational wealth; he radiated the calm intensity of someone fluent in the language of both legacy and disruption. I muttered something about my liver filing for early retirement.

Nirvana smiled. "That's why we built The Farm, my friend."

"The Farm?" I croaked.

He explained it all—a medical-grade detox and longevity retreat his family had invested in. A place in the Philippines. Clean air, vegan food, cold plunges, stem cells, the works.

I said, "After what Dragon just put me through, I need to sign up immediately."

He laughed and said, "We're always happy to host friends."

It was a perfect contrast—from the elegant chaos of Bordeaux to the clean minimalism of a Filipino wellness sanctuary—and somehow, both were equally vital parts of the journey. One filled the cup. The other emptied it. Both bonded.

As we sipped Dragon's mysterious tea, our heads began to clear remarkably fast. "Ancient Chinese wisdom," he winked, clearly enjoying his role as the group's savior.

Properly restored, we convened in the château's oak-paneled library for a crucial meeting with Dragon and his key partners to discuss specific investment details and timeline. Lawyers were instructed to begin drafting preliminary agreements, and everyone seemed aligned on moving forward aggressively.

Everything felt like it was falling perfectly into place. The next milestone would be meeting directly with Jack himself and finalizing the details of what promised to be a transformational partnership for Bitfury.

We departed Bordeaux on an exceptionally high note, confident that everything was proceeding exactly according to plan. Later, we found ourselves on a yacht sailing around Miami, greeting the sunrise with champagne toasts and absolute certainty that our rocket ship would continue its inexorable ascent.

The universe, however, had different plans.

CHAPTER 13
WHEN GRAVITY RETURNS

Men wanted for hazardous journey. Low wages, bitter cold,
long hours of complete darkness. Safe return doubtful.

—Ernest Shackleton

Things were looking phenomenal as we entered the fall of 2018. We'd successfully closed our institutional round, had serious interest for hundreds of millions in investment from Dragon's group and other strategic partners, and the time had come to launch our IPO roadshow. The confidence we'd built through our Morocco summit and subsequent meetings had created an unstoppable momentum, or so it seemed.

Val and I initiated the formal process, working closely with our French bankers, Grégoire and Pierre, to send out requests for proposal to all the leading global investment banks. In late September 2018, we issued comprehensive proposals to the top-tier institutions, inviting them to submit proposals to act as Joint Global Coordinators for our anticipated public offering.

The numbers in our pitch painted an impressive picture of just how far we'd traveled from those early days in a Kyiv café. We projected revenues for 2018 of approximately $500 million. Our global footprint had expanded to over a thousand employees across twenty countries, operating everything from cutting-edge immersion cooling data centers to enterprise blockchain solutions.

We were exploring listings on either the London Stock Exchange or Euronext Amsterdam, targeting the first half of 2019 for our market debut. The European exchanges had shown more openness to cryptocurrency-related companies than their American counterparts, where regulatory uncertainty continued to create obstacles.

> An Initial Public Offering requires months of meticulous preparation, including comprehensive financial audits, extensive legal documentation, and complex regulatory approvals. Investment banks compete fiercely for lead underwriter roles on major IPOs, as the fees and prestige can be enormous. The "bake-off" process involves banks presenting their credentials, market analysis, and proposed valuations to win the coveted mandate.

We selected six premier banks for our beauty contest, and they were absolutely dying to pitch for our business. The caliber of institutions pursuing our mandate—household names in global finance—reflected how dramatically the perception of cryptocurrency companies had evolved. The deadline for submissions was October 17, with formal presentations scheduled for our "bake-off" meetings in Amsterdam on October 30 and 31. It was an omen that this coincided with the ten-year anniversary of Satoshi writing his white paper. Here we were, looking to capitalize on a major Bitcoin story exactly a decade after the technology's genesis.

For two intensive days in Amsterdam, senior bankers flew in from London, Frankfurt, and New York to present their cases. The range of valuations was extremely comfortable—both Val and I exchanged knowing glances as banker after banker pitched, consistently valuing our business between $3.5 and $5.5 billion.

One presentation from a top-tier Western global bank was particularly compelling. They positioned us as "a pioneer and the only at-scale Bitcoin blockchain technology company" with a "massive addressable market opportunity" in the very early stages of cryptocurrency and blockchain adoption. Their executive summary painted us as the "clear market leader with sustainable competitive moats," leveraging proprietary technology and a vertically integrated business model that would be difficult for competitors to replicate.

"A well-positioned Bitfury will be extremely well-received by investors and will achieve an attractive valuation," their lead banker declared confidently, gesturing to colorful charts and projections. They highlighted our "attractive financial model with the rare combination of scale, high growth, and high margins," though they did include one cautionary note: "investors will need to be educated on the impact of crypto volatility on the financial model."

Another prestigious institution took a slightly more conservative approach, viewing "the valuation in the range of $3 billion to $4 billion," noting that "investor buy-in to 2020 targets and overall Bitcoin's cycle dynamics will be key to achieving the upper part of the range." Even their conservative estimate represented a remarkable validation of our journey.

The irony wasn't lost on me. Just two years earlier, when we were desperately seeking capital during our semiconductor crisis, we'd approached one of these same global investment banks. Their relationship bankers had been eager to help us raise capital, expressing enthusiasm for our technology and market position. But their risk committee had shut down any prospect of even taking on a Bitcoin company, viewing cryptocurrency as too speculative and reputationally risky.

Now those same institutions were competing aggressively for the privilege of taking us public. It was a powerful reminder of how rapidly perceptions could shift in our industry, though it also highlighted how dependent our success remained on market sentiment and timing.

The banks were recommending that we remain cognizant of our Chinese competitors—particularly Bitmain and Canaan's IPO timelines on the Hong Kong Stock Exchange—but not be driven by their schedules. There were "pros and cons of going first," they argued, so we should "do what is right for our business." With our "massive addressable market opportunity" and "sustainable competitive moats," they insisted we had the positioning to succeed regardless of timing.

As the final presentations concluded and handshakes were exchanged, Val and I felt a profound sense of validation. The investment banking community—the gatekeepers of public markets—was not just accepting us but actively courting us. The valuations being discussed would make Bitfury one of the most valuable blockchain technology companies in the world.

But sometime in early November, after the bankers had departed with their polished presentations and we'd conducted our internal strategy sessions, the first ominous signs of trouble began to emerge. The very crypto volatility that had warranted mere footnotes in bank presentations was about to become our greatest existential challenge.

Cracks in the Foundation

Throughout the summer and fall of 2018, Bitcoin's price had begun a stubborn, relentless decline. From the euphoric heights of nearly $20,000 just months earlier, it had dropped to $6,000, then $5,000, then $4,000, and simply refused to find a bottom. Each day brought fresh waves of selling pressure, negative headlines, and growing skepticism about cryptocurrency's future.

The massive pipeline of customers we'd built—over $2 billion in commitments that had seemed so solid during our Barcelona strategy sessions—started showing alarming cracks. We had confidently ordered chips from semiconductor foundries based on these projections, and those expensive components were now arriving just as demand evaporated.

> Bitcoin mining chips must be ordered six to nine months in advance from foundries like TSMC and UMC due to the complex manufacturing process. During boom periods, miners order aggressively based on projected demand and rising Bitcoin prices. When markets crash, those advance orders become massive liabilities—expensive chips arriving precisely when demand has disappeared and customers can no longer afford to deploy them.

I remember our crucial board meeting from the spring of 2018 with vivid clarity. Six months earlier, when we were planning our chip orders for the anticipated demand surge, we had meticulously laid out three scenarios: the base plan, base-plus, and base-plus-plus. The pipeline looked so robust, the customer commitments so solid, that the temptation was to go aggressive with our largest order scenario.

Somewhere in that process, fortunately, we decided to embrace a more conservative approach and stick with the base plan. It was our instinct that guided us toward caution, a decision that would prove to be our lifesaver. Even with our conservative approach, we had approximately 200 megawatts of chip capacity already ordered and paid for, which was a massive commitment. The difference between ordering 200 MW and our base-plus-plus plan of 600 MW would mean the difference between survival and catastrophe.

As we headed toward late fall 2018, reports from our global offices painted an increasingly dire picture. Orders that had seemed guaranteed started showing stress fractures. Customers who had committed millions began to express concerns about market conditions. The steady flow of payments that had sustained our growth suddenly slowed to a trickle, then stopped altogether.

Standing in our Amsterdam office one grey November morning, watching Bitcoin's price plummet on the monitors while our phones rang incessantly with customer concerns and cancellations, I couldn't help but remember my prescient warning from the Barcelona strategy session: "Let's be cognizant that a significant part of our financial success has been tied to the massive appreciation of Bitcoin's price."

That concern, which had felt like prudent caution during our moment of triumph, now seemed like prophecy. The mathematical reality was brutal: as Bitcoin's price fell, mining became less profitable, which reduced demand for mining equipment, which destroyed our customer pipeline. The interconnected nature of the cryptocurrency ecosystem meant that price declines created cascading effects throughout the entire supply chain.

As those expensive chips continued arriving from foundries—each shipment representing millions in sunk costs—it became increasingly clear that customers were backing out of their commitments. The pipeline we'd relied upon for our IPO projections was shrinking daily. Notifications arrived with depressing regularity: this customer cancelling their order, that customer requesting postponement, another requesting to renegotiate terms downward.

We had to scramble, and we had to scramble fast. One of our key survival strategies was to identify customers with whom we could co-invest, essentially becoming partners in deploying these chips rather than simply vendors. Instead of selling hardware, we would provide equipment in exchange for equity stakes in mining operations. The race was on to convert inventory into productive assets before the market deteriorated further.

The Dragon Deal Evaporates

The deteriorating market conditions soon reached our highest-level strategic discussions. During a tense video call with Dragon in late November, the shift in sentiment was immediately apparent. Gone was the enthusiastic deal-making atmosphere of our Bordeaux château meetings and Hong Kong cigar club discussions.

"George, Val," Dragon began, his voice lacking its usual confident energy, "after extensive discussions with Jack's team, we've decided to take a more cautious approach to the Bitcoin market at this time."

The words landed with devastating clarity. "Can you be more specific about what that means for our discussions?" I asked, though I could already sense where this was heading.

"Jack is becoming increasingly concerned about Bitcoin's trajectory and wants to hold off on any major investment in the sector," Dragon explained diplomatically. "The media narrative has shifted dramatically, and there's too much uncertainty about where the bottom might be."

The deal we'd been cultivating for the past five months—hundreds of millions in potential investment from one of China's most successful entrepreneurs—was essentially dead. Dragon mentioned he might consider a much smaller investment later, once market conditions stabilized, but the transformational partnership we'd envisioned was no longer on the table.

The speed with which sentiment shifted in cryptocurrency markets was always stunning, but 2018's bear market demonstrated just how quickly institutional interest could evaporate. Companies and investors who had been aggressively pursuing crypto opportunities during the bull market suddenly became extremely risk-averse, viewing the sector as too volatile and unpredictable for major commitments.

The intoxicating months of private jets shuttling between Bordeaux vineyards, karaoke sessions with Alibaba executives, and billion-dollar valuations from investment banks suddenly felt like scenes from someone else's life. The market had spoken with brutal, unforgiving clarity, and all our ambitious plans—the Dragon partnership, the IPO roadshow, the massive customer pipeline—were now subject to forces completely beyond our control.

The contrast was jarring and humbling. Just weeks earlier, we had been the darlings of the Bitcoin world, hosting prestigious summits in the Atlas Mountains and fielding competing offers from global investment banks. Now we were scrambling to preserve cash flow and renegotiate contracts with customers who could no longer afford our products.

Just HODL

As we approached the end of 2018, I found myself once again with my family in Dubai, seeking solace in the warm hospitality of our UAE friends during what had become an unexpectedly challenging period. The familiar luxury of the Emirates provided a stark contrast to the anxiety gnawing at me about Bitfury's future.

One evening, as Bitcoin approached a devastating $3,700—an 84 percent decline from its peak—I sat for dinner with Sheikh Ali and several other friends who had become Bitcoin believers through our years of relationship building. The conversation inevitably turned to the market carnage.

"George," Sheikh Ali said, his voice carrying genuine concern, "my uncle purchased substantial Bitcoin at $14,000 on your recommendation. He's becoming quite worried about the situation. What should we tell him?"

I looked across the table at these friends who had trusted my judgment, who had embraced Bitcoin because of my passionate advocacy, and felt the weight of that responsibility. The easy confidence I'd possessed during previous visits had been replaced by the sobering reality of a bear market that seemed to have no floor.

"Tell him to HODL," I said finally, using the crypto community's battle cry for holding through volatility. "Bitcoin has growing pains, but this technology is bigger than any single market cycle. Everything will be fine."

"HODL" originated from a misspelled "hold" in a 2013 Bitcoin forum post and became a rallying cry for long-term Bitcoin believers. During bear markets, the crypto community would use this term to encourage patience and long-term thinking rather than panic selling. The philosophy emphasized Bitcoin's revolutionary potential beyond short-term price movements.

Even as I spoke these words of reassurance, I wondered if I was trying to convince them or myself. The rocket ship that had been reaching escape velocity was now facing the harsh, unforgiving reality of financial gravity. The question that kept me awake at night was whether we had accumulated enough fuel—enough cash reserves, enough diversified revenue streams, enough strategic flexibility—to navigate the storm ahead.

Looking out at Dubai's glittering skyline from the restaurant terrace, I reflected on the cyclical nature of both markets and life. Just as I had witnessed the collapse of the Soviet system as a child, then helped build something new from those ashes, perhaps this market downturn was simply clearing space for the next phase of innovation.

But survival would require more than a philosophical perspective. It would demand the same resilience, adaptability, and relentless focus that had carried us through previous crises. The semiconductor disaster of 2016 had nearly broken us, but it had also taught us invaluable lessons about managing existential threats.

As 2018 drew to a close, with Bitcoin having lost massive value and our IPO dreams temporarily shelved, I knew we were entering another crucible period. The euphoria of recent months had been replaced by the stark reality of business fundamentals, cash management, and survival strategy.

The question was no longer how high we could fly, but whether we could maintain altitude long enough for the market winds to shift in our favour once again. Winter was coming once again to the cryptocurrency world, and only the strongest, most adaptable companies would survive to see the next spring.

CHAPTER 14

BY ENDURANCE WE CONQUER

If you're going through hell, keep going.

—Winston Churchill

As 2019 started, it became crystal clear that we had to shift into "survival mode" to restructure dramatically, and we had to restructure fast. The brutal mathematics of our situation stared us in the face with unforgiving clarity: we were burning through $10 million per month in cash with rapidly dwindling reserves and a customer pipeline that was evaporating by the day.

The contrast with just nine months earlier was jarring. During our euphoric Barcelona strategy sessions, we had been planning aggressive expansion, implementing OKRs to manage our growth, and fielding multiple billion-dollar IPO valuations. Now, we were facing the stark possibility of bankruptcy if we didn't act decisively within weeks.

Val called an emergency executive meeting in our Amsterdam offices in January. The atmosphere was heavy with tension as he laid out the stark reality to our directors, many of whom had grown accustomed to hearing success stories and expansion plans during our monthly gatherings.

"Fellas, we're facing our most serious challenge yet," he began, his voice steady but grave as he looked around the table at faces that reflected the weight of our situation. "We're burning ten million dollars monthly, and if we don't act decisively, we'll run out of cash in less than six months."

I nodded grimly, feeling the responsibility for every person employed by Bitfury across our global operations. "We need to cut to the bone. Everything non-essential has to go. This isn't about preserving comfort—it's about survival."

The room fell silent as the implications sank in. These weren't theoretical business school case studies we were discussing; these were real decisions that would affect hundreds of families and determine whether the company we'd built over nearly a decade would survive to see another year.

As the crisis deepened and sleepless nights became my new normal, I found myself returning to one of my most treasured books: *Endurance: Shackleton's Incredible Voyage* by Alfred Lansing.[10] I had read it multiple times over the years, but now, facing our own seemingly impossible situation, Shackleton's story took on profound new meaning.

Ernest Shackleton's 1914 Antarctic expedition became legendary not for reaching its destination, but for survival against impossible odds. When pack ice crushed their ship Endurance, Shackleton kept twenty-seven men alive for nearly two years in one of Earth's most hostile environments through unwavering leadership, relentless optimism, and an absolute refusal to abandon anyone. His family motto: "By endurance we conquer."

Late at night in my Amsterdam hotel room, as I pored over restructuring plans and cash flow projections that seemed to grow more dire with each iteration, I would pause to reread passages about how Shackleton maintained morale and made life-or-death decisions in the Antarctic wasteland. The parallels were striking—we too were trapped in an unforgiving environment, with dwindling resources and no clear path to safety.

The book became my nightly companion, a source of perspective when the weight of difficult decisions threatened to overwhelm me. Shackleton's unwavering optimism in the face of impossible odds, his ability to make crucial decisions quickly without complete information, and most importantly, his absolute refusal to abandon any member of his crew—these lessons guided me through our darkest months.

One passage particularly resonated: "Optimism is true moral courage." As we faced the prospect of laying off hundreds of employees while maintaining hope for our company's survival, Shackleton's example reminded me that leadership during a crisis requires projecting confidence even when the outcome remains uncertain.

The first and most painful adjustment was downsizing our workforce dramatically. We had grown to over a thousand employees during our euphoric expansion, but now we faced the excruciating decision to let hundreds of talented people go. Each termination felt deeply personal—these were colleagues who had believed in our vision and worked tirelessly to build something revolutionary.

The conversations were among the most difficult of my professional life. Looking into the eyes of talented engineers, dedicated marketers, and passionate project managers—many of whom had relocated their families to join our global mission—while explaining that we could no longer afford their positions required every ounce of emotional strength Val and I could muster.

For all the senior executives who remained, we implemented salary cuts of 50 percent. "Drastic times call for drastic measures," Val told the executive team during one particularly somber meeting. Leading by example, we wanted to demonstrate that everyone was sharing the burden of survival.

Our goal was ambitious but necessary: downsize first to a $2 million monthly burn rate, then push it down to just $500,000. Every line item, no matter how small, required Val's personal approval. We established an executive committee that convened daily via Zoom to monitor our cash position and make rapid adjustments as needed.

The second major strategic decision was equally painful: we would spin off all non-core projects to become self-funded entities and would attract outside investors, essentially cutting away parts of the company we had lovingly built over years of development.

First, we examined our software business. Project Crystal, our KYC/AML intelligence platform, had shown promise in combating financial crime but wasn't generating sufficient revenue to justify its overhead during our crisis. We found a capable CEO to run it as an independent entity and executed the spinout, raised outside funding, and let it develop by itself, hoping it could thrive with focused leadership and reduced overhead.

We dramatically downsized the Exonum team as well, recognizing that despite our passionate belief in enterprise blockchain applications, there wasn't enough immediate market traction to justify the investment during our survival period. Lightning development was reluctantly put on hold. Our liquid cooling immersion technology, which had been a source of great pride and innovation, also had to be spun out.

"Joe's the right person for this challenge," I told the team as we finalized the LiquidStack spinout with Joe Capes, a veteran executive from Schneider Electric who would rebrand and lead the new company. "If anyone can turn our cooling technology into a viable business, it's him."

We also made the decision to spin out Axelera, the AI acceleration company that Fabrizio del Maffeo had been developing with remarkable technical innovation. "Fabrizio, you've built something incredible," I said as we discussed the transition. "But now it needs room to grow independently, with dedicated resources we simply can't provide during this period."

Each spinout felt like saying goodbye to a child, but we consoled ourselves that these technologies would have better chances of success with focused teams and appropriate funding than they would have staying within a cash-strapped parent company.

The biggest challenge, however, was our supplier obligations—a situation that threatened to destroy us regardless of how much we cut operating expenses. We had ordered $150 million worth of chips from UMC in Taiwan during the height of the 2018 boom, and those chips were arriving precisely as our customers were canceling orders en masse.

This crisis required our most experienced diplomatic intervention. Dr. Jackson Hu, who had been instrumental in our earlier TSMC negotiations during the 16 nm crisis, once again proved absolutely critical to our survival. Jackson stepped up to handle what would become one of the most complex and crucial negotiations in Bitfury's entire history.

"Jackson, we need you to work your magic with UMC," I told him during an emergency call, knowing that our entire future might depend on his ability to restructure these obligations.

Jackson flew to Taiwan and spent weeks in intensive, around-the-clock negotiations with UMC's executive team. Through his patient diplomacy and deep industry relationships, we managed to negotiate crucial breathing room, restructuring the payment terms to give us time to deploy the chips ourselves rather than relying on our vanishing customer base.

Without Jackson's intervention, the UMC situation alone could have bankrupted us, regardless of any other survival measures we implemented. His work quite literally saved the company.

But the fundamental problem remained: chips were accumulating on our shelves like expensive paperweights, each one representing sunk costs we desperately needed to recover. The situation was exacerbated by our competitor Bitmain's desperate strategy. Having raised over $1 billion the previous summer from Sequoia China and other mainland venture capital firms, Bitmain had ordered massive quantities of wafers during the boom, becoming one of TSMC's top five customers.

However, when Bitcoin's price collapsed, their demand evaporated as well, and they began dumping chips on the market at fire-sale prices, driving industry prices down by 90 to 95 percent. It was a classic race to the bottom, with desperate companies destroying industry economics in their scramble for survival.

"It's a complete race to the bottom," Val observed as we watched chip prices crater in real time. "Perfect storm of oversupply and collapsing demand."

"Bitmain's desperation is destroying the entire market," I replied, recognizing that our survival would require finding creative solutions beyond simple price competition.

The Kazakhstan Gambit

As Bitcoin's price continued its relentless slide, another blow landed when Georgian electricity prices began climbing sharply. Our long-time operational base—where we'd built our first major facilities—was becoming increasingly uneconomical for mining. But sometimes prior decisions reveal their genius only in crisis: our BlockBox containerized mining solutions, originally designed for flexibility, had now become our salvation. These modular units could be unplugged, loaded onto trucks, and relocated wherever power was cheapest.

This was where thinking like nomads rather than settlers paid unexpected dividends. A year earlier, with typical Bitfury foresight, we'd begun cultivating opportunities in Kazakhstan. We'd established an office in Almaty and were already executing high-level blockchain projects with the government—not mining, but software solutions that built trust and relationships.

Our man on the ground was Timur, a brilliant young director who understood that success in Kazakhstan required more than just business acumen. He'd spent months building genuine relationships with officials, learning the nuances of local business culture, and identifying opportunities others missed. While we'd hired him to run software projects, his real value was about to reveal itself in ways we never anticipated.

"I've been talking to energy officials here," Timur called one evening, his voice crackling over WhatsApp. "Kazakhstan has massive power surpluses from Soviet-era infrastructure. They're practically begging for large-scale consumers. And George, the prices they're quoting—it's like stepping back in time."

Kazakhstan's vast energy resources, including substantial oil, gas, and renewable capacity, combined with relatively progressive policies toward cryptocurrency, made it an attractive destination for mining operations seeking low-cost power. The country's geographic position between Europe and Asia also provided strategic advantages for global operations.

Timur had been mandated to identify low-cost energy locations, and in remarkably short order, he identified a 100-megawatt opportunity at approximately 2.5 cents per kilowatt-hour—roughly half the cost of our Georgian operations. With that information, our operations team, headed by always charging Vadym, executed a logistical masterpiece, moving containers to Kazakhstan and not only stopping our financial bleeding but actually generating additional cash flow.

Through our expanding network in Kazakhstan, we also identified a potential customer who wanted to deploy close to 100 megawatts of mining capacity. This could be our salvation—a way to deploy our accumulating chip inventory and generate desperately needed cash flow to stabilize our finances.

Val flew to Kazakhstan with our development team, exploring various creative ways to structure the deployment. The meetings went exceptionally well, the economics were attractive for all parties, and we reached a handshake agreement that seemed to solve our most pressing problems.

"This could be exactly what we need," I told Val during one of our daily check-in calls. "If we can get this Kazakhstan deployment online, it gives us breathing room with the chip inventory and provides the cash flow we need to survive."

But just as we were finalizing contracts and preparing for deployment, the customer developed cold feet about Bitcoin's volatility and backed out of the deal at the last moment.

"I'm sorry, Val," their representative said during what should have been our final meeting. "Our board has decided Bitcoin is too risky given current market conditions."

In retrospect, given how attractive the energy pricing was and Bitcoin's subsequent recovery, we calculated that the investor would have made hundreds of millions of USD in profits by holding firm and proceeding with the deployment. But fear had overtaken greed, and we were left scrambling for alternatives once again.

"Not to worry, Val," I told him with complete conviction. Having lived through the 16 nm debacle, I considered this challenge less daunting and had full confidence we'd dig ourselves out of this hole. "We'll find another solution."

As summer 2019 approached, the reality became stark and unavoidable: we were down to just a couple of million dollars in cash—a dramatic fall from the over $200 million we'd held just a year earlier. Our situation was desperate enough that I began making rounds to existing investors, hat in hand, seeking emergency funding to keep the lights on.

The response was universally and brutally negative.

"George, we wish we could help," one major investor told me with uncomfortable frankness during a meeting in his London office, "but nobody wants to throw good money after bad in this market. Bitcoin might never recover to previous levels."

Those investor meetings were humbling in the extreme. People who had celebrated our success and competed for allocation in our funding rounds just months earlier now looked at us with barely concealed pity. The speed of the reversal was breathtaking—from unicorn status to potential bankruptcy in less than twelve months.

The venture capital ecosystem that had once courted us was now treating cryptocurrency as radioactive. Partners who had rushed to attend our blockchain summits were now avoiding our calls, afraid that association with a struggling crypto company might damage their reputations with limited partners.

As a last resort—just as we had done during our earlier TSMC crisis—we went to our founding shareholders and angel investors. Val and I, along with our core team, pooled our personal life savings to provide emergency funding for Bitfury's survival. It was our second time putting everything on the line for the company we'd built.

"This is it," I told Val after we secured the emergency funding from our personal resources and those of our most loyal supporters. "This is the final lifeline, and it has to last us until the industry recovers. If we can't make it work with this, there won't be a next time."

There were countless sleepless nights during this period, each decision carrying life-or-death consequences for the company and the livelihoods of everyone who remained. But having weathered the TSMC crisis years earlier, and drawing strength from Shackleton's example of leadership under impossible pressure, I maintained absolute conviction that if we managed our cash carefully and made smart strategic decisions, we could survive this storm as well.

Slashing Cash Burn by Ninety-Five Percent

We implemented extreme cost controls that were essential for survival. Every single expense, no matter how trivial, required Val's personal approval. We developed creative ways to restructure payments and push out obligations, essentially stretching every dollar as far as possible.

Our sizable holdings in Hut 8 shares, though also depressed in the bear market, provided some strategic ammunition. We could sell shares periodically to generate additional cash flow, though we had to be careful not to flood the market and further depress the stock price.

"It's ironic," I told Val during one particularly difficult week as we reviewed our Hut 8 position, "our public company spinout, which seemed like a nice-to-have diversification play during the boom, is now helping keep us alive during the bust."

"Sometimes the side projects become the main event," he replied with characteristic pragmatism.

The Hut 8 listing on the Toronto Stock Exchange, combined with the emergency shareholder support and our creative financial management, became the magic combination that allowed us to weather the storm. We managed to cut our workforce by over 90 percent and monthly cash burn from $10 million to less than $500,000.

One of our European investors could not believe what he saw. "Never in a hundred years would I see anything like this done at a European company," he said, shaking his head in amazement.

"We are not a European company," I replied. "We are Bitfury."

The diversification we'd built during good times was now paying survival dividends during the crisis.

Despite all the layoffs, the spinouts, and the financial constraints, we maintained our tradition of holding an annual summit on Necker Island. The June 2019 gathering wasn't as intense as in previous years, but it remained a valuable convergence of minds who understood that innovation continues even during downturns.

The three-day program reflected the sobering times, but there were moments of pure Necker magic that reminded us why we kept coming back. It was during one of these afternoons that we witnessed something that would become legendary in our circle.

"Nick's going for it," Bill said, almost offhandedly, as we gathered on the upper deck of the Great House. We turned toward the far edge where Nick Jacobsen, kiteboarding legend and certified lunatic, was barefoot on the ledge, eyes on the horizon, kite already catching the wind.

"You've got to be kidding," someone whispered behind me.

But I knew better. "This is Necker," I said. "He's definitely doing it."

And then he did—Nick launched off the balcony, kite stretched wide against the late afternoon light, carving a perfect arc through the air before slicing into the turquoise water below. A moment of stunned silence gave way to roars and laughter as champagne bottles popped and cameras went wild. Bill turned to me, beaming:

"Now that's what I call a leap of faith."

In a week defined by visionaries talking about decentralization, freedom, and breaking through old systems during one of crypto's darkest hours, Nick's flight was the perfect metaphor: bold, risky, beautiful. Proof that when the wind's right and the conviction is strong, you jump.

Rachel and Kezzia, our Heads of PR and Events respectively, had worked tirelessly to organize the summit's complex logistics, coordinating schedules across time zones and managing the intricate dance of getting heavyweight speakers to two different islands. Their meticulous planning showed in every seamless transition between sessions.

The morning's "New Governments" panel brought together heavyweight voices. Roger Ferguson, the former Vice Chairman of the Federal Reserve, who led a $1.3 trillion asset manager, Teachers Insurance and Annuity Association of America (TIAA), brought gravitas with his insights on monetary policy and financial stability that few in crypto could match. Alongside him, Caitlin Long, the Wall Street veteran turned Wyoming Bitcoin advocate who'd spent over two decades at Morgan Stanley, shared hard-won insights about navigating regulatory headwinds. Her work getting Wyoming to pass Bitcoin-friendly legislation offered a rare bright spot in an otherwise challenging regulatory landscape. Annette Nazareth, Bitfury advisor and former SEC Commissioner who'd helped oversee market regulation during the 2008 financial crisis, added a crucial perspective on how regulators think during times of market stress.

The panel at Sir Richard's other island, Moskito, on "Corporations and Blockchain," led by GBBC CEO Sandra Ro, featured David Treat from Accenture discussing enterprise blockchain adoption. Adam Caplan, SVP of Salesforce, and our Brazilian friend Veronica Serra—a serial entrepreneur who'd built multiple startups across Latin America—explored how corporations were navigating the complex regulatory landscape.

After the panel, Veronica caught me by the pool. "George, this downturn is actually creating numerous opportunities in Latin America," she said, her enthusiasm undimmed by the market conditions. "The banks are so inefficient there that even with crypto winter, blockchain solutions still make economic sense. We're seeing real adoption, not speculation."

"That's what we need more of," I agreed. "Real use cases that solve actual problems."

"Exactly. When the hype dies, the builders remain," she smiled. The conversations felt more grounded in reality than in previous years.

Sir Richard pulled me aside during one of our traditional morning tennis matches, the Caribbean sun providing a welcome contrast to the gloom of our recent months.

"George, I heard you guys have weathered quite a storm," he said, toweling off after a particularly competitive game.

"We're still standing, Sir Richard," I replied, grateful for his continued support. "The team that's left is stronger for it. We've cut the fat, kept the muscle."

"That's the spirit," he nodded. "The entrepreneurs who survive the downturns are the ones who thrive when things turn around."

His encouragement meant more than he probably realized. Having survived the worst of the restructuring and seeing Bitcoin's price beginning to show signs of life, there was cautious optimism beginning to emerge from the wreckage.

Val, Bill, and I had to leave Necker earlier this time, as we flew to the Greek island of Patmos for the wedding of our dear friends Lars and Elomida. It was a beautiful celebration of love and partnership, and remarkably, Bitcoin touched $10,000 during the festivities—a dramatic recovery from the $3,700 lows that had nearly destroyed us.

The timing of Bitcoin's recovery coincided with Facebook's announcement of Libra (later renamed Diem), which generated massive mainstream excitement about digital currencies. This institutional validation helped restore confidence in the sector and attracted new waves of investment and development.

Sitting at the wedding reception, watching the sunset paint the Aegean Sea in brilliant colors while Bitcoin crossed the psychologically important $10,000 threshold, felt symbolic of our own recovery and renewal.

"Look at that," I said to Bill Tai, showing him the price on my phone with genuine amazement. "The tide is finally turning."

At the wedding, we finally got to meet and hang out with Melanie Perkins and Cliff Obrecht, the founders of Canva, whom Bill and Lars had supported during their own challenging early days in Australia. Melanie shared the incredible story of how they raised their $3 million seed round after attending Bill's MaiTai kite surfing camp in Hawaii—a tale that perfectly embodied the entrepreneurial spirit we all admired.

"I had to learn to kite surf to get into Bill's network," Melanie laughed as we grabbed cocktails at the reception. "It's not something I would normally try, but when you don't have any connections, you just have to wedge your foot in the door and wiggle it all the way through."

The determination required to learn an entirely new extreme sport just to access investor networks was exactly the kind of audacious persistence that defined successful entrepreneurs. After facing more than one hundred rejections from venture capitalists, Melanie and Cliff had found their breakthrough through Bill's unique combination of kite surfing and entrepreneurship—a perfect example of how unconventional networking could lead to transformational opportunities.

"Congratulations on Canva's incredible success," I told Melanie during dinner, genuinely impressed by how they'd built such an impactful company. "Bill told us about your journey—it's inspiring to see how you've scaled from a startup to global impact."

"Thank you," she replied graciously. "I heard you've been through quite a battle yourselves with the crypto winter. These survival stories are what truly bond entrepreneurs together."

Her words resonated deeply. The shared experience of near-death corporate experiences created bonds that transcended industry boundaries.

As 2019 wound down, I had some interesting adventures that helped put our business challenges in proper perspective. Marat invited us to the Burning Man, where I had the opportunity to reconnect with Sergey Brin in the surreal, transformative environment of the Nevada desert festival.

Burning Man represents a unique cultural experiment in radical self-expression and temporary community building. The festival's principles of gifting, decommodification, and radical self-reliance often provide tech leaders with a perspective on values beyond pure commercial success.

"We're working on AI acceleration technology that might interest Google," I told Sergey as we spent time together in his beautifully designed camp in the middle of the desert, surrounded by incredible art installations and fellow explorers.

"Come see us after the festival," he said with genuine interest. "Let's compare notes on what you're building."

Later that day, we all gathered to watch the traditional burning of the Man—a spectacular ritual that marks the festival's climax. As I watched the massive wooden figure consumed by flames, I couldn't help but think of all the challenges we had overcome and the lessons learned about ourselves and about human nature. It was a deeply rewarding experience, and I felt blessed to be part of that transformative community.

After a much-needed detour to decompress at Lake Tahoe, we drove to Google headquarters in Mountain View, where our chip R&D head, Vlad, presented our AI acceleration concepts to Sergey's top engineering team. It was clear they were already focused on their TPU architecture, which represented a different approach from ours, so we agreed to stay in touch as both companies developed their technologies.

But as we were leaving the building, Sergey looked at us with genuine admiration that felt earned through our survival journey.

"You guys have built a very solid foundation," he said thoughtfully. "That Axelera project you spun out during your restructuring could become something quite significant."

His words would prove remarkably prophetic—Axelera would indeed grow into one of Europe's leading AI companies, eventually approaching unicorn valuations and validating our decision to spin it out when we couldn't provide adequate resources.

Antarctic Conditions to Spring

As the year wound down, I found myself at Art Basel Miami for Marat's fortieth birthday celebration—a fitting way to mark both his milestone and our company's survival. During the party at the stylish Delano hotel, I met Peter Tuning, a renowned digital artist whom I'd first encountered at Alan Howard's Bitcoin gathering at Lake Como.

Peter had created stunning exhibitions exploring the intersection of technology and art, and I'd commissioned a Bitcoin-themed painting from him that captured the revolutionary spirit of our industry.

"Peter, wouldn't it be incredible to have a functioning Bitcoin mining container right here in Basel as an art installation?" I suggested. The idea had emerged during the celebration from our experience with portable mining solutions.

His eyes lit up with creative possibility. "That's a fantastic concept! A fusion of functional technology and artistic expression—something I'd absolutely love to work on."

The idea of making our industrial technology into art felt symbolic of how we'd transformed our challenges into opportunities throughout the crisis.

Later, we found ourselves on a yacht sailing around Miami, greeting another sunrise with cautious optimism. Bitcoin had stabilized around $7,200—not the euphoric heights of the previous peak, but a sustainable level that allowed rational business planning.

The worst was clearly behind us. We had restructured successfully, moved operations to Kazakhstan for better economics, used our Hut 8 shares strategically to manage cash flow, and most importantly, we had survived another existential challenge.

Looking back at 2019, I realized it had been one of the most challenging yet formative years of my professional life. We had faced the abyss and found a way back through discipline, creativity, and sheer determination. The lessons learned—about leadership under extreme pressure, the critical importance of preserving cash, the value of true partnerships, and the resilience required to weather any storm—would serve us well in whatever battles lay ahead.

The crypto winter was ending, and spring was beginning to show its first green shoots. Bitcoin was demonstrating signs of sustained life, our operations were stabilized and efficient, and we had proven to ourselves and our stakeholders that Bitfury could survive anything the market threw at us.

As I sat down with my family on New Year's Eve 2019, I opened my worn copy of Shackleton's story one more time. The inscription I had written to myself during our darkest months caught my eye in the lamplight: "By endurance we conquer."

Those words had guided us through the Antarctic conditions of the crypto winter. We had kept our crew together, made the hard decisions necessary for survival, and emerged stronger and more resilient than before.

The rocket ship had returned to earth, been stripped down and rebuilt with hard-earned wisdom, and was ready for launch once again. This time, we would be prepared for any weather the journey might bring.

CHAPTER 15
PHOENIX RESURRECTED

If you hang around the barbershop long enough, you'll get a haircut.
—Denzel Washington

As we entered 2020, it became crystal clear that we needed to execute something transformational to get back into the major leagues. During the brutal restructuring of 2019, we had spent considerable energy hunting for strategic locations in the Western Hemisphere, particularly North America. Despite the carnage of the crypto winter, we sincerely believed that Bitcoin would eventually recover and the excitement would return, and when that inevitable moment arrived, we needed to have tangible, revenue-generating assets ready to be monetized.

Our long-term vision remained unchanged: we would eventually complete our IPO and list on US capital markets, fulfilling the dream that had been temporarily derailed by the 2018-2019 bear market. But first, we needed to rebuild our foundation with strategic assets in America. More than ever, I was convinced that the United States represented the right geography to capitalize the business, and in the next Bitcoin bull run, we had better be prepared well in advance.

The lessons of 2019 had taught us that survival demanded building sustainable competitive advantages that could weather any storm. We had learned to operate lean, but now it was time to grow smart.

As part of our Series C institutional round with Korelya Capital, we conducted extensive due diligence meetings with potential strategic investors. One of the most intriguing conversations had been with Total Energy's private equity arm. Although the fund didn't ultimately invest in our round, we were extremely impressed by one of their young directors, Samy Biyadi, who demonstrated remarkable knowledge about renewable energy markets and global power dynamics.

"This guy really understands the energy landscape at a level most people don't," I told Val after our extensive meeting with Total's team. "He could be exactly what we need to execute our North American strategy."

> The global energy transition was accelerating rapidly in 2020, driven by falling costs of renewable technologies and increasing corporate commitments to carbon neutrality. For Bitcoin mining companies, this represented both opportunity and necessity—the industry needed to address environmental concerns while capitalizing on the abundance of stranded renewable energy worldwide.

When we successfully closed our institutional round, we made sure to maintain contact with Samy throughout the process. As we began strengthening our energy team to scout predominantly American opportunities, we extended an offer for him to join us as head of energy development.

"Samy, we're building something transformational here," I explained during our dinner meeting in Paris. "We need someone who understands both traditional energy markets and the revolutionary future we're creating with Bitcoin mining. You could be instrumental in securing the energy infrastructure that powers the next phase of this industry."

It proved to be one of our most strategic hires—Samy would become absolutely key in helping us identify and secure energy locations throughout the United States, bringing a level of sophistication to our energy strategy that would prove crucial for our growth.

With Samy methodically on location scouting, we systematically searched the entire United States for optimal opportunities—from the renewable-rich landscapes of Alaska to the industrial heartlands of Illinois and Ohio. But one region quickly emerged as particularly promising: West Texas.

Samy immediately recognized that Texas offered a uniquely attractive opportunity to deploy large-scale Bitcoin mining operations with unmatched economic advantages.

"George, the energy market in Texas is absolutely perfect for what we're trying to accomplish," he explained during one of our daily strategy calls, his enthusiasm evident even through our video connection. "You've got deregulated markets, abundant renewable energy capacity, and grid operators who actually understand flexible load management."

We began working around the clock to secure energy contracts and development deals throughout Texas. The state's unique energy profile—featuring massive wind and solar capacity that often produced excess power during optimal conditions—created near-perfect conditions for Bitcoin mining operations that could scale up and down based on grid needs.

> Texas's deregulated electricity market and abundant renewable energy resources made it an ideal location for large-scale Bitcoin mining. The state's Electric Reliability Council of Texas (ERCOT) operated an energy-only market where Bitcoin miners could serve as a flexible load, consuming excess renewable energy when available and shutting down during peak demand periods. This symbiotic relationship helped stabilize the grid while providing miners with cost-effective power.

Our Texas strategy represented more than just finding cheap electricity. We were positioning Bitfury to become an integral part of America's energy infrastructure, providing grid services while building a sustainable foundation for our mining operations.

Nurturing the Spinouts

While aggressively pursuing our American expansion, we simultaneously continued nurturing the companies we had spun out during our survival period. Each of these entities was showing promising signs of independent growth, validating our decision to give them focused leadership and dedicated resources.

Crystal was gaining significant traction in the compliance space, with new cryptocurrency exchanges and enforcement agencies signing up for their KYC/AML intelligence services. The regulatory environment was becoming increasingly sophisticated, creating strong demand for their forensic blockchain analytics.

"The regulatory landscape is evolving rapidly," I observed during a Crystal board meeting. "Every exchange and financial institution needs better compliance tools to satisfy regulators. You're positioned perfectly to capitalize on this trend."

We managed to attract substantial third-party financing to expand Crystal's capabilities, allowing them to compete effectively with established players like Chainalysis while maintaining our strategic relationship.

Axelera was also making impressive progress in the AI acceleration space, announcing the opening of new offices while assembling a strong foundation to attract outside investors. The CEO, Fabrizio, was doing an excellent job growing the AI business and building partnerships with major technology companies.

"The AI acceleration market is heating up dramatically," Fabrizio reported during one of our quarterly reviews. "We're seeing strong demand from multiple verticals—autonomous vehicles, data centers, edge computing applications. The spinout decision was absolutely the right move."

LiquidStack was equally impressive, securing significant outside capital from strategic investors while rapidly scaling its immersion cooling operations. The company was perfectly positioned for the burgeoning data center expansion driven by cloud computing and AI workloads.

Unfortunately, we had to make the difficult decision to mothball both the Exonum blockchain platform and the Lightning Peach payment project. Despite our technical achievements, we realized there simply weren't enough paying customers at that stage of market development.

"This is one of the hardest decisions we've made," I told the development teams during an emotional all-hands meeting. "We were probably just extremely early with those technologies. There's definitely option value there for the future, but sometimes even great technology needs to wait for market readiness."

The experience reinforced our learning that timing in technology markets is often more important than technical superiority—a lesson that would guide our future investment decisions. But it was comforting to see that all of our software developers had no problem finding employment quickly, being recruited by other top blockchain projects, and ending up making a significant impact in the field.

In February 2020, I flew to Abu Dhabi for the Milken Institute's Middle East conference at the invitation of our dear friend from the Necker Summit, Staci Warden. The region was beginning to show encouraging signs of rejuvenation after the prolonged crypto winter, and I caught up with numerous industry veterans who had also survived the brutal downturn.

I participated in a panel discussion alongside our investor Mike Novogratz, CEO of Galaxy, and Jonathan Levin, CEO of Chainalysis. The conversation was particularly poignant for me, as it highlighted one of our more significant missed opportunities.

It was ironic—just four years earlier, Marat had brought us an acquisition opportunity to purchase close to 40 percent of Chainalysis at what now seemed like a ridiculously low valuation. At the time, we were focused on other priorities and passed on the deal. Now here they were, already a unicorn with a rapidly expanding valuation and becoming a formidable competitor to our own Crystal platform.

"Sometimes timing is everything in this business," I reflected to Mike after our panel concluded. "We had the opportunity to acquire a major stake in Chainalysis when they were tiny, but we were concentrated on other strategic initiatives."

"That's the nature of venture investing," Mike replied with characteristic pragmatism. "You can't pursue every opportunity. The key is learning from those decisions without dwelling on them."

Later that evening, I attended a reception organized by our UAE sheikh hosts. To my surprise, I found myself in conversation with Paris Hilton and her then-fiancé Carter Reum, who turned out to be actively investing in the space, including funding our friend Elizabeth Stark's venture, Lightning Labs.

"People think I'm just the party girl," Paris said with a knowing smile, "but I've been a fan of Bitcoin for years."

"That's smart," I replied. "We are in a bear market now, but one day we'll be headed for a million."

Our friend Harry Yeh was also attending the conference. By this time, he had relocated full-time to Abu Dhabi and had become one of the first cryptocurrency entrepreneurs to establish serious digital asset business relationships within Abu Dhabi's sophisticated investment community.

After the reception, we spent the rest of the evening on his yacht Babylon, enjoying dinner while reminiscing about all the adventures we'd shared throughout the years. The conversation naturally turned to how the industry had evolved and how we had all managed to survive the brutal downturn that had claimed so many companies.

"You know what I've learned through all of this?" Harry said as we watched Abu Dhabi's glittering skyline from his deck, the lights reflecting off the calm waters. "The companies that survive these cycles aren't necessarily the best funded initially—they're the most adaptable and resilient."

"Absolutely true," I agreed, thinking of our own transformation from a growth-focused startup to a lean survival machine and now back to strategic expansion. "We're all still here because we learned to pivot quickly when circumstances demanded it."

This turned out to be my final international outing for quite some time. Little did I know that my typical 250-days-on-the-road travel regimen would come to an abrupt stop due to the COVID-19 global pandemic that was about to sweep the world.

The Paul Tudor Jones Moment

Back in April 2020, just weeks before Bitcoin's third halving, I tweeted: "In less than 30 days #bitcoin will become the most scarcely issued commodity in the world, beating Gold. Let that sink in."

At that moment, Bitcoin was trading around $6,800—a price that now seems surreal. Few fully grasped what was about to unfold. Bitcoin's issuance rate was about to drop below gold's, mathematically guaranteeing its scarcity with every block. While central banks were printing trillions in response to COVID, Bitcoin was doing the opposite—cutting supply. That asymmetry between ever-expanding fiat and provable digital scarcity is what fuels the Bitcoin thesis. I saw it then. The market realized it soon after.

In May, Bitcoin crossed the psychologically important $10,000 threshold, and the much-anticipated halving event occurred around the same time, reducing mining rewards and tightening supply dynamics exactly as I had predicted. But what I considered one of the most significant developments happened when Paul Tudor Jones, the legendary macro investor, published a detailed thesis explaining why Bitcoin made compelling sense as an institutional investment.

The timing was no coincidence. Tudor Jones, who had built his fortune understanding commodity flows and scarcity dynamics, recognized exactly what I had tweeted about weeks earlier: Bitcoin was becoming the hardest money ever created.

For me, this represented the most important milestone in Bitcoin's journey toward institutional adoption. Here was someone of incredible caliber and reputation from the traditional financial world—a man who had made billions of dollars in commodity and macro trades—coming out publicly with a sophisticated thesis on why Bitcoin deserved a place in institutional portfolios.

Paul Tudor Jones's endorsement of Bitcoin in May 2020 marked a watershed moment for institutional adoption. In his investor letter, Jones compared Bitcoin to gold as an inflation hedge and allocated a small percentage of his fund to Bitcoin futures. As the founder of Tudor Investment Corporation and one of the most respected macro traders in history, his endorsement carried enormous weight with institutional investors who had previously dismissed cryptocurrency.

"When someone of Tudor Jones's caliber and reputation enters the space, you know something fundamental has shifted in the market," I told Val during one of our strategy calls.

I immediately reached out to our trusted advisor, Jim Newsome, who had known Paul for many years through commodity market circles. "Jim, Paul has finally embraced Bitcoin in a major way," I texted him excitedly.

"Absolutely, this is genuinely major news," Jim replied almost instantly. "This confirms what I've thought all along—once the traditional finance titans start moving in, institutional adoption becomes inevitable."

I also texted Don Wilson at DRW, and he confirmed the same sentiment from the professional trading community. For me, this represented the real turning point in Bitcoin's institutionalization—not the retail speculation or Silicon Valley venture capital enthusiasm, but serious Wall Street money recognizing Bitcoin's fundamental potential as a portfolio asset.

And I was absolutely right. This moment would prove to be the beginning of an institutional flood that would transform the entire cryptocurrency landscape.

As market momentum returned and institutional interest accelerated, we prioritized developing sophisticated sales capabilities for our blockchain infrastructure solutions. One of our most strategic hires during this period was Tyler Page, who brought an extensive background in capital markets and legal training to our team.

Tyler's unique combination of technical understanding and regulatory expertise made him invaluable for communicating with institutional clients who required both performance and compliance.

"Tyler, we need someone who can speak fluently in the language of institutional clients," I explained during his recruitment process. "You understand both the underlying technology and the complex compliance requirements that these sophisticated customers demand."

Tyler joined us as head of digital asset sales, and he immediately became instrumental in advancing our solutions to sophisticated customers across North America. With Tyler leading our institutional sales efforts, we began generating significant revenue from mining capacity sales in Canada while simultaneously developing several hundred megawatts of capacity in Texas.

These Texas assets were being strategically positioned for either potential client sales or eventual inclusion in IPO assets, depending on market conditions and strategic opportunities.

Simultaneously, with Tyler overseeing predominantly North American sales, we launched our first institutional fund in Japan, providing Japanese investors with access to the digital asset mining asset class through a properly regulated structure.

Our Tokyo team, led by the capable Katsuya, was steadily growing the business and making impressive traction in the sophisticated Japanese institutional market.

"The Japanese market demonstrates remarkable sophistication when it comes to digital assets," Katsuya reported during our quarterly business review. "There's genuine institutional demand here for properly structured mining exposure with appropriate risk management."

The SPAC Opportunity

During this period, the SPAC (Special Purpose Acquisition Company) industry was experiencing dramatic growth and mainstream acceptance. What I noticed was the massive amount of SPAC capital that had begun flowing into various business sectors, creating new pathways to public markets.

The COVID pandemic, rather than hindering our operations, actually played to our strengths—we had been essentially a distributed, Zoom-enabled company long before the pandemic forced global remote work adoption, so the transition felt natural and seamless.

> Special Purpose Acquisition Companies (SPACs) became the preferred method for companies to access public markets in 2020. Rather than the traditional, lengthy IPO process, companies could merge with publicly traded shell companies that had already raised capital, allowing for faster access to public markets with reduced regulatory complexity and timeline uncertainty.

What we observed during the COVID era was a massive SPAC boom, and I immediately recognized this could be perfect for our US expansion strategy and long-term public market ambitions.

I reconnected with one of the global investment banks from our previous IPO discussions and pitched the SPAC concept with renewed enthusiasm.

"Listen, we have substantial US energy assets under active development," I explained to their managing director during a video conference. "There's clearly a tremendous opportunity to take these revenue-generating assets and structure them under the umbrella of a US SPAC."

Initially, they expressed a strong interest in the concept. We invested months in detailed discussions, legal structuring, and due diligence processes. But eventually, I realized this bank was exhibiting the same bureaucratic foot-dragging that had characterized our previous experiences with large financial institutions.

The familiar pattern of risk committee paralysis was emerging—the same institutional dynamics that had torpedoed previous opportunities when we needed decisive action.

"Look, you either commit to executing this deal or you don't," I finally told the managing director in what amounted to an ultimatum. "We can't spend indefinite time in due diligence limbo while market windows close."

When they continued stalling and introducing additional bureaucratic obstacles, it became clear this was yet another case of big bank institutional inertia trying to undermine an innovative opportunity. I had learned from previous experiences that sometimes you need to cut your losses quickly.

Enough was enough—we immediately put all discussions with that bank on indefinite hold.

However, during these extensive discussions, we had thoroughly tested and validated the SPAC concept using our US energy contracts and operational assets. The market reception from other parties had been overwhelmingly positive, confirming that this could become something genuinely significant.

Then, one day while casually scrolling through social media, I noticed that one of my entrepreneur contacts, George Arison, had successfully completed a SPAC transaction for his car retailer company, Shift.

The coincidence was too perfect to ignore. I immediately reached out to him.

"George, congratulations on the successful SPAC execution. Who were your investment bankers for the transaction?" I texted him instantly.

Within a couple of hours, I found myself on a video call with Dan Nash and his team at Wells Fargo Securities. The contrast with our previous banking experience was immediately apparent—this team moved with purpose and understood innovative deal structures.

"Dan, here's what we're building," I explained during our first comprehensive call. "We have substantial Bitcoin mining assets under development in Texas and other strategic locations. The SPAC structure could be perfect for bringing institutional capital into this rapidly growing space. And we have an ideal CEO candidate for this venture—our head of digital asset sales, Tyler Page."

Dan's team operated with impressive speed and decisiveness. Wells Fargo, as a West Coast-headquartered bank with more technology-forward thinking, immediately grasped the opportunity and moved quickly to approve our engagement.

"This is exactly the kind of innovative, forward-thinking deal we want to be involved with," Dan told me with genuine enthusiasm. "Let's move at full speed on this project."

Wells Fargo's approach to the SPAC market reflected the bank's West Coast technology focus and willingness to embrace innovative financial structures. Unlike more conservative East Coast institutions, Wells Fargo had developed expertise in SPAC transactions and understood how to navigate the regulatory and market dynamics efficiently.

We immediately began working at maximum intensity on what promised to be a transformative opportunity for Bitfury's growth and public market access.

Ready for Launch

After surviving the brutal crypto winter of 2018-2019, executing a painful but necessary restructuring, and methodically building new capabilities in energy procurement and institutional sales, we were finally positioned to make our decisive move back into the major leagues.

The recovery wasn't simply about Bitcoin's price returning to $10,000. It represented our successful transformation into a more resilient, diversified business model that could weather future market storms while capitalizing on the inevitable institutionalization of digital assets.

What hadn't killed us had indeed made us stronger, more focused, and better prepared for sustainable growth. Now it was time to prove it on the largest possible stage.

Standing on the terrace of my home at the end of 2020, looking out at a world transformed by pandemic disruption and accelerated digital adoption, I reflected on the extraordinary journey we had navigated. From the euphoric heights of 2018 through the brutal restructuring of 2019 to this moment of strategic positioning, we had learned lessons that no business school curriculum could teach.

The Shackleton principles we'd embraced during our darkest moments had proven prophetic—endurance, adaptability, and commitment to something greater than ourselves had carried us through when many others had fallen. The samurai code of honor and discipline guided our decision-making when easy paths would have led to destruction.

As Bitcoin approached new all-time highs and institutional adoption accelerated with unprecedented momentum, we were no longer the scrappy startup fighting for recognition and legitimacy. We had evolved into battle-tested veterans with the scars and wisdom to prove it, positioned to capitalize on the next phase of the digital asset revolution with strategic advantages earned through survival.

The rocket ship was fueled and ready for launch once again, but this time, we had learned to build for both the inevitable journey to the stars and the eventual return to Earth. The foundation was solid, the strategy was clear, and the team was prepared.

It was becoming obvious to everyone that we were going to win after all.

PART IV

AND THEN YOU WIN

ნაწილი IV: და შემდეგ შენ იმარჯვებ

CHAPTER 16

SPAC IT, BABY

Success is not final, failure is not fatal:
it is the courage to continue that counts.

—Winston Churchill

The contrast between Wells Fargo and our previous banking experience was like stepping from a dimly lit cave into brilliant sunshine. Where the East Coast institution had drowsed through months of committee meetings and risk assessments, Dan's team moved with the precision of a Swiss chronometer.

"George, we've reviewed your materials," Dan announced during our second call in December 2020, his voice crackling with the kind of energy I'd learned to associate with deals that actually happen. "We love the story. Let's get this SPAC launched."

I was extremely happy. After years of bureaucratic warfare with traditional finance, hearing decisive action felt almost surreal. This wasn't the familiar dance of "we're very interested, but..." followed by months of foot-dragging. This was a California efficiency meeting Bitfury determination. Few of the top-tier banks had even told me privately there was zero chance we would get the deal done. My goal was to prove them wrong. Once again.

Val, dialing in from the UAE, where he had made his permanent base, was equally excited. "That's it? No six-month due diligence marathon?"

"Definitely not," I replied, still processing the speed. "Welcome to the West Coast way of doing business."

The timing was approaching perfection. Bitcoin had not only recovered from its $3,700 apocalypse but was charging past $20,000 toward uncharted territory. Paul Tudor Jones had opened the institutional floodgates, and now companies like MicroStrategy, led by savvy Michael Saylor, were adding Bitcoin to their corporate treasuries as if it were as conventional as cash or bonds.

> The institutional adoption wave represented a seismic shift in market dynamics. Unlike previous Bitcoin bull runs driven primarily by retail speculation and early adopter enthusiasm, this cycle was being powered by sophisticated institutional capital seeking portfolio diversification and inflation hedges. The Federal Reserve's unprecedented monetary expansion in response to COVID had created a perfect storm of currency debasement fears and asset price inflation that made Bitcoin's fixed supply increasingly attractive to professional money managers.

The SPAC boom was equally explosive. Celebrity-sponsored acquisitions were raising hundreds of millions, and anything connected to Bitcoin or blockchain was trading at valuations that would have seemed fantastical just months earlier. As Bill—an avid kite surfer—commented, "We were surfing multiple waves simultaneously."

Assembling the Dream Team

Ideas are one thing, execution is another. As we started the process in late 2020, it became apparent that we needed an experienced legal advisor for what would be an incredibly complex transaction involving numerous international banks, law firms, and accounting outfits. There were countless moving parts, and I insisted we bring on an experienced legal counsellor—my old friend Chris Allen, who was a partner at Latham Watkins and recently retired from the firm. I had tried to bring him in in previous years, but the timing had never been right until now. Chris would join and bring aboard the leading US IPO and capital markets firm, Latham Watkins, as our legal counsel. The decision, in retrospect, was crucial to our success in launching the SPAC.

> The complexity of SPAC transactions in 2020–2021 had reached extraordinary levels. Beyond the traditional challenges of mergers and acquisitions, these deals required navigating an intricate web of securities regulations, PIPE (Private Investment in Public Equity) structuring, and the unique governance issues that arose when blank-check companies merged with operating businesses. The regulatory environment was evolving rapidly, with the SEC issuing new guidance almost monthly as the SPAC boom tested the boundaries of existing frameworks. Our deal would be pushing boundaries on all fronts.

I had known Chris for twenty years, and he was a trusted friend. With his massive experience, he knew very well what it took to get these high-level deals over the line. In fact, we had initially met through work and partnered on many deals in my earlier professional years back in the early noughties, so I knew very well what he could bring to the table. More crucially, Chris knew how to work with senior counterparts at the firm and how to stay on top of things. With our window of opportunity unknown (and potentially short), smooth deal execution and management on our side was essential. It was vital for us to recruit him.

"Chris," I explained during our initial call just after Christmas 2020, "We have a unique opportunity here to capitalize our US assets, but we need a legal expert like you to help with the project. I know you have been enjoying your semi-retirement and lockdown gardening, but it's time to get back in the saddle, mate."

After a night's deliberation, Chris called back. "I'm in. When's the first conference call?" We laughed (and still do) about how in the early days of my engagement in Bitcoin and Bitfury, I would send him screenshots saying, "Mate, you gotta buy this now," when the price was still in the low hundreds. He was sold on the concept, but, like many folks before and since, he failed to act on it. This was his chance to put it right. He was pumped by the chance to combine his skillset with Bitfury and the crypto scene, which he had been following vicariously for so many years through me.

We had a call with Val, who was visibly impressed by Chris's background. We realized the SPAC train was moving fast, and we needed someone of his caliber ASAP.

Bringing Chris aboard would prove to be one of the key decisions of the entire process. There would be countless sleepless hours spent on structure, legal documents, risk assessment, working with Latham, working with Wells Fargo, and outside accountants, the SEC process, PIPE negotiations, governance—the list was endless. This was proper top table transactional stuff, and we at Bitfury had to be credible and on our A game. Chris, being based in the UK, was running the exercise and staying on top of things, serving as our legal quarterback throughout the process.

One of the first things Chris told me and Val was that the deal would simply not happen without top-tier legal counsel who really knew their way around these public deals and, crucially, the SEC.

The SPAC deal we contemplated was bold. There would for sure be many tricky twists and turns in the process, needing complete alignment and trust between the client and the law firm. Consequently, he brought in the very capable Latham team, headed by David Stewart, to help get the deal done. I'd also known David for many years, having worked with him on some large deals, and knew how capable he was. All in all, I was very happy with this team in place to guide us and manage all legal aspects of the deal and SEC approvals.

Our selection of Tyler Page as CEO for what would become Cipher Mining represented one of our most fruitful strategic decisions as well. Tyler brought something unique to the table: finance and legal expertise coupled with a deep operational understanding of Bitcoin mining economics. Tyler had been with Bitfury for some time, so he was a known quantity to us. He was smart, fully on top of his brief, and had a very likable, positive, and energetic personality that we knew would go down well with the banks and prospective SPACS. He was another crucial piece in the jigsaw puzzle.

The Bitcoin mining industry from 2020 to 2021 was undergoing a profound professionalization. Gone were the days when operations could be run from garages or abandoned warehouses with jury-rigged cooling systems and improvised electrical setups. Institutional investors demanded sophisticated risk management, comprehensive regulatory compliance, and operational transparency that matched traditional infrastructure businesses. This evolution required leaders who could speak fluently to both technical mining operations and institutional capital markets—a rare combination that Tyler embodied perfectly.

"Tyler," I said during one of our final preparation meetings, "This is your moment. Let's get this done."

Tyler had that focused intensity I recognized from our early Bitfury days, the kind of laser-sharp determination that separates successful entrepreneurs from talented employees. During our due diligence process, he'd demonstrated an ability to translate complex mining operations into language that institutional investors could understand and trust.

"The beauty of our model," Tyler explained during a practice pitch session, "is that we're not just buying machines and hoping for the best. We're building a sophisticated energy management business that happens to mine Bitcoin. Operational excellence will be our competitive moat. That, along with locking in the industry record low energy prices at scale."

His background as a lawyer at Davis Polk was particularly valuable. Unlike many Bitcoin entrepreneurs who had learned compliance through painful trial and error, Tyler understood regulatory requirements intuitively, speaking fluently in the language of audit committees and institutional compliance officers. His multi-year experience on Wall Street—first at Lehman Brothers and Goldman Sachs before leading sales for the fund solutions business at Guggenheim Partners and then at Stone Ridge and NYDIG—meant he was also excellent at speaking the language of investors, understanding their concerns, and addressing them with the kind of sophisticated financial analysis that institutional capital demanded.

The contrast with our early days was remarkable. When Val and I first appeared on CNBC in 2014, we were evangelizing to a skeptical world about this strange thing called Bitcoin mining. Now, Tyler would be presenting to investors who were already convinced of Bitcoin's legitimacy and hungry for professionally managed exposure to the space.

Tyler brought in two seasoned executives to complete the C-suite: Patrick Kelley, who would run operations given his experience at D.E. Shaw and Citadel, and Will Iwaschuk, who would run legal and corporate. Through the network of my Johns Hopkins friend Neil Keegan, who ran the successful PE fund Marlinspike, we found the company CFO, Ed Farrell, who had just retired as CFO of the $800 billion asset management behemoth Alliance Bernstein.

"Neil," I called him one afternoon, "we need someone with serious public company CFO experience. Someone who can speak Wall Street's language but understands our technology vision."

"I've got just the guy," Neil replied without hesitation. "Ed Farrell from Alliance Bernstein. He's been looking for his next challenge, and this could be perfect timing."

The call with Ed went exactly as I'd hoped. Here was someone who had managed finances for one of the world's largest asset managers, yet was intrigued by the revolutionary potential of Bitcoin infrastructure.

And to provide governance oversight and regulatory credibility, we nominated our board advisor, Jim Newsome, to serve as Chairman of the Board, a position he holds to this day. Jim's experience as former Chairman of the CFTC brought institutional gravitas and regulatory expertise that would prove invaluable as we navigated the complex waters of Cipher becoming a US public company.

We also nominated longtime Bitcoiner and Necker summit participant Caitlin Long to the Board. When I called her with the proposal, she didn't hesitate.

"George, I would be delighted to join the effort," she said.

"We need someone who understands both Wall Street and Bitcoin," I explained. "You're one of the few who truly gets both worlds."

Building the Texas Empire

While Tyler assembled our management team, Samy was executing a masterpiece of strategic positioning across Texas. The state's deregulated electricity market had created opportunities that simply didn't exist anywhere else in the world.

"The genius of the Texas grid," Samy explained during one of our strategy sessions, his enthusiasm infectious even through Zoom, "is that Bitcoin mining becomes a grid stabilization service. We consume excess renewable energy when it's abundant and shut down during peak demand. Everyone wins."

This wasn't just about finding cheap electricity—though our contracted rates were extremely competitive. We were positioning ourselves as partners to grid operators, providing valuable flexibility services while building sustainable competitive advantages.

Texas's ERCOT grid offered a unique opportunity where Bitcoin miners could serve as a flexible load, consuming excess renewable energy when abundant and shutting down during peak demand—a symbiotic relationship that stabilized the grid while providing miners with cost-effective power and additional revenue streams. Unlike other states where regulators viewed Bitcoin mining with suspicion, Texas officials understood the economic benefits of attracting large-scale industrial operations. The state's business-friendly policies, abundant land, and proximity to major renewable projects created an ideal environment for the massive mining operations that institutional investors demanded, representing a fundamental evolution in how Bitcoin mining could enhance rather than simply consume energy infrastructure.

The development pipeline we'd assembled was massive. Several hundred megawatts of potential capacity with contracts were structured to provide both operational flexibility and attractive economics. Each site had been selected not just for power costs but for grid proximity, renewable energy access, and local regulatory support.

It was set up very well, but we had a serious challenge to address. To go to final contracts with our energy providers, we had to put up tens of millions of dollars as collateral. This was one of many similar chicken-or-egg challenges that we had with taking the US assets public—we needed to go public to have the money to secure the final contracts, but it might be tough to convince investors to partner with us in an offering if we did not yet have final contracts. As with many other issues on the entrepreneurial journey, we had to keep moving forward and figure it out.

The SPAC Hunt

Next, we needed to secure an auditor, and after a few phone calls, we got Marcum on board. Well, perhaps it wasn't that easy. The project had no revenue, no profits, and it was just about to be conjured into existence. All we had were agreements to enter energy contracts and the brand reputation of Bitfury. We were literally about to form the company and have the auditor review our first two weeks of operations and financial statements—essentially just a page of zeros. Needless to say, this was very atypical. Our bankers at Wells Fargo did not want to proceed with marketing until they had a clear indication from an auditor that a PCAOB-level audit (required of public companies) would be forthcoming for the new entity. We were at an impasse with Bitfury's auditor. I will let Tyler give his version of the story:

> *I had always been impressed with the resilience of the Bitfury team. Bitcoin mining had been a digital wildcatting business with wild swings from boom to bust, and to survive as long as they had meant that they had grit and could come up with crafty solutions to problems. Unfortunately, along the way, those creative solutions didn't always sit well with their service providers. Bitfury's well-known, big-name auditor was pretty fed up with them when I was introduced to the relationship partner in late 2020. He was a stuffy Dutch gentleman who suggested that there was no way we could spin off these assets to do a SPAC, mostly because no investors would ever want such a thing. Furthermore, while he needed at least six months to evaluate such a deal, he was confident that his firm would not be associated with such a transaction and that I was "not allowed" to do it. I took that personally and absolutely lost my mind while showering him with a profanity-laced tirade, suggesting that he had no idea what he was talking about, worked for us, and that we would simply find a different auditor. He assured me that it would not be possible. Trying to calm myself, I conjured my favorite phrase from Louis XIV and simply replied, "I shall see," and then hung up on him.*

The next day, I scrambled to connect with as many auditors as possible. After a few weeks of preliminary calls where I definitely felt like the fat kid asking skeptical girls to the prom, luck shone on us when we met Marcum. It just so happened that Marcum was a leader in both Bitcoin mining and SPAC audits. They were also commercial and understood our challenges. After some quick background checks, they took us on as clients and have remained with us ever since.

With the auditor problem solved, we could proceed with finding a SPAC acquirer.

> The SPAC market in late 2020 had become a feeding frenzy of unprecedented proportions. Special Purpose Acquisition Companies were raising capital at rates that dwarfed traditional IPO activity, driven by a combination of low interest rates, abundant liquidity, and investor hunger for exposure to high-growth sectors. The structure allowed companies to go public with forward-looking projections that wouldn't be permitted in traditional IPO processes, making it particularly attractive for early-stage technology businesses with ambitious growth plans but limited historical financial performance.

Now came the crucial step: identifying a SPAC. We pitched a few proposals, but after careful consideration, we narrowed it down to a few finalists and began spending time with one high-profile SPAC that showed strong interest. But as time progressed, we felt that the high-profile SPAC was dragging its feet.

Enough was enough. Speed was important. We decided to drop them and switch to Good Works—a SPAC that had very fast-moving sponsors who also appreciated the opportunity and realized that the SPAC window might not last forever. We were fully aligned.

On the call with Good Works CEO, Cary Grossman, I felt a close connection and sync on the appreciation that speed was vital. That would prove to be a crucial bet that would lead us to success.

> The SPAC boom created a unique temporal dynamic where timing often mattered more than terms. Market conditions were changing rapidly, and sponsors who understood this urgency had significant advantages over those who approached deals with traditional due diligence timelines. The most successful SPAC sponsors in this era were those who could move decisively while maintaining appropriate risk management—a balance that required both speed and sophistication.

One of the sponsors of Good Works, Doug Wurth, also happened to be a former senior executive at JPMorgan, and through him, we brought in JPMorgan's capital markets team for the PIPE transaction. In a SPAC merger, the investors in the SPAC have the right to redeem their shares at $10 per share before the consummation of the merger with the target company. Thus, if the investors don't like the deal, they can effectively get their money back.

As a result, valuations could get stretched to big numbers in SPAC transactions because there wasn't always a guarantee that the investors would stick around. Because of this, most SPAC mergers were typically accompanied by concurrent equity raises via a PIPE. As the investors in the PIPE were specifically buying at the stated valuation and could not back out, the PIPE investors really validated the valuation of the merger and provided guaranteed cash. In our case, without that PIPE support, the SPAC merger would not accomplish the purpose of raising cash to build the US business.

We were running a hundred miles an hour to put the merger deal together with countless hours of work while simultaneously pulling together an equity pitch for PIPE investors to try and prove that a greenfield company with nothing more than some letters of intent for power, our good name, and a few hard-working employees was worth two billion dollars. Weekends blurred into weekdays as we refined the pitch and progressed toward signing the deal.

The Institutional Avalanche

As we started moving into the spring, something extraordinary happened: institutional FOMO reached critical mass. Tesla announced a

$1.5 billion Bitcoin purchase. Coinbase went public via direct listing. Even JPMorgan, whose CEO had once called Bitcoin a "fraud," was launching cryptocurrency services for clients.

> The institutional adoption wave of early 2021 represented a tipping point that had been building for years. The COVID pandemic accelerated digital transformation across every sector of the economy, making blockchain technology and digital assets seem less like speculative experiments and more like inevitable infrastructure. Central bank monetary policies worldwide created unprecedented levels of liquidity in financial markets, forcing institutional investors to seek new asset classes and yield opportunities.

"This is what we've been waiting for," I told Val as we watched Bitcoin obliterate $40,000, then $50,000, with the relentless momentum of a rocket achieving escape velocity. "The institutional adoption isn't coming—it's here."

The timing for our SPAC was approaching perfection. Investors were desperate for exposure to Bitcoin and blockchain technology, but most pure-play opportunities were either private or trading at extreme valuations. We offered something different—a professionally managed, institutionally-backed Bitcoin mining operation with significant growth potential and actual operational assets.

MicroStrategy's Michael Saylor had become the poster child for corporate Bitcoin adoption, making increasingly bold statements about Bitcoin as digital property. His company's stock price moved in lockstep with Bitcoin, creating a template for how traditional companies could gain cryptocurrency exposure.

> The MicroStrategy phenomenon had created a new category of public company—the "Bitcoin proxy" that allowed traditional equity investors to gain cryptocurrency exposure through familiar investment vehicles. This model was particularly attractive to institutional investors who faced regulatory or operational constraints that prevented direct Bitcoin ownership, but could easily purchase shares of public companies with Bitcoin treasury strategies.

"Look at MicroStrategy's premium to Bitcoin," I observed to Tyler during one of our market analysis sessions. "Investors are paying a huge premium for managed Bitcoin exposure through a traditional equity structure. We can offer similar benefits with actual operational leverage."

The Cipher Connection

While we were working on the SPAC and PIPE transactions, we still had no name for the company. Listing it as "Bitfury USA" didn't feel right. It lacked spark, originality, and the story we wanted to tell. So I went back to the drawing board.

Then, during one of my walks, it hit me.

Why look far when we could look to the very root of our motivation—Alan Turing. After all, it was Turing at Bletchley Park who cracked the Enigma cipher, helping win the war and laying the foundations of modern computing. That same wartime effort gave us the inspiration for Hut 8—so I thought: what else could it produce?

I kept coming back to the word cipher. It was simple, powerful, and loaded with meaning: encryption, code, mystery, computation. Everything we were building.

And just like that, Cipher Mining was born from Turing's brilliance, through Bletchley Park, to the new frontier of digital infrastructure.

Needless to say, everybody loved the idea.

The naming choice reflected a deeper truth about our industry's evolution. Bitcoin mining had always been fundamentally about cryptography—the mathematical processes that secure the network and validate transactions. By choosing "Cipher," we were acknowledging both the technical heritage of our work and the sophisticated computational challenges that separated professional mining operations from amateur enthusiasts.

Having successfully buttoned down the SPAC component of the deal, we immediately turned to the PIPE funding. As markets were getting exuberant, we realized we really needed to work around the clock. The deal started coming together as we worked through all our contacts, calling up all the Bitcoin OG funds to participate. JPMorgan was working their contacts, and so was Wells Fargo.

> The fundraising environment in early 2021 was unlike anything the crypto industry had previously experienced. Traditional venture capital firms that had avoided digital assets for years were suddenly scrambling to deploy capital in the space. Sovereign wealth funds and pension systems were conducting their first serious evaluations of cryptocurrency investments. This created both tremendous opportunities and intense competition for quality deals.

The whole deal was done over Zoom calls. Tyler and the team were pitching investors for entire weekdays, doing dozens of pitches. Markets had been booming, and as we went through the roadshow for the PIPE fundraising, I felt good as the book got oversubscribed and indications of interest far exceeded our target with a week to go. As we entered the final week of marketing, on the morning of March 3, I woke up to a message from JPMorgan that they had great news on securing two large cornerstones for $150 million and that the book was filling up fast.

We spent the next twenty-four hours watching the book continue to fill up with smaller investors. We were ready to officially secure PIPE commitments and sign the final deal to complete the acquisition and go public.

Then the most unprecedented thing happened. On March 4, I woke up to *WSJ* headlines: "Stock selloff accelerates. Treasury yields jumped as the latest comments from Federal Reserve Chairman Powell did little to reassure investors about rising interest rates."

I said to myself: "Oh, no! Not Powell again!"

The JPMorgan team texted me: "George, we need to Zoom ASAP. Deal may be in jeopardy!"

Just a day before we were scheduled to sign the deal and secure the final commitments to fund the PIPE, the fundraising markets began to seize up. Our book of interest went from over two times oversubscribed to failing to meet our minimum cash fundraising target. I could not believe that this was happening when we were so close. At this point, everyone's scrappy instincts kicked in, and we worked all our contacts, calling in favors around the world, asking for funds to come in against an ugly market backdrop. After a stressful twenty-four hours working around the clock, at 5:00 a.m. the morning of our signing date, we rallied enough of our contacts to just barely hit our targets and sign the deal.

We announced the deal early in the morning on March 5. It was one of the biggest SPACs and one of the biggest raises in the history of Bitcoin mining. I tweeted out: "BREAKING: We just raised close to $500 million for Bitcoin mining operations in Texas. The new era of Bitcoin mining is upon us."

I got major congratulatory notes from everybody. Saylor pinged me: "Well done. Great for the industry." "Amazing accomplishment and proof of your perseverance," Jack Yee wrote me from Asia. Indeed, it was an amazing achievement. We had taken commitments for energy contracts and our brand name and capitalized them into a massive $2 billion valuation, launching Cipher Mining. Unbelievable. If this was not the embodiment of impossible is nothing, I don't know what is.

After the deal was announced, and our initial celebrations subsided, the documents were given to the SEC for approval, which would take another six months of discussion. We thought it was a done deal, but as always, there would be some unturned stones, and we'd have to fight quite a bit together alongside Latham senior partners against Bitcoin-sceptical SEC bureaucrats to get this transaction done by the deadline stipulated for early September.

But that's another story for another chapter.

CHAPTER 17

THE WESTERN PIVOT

*Do not go where the path may lead,
go instead where there is no path and leave a trail.*

—Ralph Waldo Emerson

As soon as we closed the SPAC deal, everybody was euphoric. The social media was buzzing with congratulations, phones were ringing nonstop with jubilation, and the team was celebrating what felt like our ultimate victory. But while everyone else was basking in the success, I couldn't shake the words of my childhood basketball idol, Michael Jordan: "We celebrate championships, but the next day we're back in the gym."

So the next day, March 6, I sent out an email to the executive team that would set our next chapter in motion:

"Team—incredible work on Cipher. But we can't rest on this victory. I think we must move fast and carve out our non-US Bitcoin mining operation and list the entity in London. The window is open, and we need to capitalize on our momentum. Let's discuss ASAP."

In his typical fashion, Val loved the idea. So within a few days, we had formulated a request for proposal to several banks for what we christened "Project Colossus"—another inspiration from Alan Turing's Bletchley Park, where the Colossus computer had helped crack

Enigma codes during World War II. If Cipher was our breakthrough into American markets, Colossus would be our assault on European capital markets.

> The naming pattern reflected our deep appreciation for the cryptographic pioneers who had laid the foundation for everything we were building. Turing's wartime innovations had not only helped win the war but had established the theoretical framework for modern computing and, by extension, cryptocurrency mining. Each project name connected us to that legacy of breakthrough thinking and relentless innovation.

As always, we needed to find a CEO for the project and find one fast. Actually, I had a perfect candidate in mind: my old friend from the private equity days when I was at York. Boris Erenburg, a Stanford grad, was at Spinnaker, and I'd kept close contact with him. Boris had watched my Bitcoin journey from early on after I orange-pilled him, and we were always in touch.

When I contacted him about the idea after our Cipher success, Boris loved it! "I'm in," he said without hesitation.

> Boris brought exactly the kind of pedigree that London's institutional investors would respect. As an executive vice president and portfolio manager in PIMCO's London office, he was responsible for sourcing, underwriting, and managing emerging markets special situations and direct investments for PIMCO's public and alternative funds. His background represented the perfect blend of traditional finance credibility and entrepreneurial appetite for emerging opportunities.

Based in London, together with Chris Allen, I believed they would form a great alliance for the project. Here was someone who understood both traditional finance and emerging markets, who had the credibility to speak with London's most sophisticated investors, and who was excited about the transformative potential of cryptocurrency infrastructure.

The London financial ecosystem required a different approach than the New York markets. The City's institutional investors were more globally oriented, but they also demanded sophisticated financial analysis and a deep understanding of complex cross-border structures. Boris's emerging markets background and international experience made him ideally suited to navigate these requirements while building credibility for our Bitcoin mining proposition.

Project Colossus Takes Flight

With Boris aligned, we sent out RFPs to banks with a message that demonstrated our newfound confidence and ambition:

> Fresh off the success of raising capital for Cipher Mining, Bitfury is now planning to conduct an Initial Public Offering of its Eurasian cryptocurrency mining assets (Project Colossus) on the London Stock Exchange (LSE). We contemplate to raise around $500 million in primary capital to fund the growth of the company. Bitfury is inviting a limited number of banks, on a confidential basis, to submit a proposal to act as lead syndicate member for the potential IPO and to provide advice and recommendations on a range of factors concerning the structuring, preparation, marketing, and consummation of the IPO.

We ended the message by giving banks two weeks to analyse the proposal and submit results to the executive committee.

The vision we outlined to banks was ambitious yet compelling: we would position ourselves as the "Eurasian Sustainable Bitcoin Mining Champion" traded on the LSE. The project would leverage our existing mining operations in Norway and Kazakhstan as the foundation, with plans to expand to a massive 660 MW of total capacity, mostly in Scandinavia, and aim to have computational power of 35 exahashes.

Project Colossus represented the perfect counter-narrative to the environmental FUD (Fear, Uncertainty, and Doubt) plaguing the industry. By emphasizing computational infrastructure powered entirely by renewable sources—hydro power in our existing facilities and flare gas from new greenfield projects in Kazakhstan—we could position Bitcoin mining as an environmental solution rather than a problem. The geographic diversification across Eurasia would provide both operational resilience and regulatory arbitrage, while the scale would make us a major player in the global mining ecosystem.

Our key differentiators were strategically crafted: power sourced only from renewable sources, best-in-class Bitcoin mining equipment for efficiency and reliability, and strong operational excellence. The combination would create a compelling investment proposition, resilient to Bitcoin price volatility, while capitalizing on the institutional wave of digital asset adoption.

With key assets located across Eurasia—Scandinavia's abundant hydro power and Kazakhstan's flare gas energy—the project would be a unique offering on the LSE and represent an unparalleled opportunity for institutional investors to ride the digital assets wave.

In a couple of weeks' time, we started receiving feedback from investment banks that the deal was very much doable. One global bank's response particularly captured the excitement:

We believe that Project Colossus will represent a unique opportunity for the European institutional investors to get exposure to crypto mining and the broader, rapidly evolving Bitcoin ecosystem. The Project is expected to create the largest Bitcoin mining champion outside of the US and the second largest Bitcoin miner globally.

The final page of the pitch deck was a valuation analysis and a preliminary valuation that stood in the range of $1.5 to $2 billion. I looked at Val and Boris. This clearly was a very juicy prospect. We were all aligned.

The banks' enthusiasm validated everything we had believed about the European opportunity. Unlike the US market, where multiple Bitcoin mining companies were already public or preparing to go public, Europe represented a largely untapped institutional market with only Argo Blockchain as meaningful competition. Our scale advantage, which was three times larger than the only European competitor, combined with our operational track record and sustainable energy focus, created exactly the kind of investment thesis that institutional investors were seeking. The story positioning was particularly astute, suggesting that Project Colossus would become the reference point for European crypto investment.

So after a short consideration, we selected a leading global bank and created a working group with Boris at its helm, and started putting the deal together. The momentum was building, the market conditions were solid, and we had institutional demand. Everything seemed to be aligning for our second major capital markets success in less than six months.

This ambitious thinking represented how quickly our world had transformed. It was a major milestone that seemed to unlock doors that had been sealed shut during the crypto winter. We started seeing the Bitfury story become appealing again. Suddenly, former investors who had ghosted us during our darkest hours were approaching with renewed interest, discussing the potential for multiple IPO opportunities. And all of a sudden, there was a line for Bitfury secondaries with many new investors eager to participate in the ride.

The venture capital ecosystem has an almost magnetic quality—success attracts more success, while failure tends to compound isolation. Our SPAC victory had shifted us back into the category of "winning" companies, which changed everything about how potential partners, investors, and employees viewed us. The same fundamental business that had struggled to raise capital eighteen months earlier was now being courted by the same institutions that had previously ignored our calls.

The timing couldn't have been more dramatic. Bitcoin had recovered to a full $60,000, and a company that barely a year ago was on the verge of bankruptcy, yet again was suddenly being talked about as being valued in the billions again. The speed of the transformation was breathtaking.

A few weeks after we announced the Cipher deal, our longtime investor, François, introduced us to Bertrand des Palliers, a very experienced banker who had worked at leading global banks. His idea was to bring in institutional investors and help capitalize Bitfury with an IPO on the US capital markets.

Val and I had a few discussions with Bertrand and then followed up with a first face-to-face meeting with him in Dubai. It was still during COVID times, so movement was somewhat limited, but the UAE had handled the pandemic extremely well. There was regulatory oversight, but also a certain freedom where you could fly in, get tested, meet up, and conduct business. Dubai was the perfect location for this kind of high-level discussion.

The COVID pandemic had created a unique business environment where certain jurisdictions like the UAE became havens for international deal-making. Their combination of efficient testing protocols, business-friendly policies, and world-class infrastructure made Dubai an ideal location for the kind of complex financial discussions that required face-to-face interaction. Unlike many Western cities that remained locked down or heavily restricted, Dubai had struck a balance between health safety and economic activity that attracted global business leaders seeking to conduct serious negotiations.

I was genuinely impressed meeting Bertrand. His multi-decade experience of raising capital showed, and his sharp mathematical mind grasped the value and scarcity aspect of Bitcoin. At our meeting at the Palm Waldorf Astoria, Bertrand presented us with various models for Bitcoin and Bitcoin mining, presenting a compelling case for Bitfury achieving a multi-billion-dollar valuation.

We also learned about Bertrand's close relationship with Rajeev Misra, who was running SoftBank's Vision Fund and was one of the global deal-makers in the tech investment space. The idea was that we would utilize the connections of Bertrand and Rajeev to put together a team to drive the operations forward and capitalize Bitfury in a major way. This was music to our ears.

> SoftBank's Vision Fund had emerged as one of the most influential technology investors globally, with the resources and appetite to write checks that could transform entire industries. Rajeev Misra's reputation in the venture capital community was built on identifying and scaling transformative technology companies across multiple sectors. Having access to this level of institutional capital and strategic expertise represented exactly the kind of partnership that could accelerate Bitfury's evolution from crypto startup to major technology platform.

The Bukele Bombshell

While we were setting our sights on capitalization, something even more profound was happening in the Bitcoin world. On June 4, my phone lit up with messages from the Bitcoin 2021 Conference in Miami.

"Turn on the livestream NOW," Marat texted urgently.

I opened the stream to see Jack Mallers on stage, and you could feel the electricity even through my phone screen. Jack—the young, passionate founder of Strike who had been quietly working on Bitcoin adoption in El Salvador through the Bitcoin Beach project—was practically vibrating with excitement. His boyish face, usually animated, was now absolutely radiant with the weight of what he was about to reveal.

"I have a message for you all from a very special friend," Jack said, his voice cracking with emotion.

The massive conference screen behind him flickered to life, and suddenly President Nayib Bukele of El Salvador appeared. The thirty-nine-year-old president, wearing his signature backwards baseball cap in the pre-recorded message, looked directly into the camera with a confidence that suggested he understood the historical magnitude of his words.

"My name is Nayib Bukele, president of El Salvador," he began in accented but clear English. Then, with perfect timing: "Next week, I will send to Congress a bill that will make Bitcoin legal tender in El Salvador."

The conference hall exploded. Through my phone, I could see people leaping from their seats. Jack Mallers, still on stage, broke down in tears—months of secret work had culminated in this world-changing moment. Bitcoin Twitter went supernova. I sat in my Dubai office watching history unfold in real-time. A sovereign nation was about to adopt Bitcoin as legal tender.

"Val," I called immediately, "remember what you said in that Kyiv banya? About governments hoarding Bitcoin being our ultimate success metric?"

"Don't tell me..." Val's voice trailed off as he processed the news.

"It's happening. Not just hoarding—full legal tender status."

The speed was breathtaking. By June 8, El Salvador's Legislative Assembly had passed the Bitcoin Law. Bitcoin would be accepted for all debts, public and private. Taxes could be paid in Bitcoin. Every business would need to accept it.

A few weeks later, I found myself in Tbilisi having dinner with Remi at our favorite Georgian restaurant, Kahelebi. The Bukele news had triggered a wave of nostalgia and, frankly, frustration about missed opportunities.

"Remember those meetings?" Remi said, raising his glass of a fine Georgian amber wine with a rueful smile. "We spent months trying to convince them. Charts, presentations, economic models..."

"$100 million," I replied, shaking my head. "That's all we asked. Just $100 million from our country's bank reserves when Bitcoin was at $200."

"They looked at us like we were trying to sell them magic beans," Remi laughed bitterly. "And now look—Bukele just made his entire country a Bitcoin nation."

The math was painful to contemplate. That $100 million investment we'd proposed would be worth $30 billion. Georgia's entire external debt stood at $17 billion. One bold decision could have transformed the nation's financial future.

"You know what kills me?" I said, cutting into my river trout. "We weren't asking them to bet the country like Bukele. Just a small allocation. A hedge. An experiment."

"Gaumarjos to the leaders who see the future," Remi toasted with irony. "And to those who don't—may they learn from others' courage."

That night, still fired up from our conversation, I pulled out my phone and tweeted what I was feeling:

Few years back, when #bitcoin was at $200, I lobbied Georgian Government officials to invest up to $100 mln into #BTC from Reserves. No one listened. Had they listened, the ENTIRE EXTERNAL DEBT of $17 BLN would have BEEN PAID OFF by now. The world needs more of @nayibbukele

Within hours, the tweet exploded. Thousands of likes, retweets, and comments from around the world. But it was Mike Belshe's response that made me laugh despite my frustration:

"So the country should blame the entire mass of debt on your lack of persuasiveness :-)"

I had to smile. Mike, the BitGo CEO who'd helped secure billions in Bitcoin for institutions, knew exactly how hard it was to convince traditional authorities about Bitcoin's potential. His joke cut through my frustration with the gentle ribbing only possible between battle-tested Bitcoin veterans.

But then something remarkable happened. My tweet had opened a floodgate of similar stories from Bitcoin OGs around the world. Tuur Demeester chimed in:

"Reminds me of Trace Mayer's efforts in Africa/Ghana"

Soon, Trace's own story emerged—how he'd worked with Papa-Wassa Nduom, the Vice President of Group Nduom, to convince the Central Bank of Ghana to allocate just one percent of their reserves to Bitcoin. The same polite dismissals, the same missed opportunity.

Santiago Siri's name came up as well—his 2014 pitch to Argentina's government when their economy was struggling. He'd presented a detailed plan for Bitcoin adoption that could have transformed their monetary crisis into an opportunity. They'd chosen traditional IMF loans instead.

The pattern was universal and heartbreaking. In every corner of the globe, Bitcoin evangelists had approached their governments with data, models, and passionate arguments. From Africa to South America, from Eastern Europe to Southeast Asia, the story was the same: visionaries trying to gift their nations a lifeboat, only to be dismissed as dreamers.

"It's like we were all Cassandras," I texted Val, watching the stories pour in. "Cursed to see the future but unable to make anyone believe us."

"Until Bukele," Val replied. "He didn't need convincing. He just acted."

The responses to my tweet became a kind of group therapy session for Bitcoin OGs. Each story of rejection was also a story of vindication. We hadn't been crazy. We'd been early. And the difference between those two things, as I'd learned repeatedly, was simply surviving long enough to be proven right.

What struck me most was the modesty of our asks. We weren't suggesting these countries bet everything like El Salvador. Trace wanted one percent for Ghana. Santiago proposed a small pilot program for Argentina. I'd asked for less than two percent of Georgia's reserves. These weren't radical proposals—they were prudent hedges that would have transformed national balance sheets.

"You know what this means?" Val texted the next day, having watched the Twitter storm unfold. "Every one of these stories is proof that Bitcoin adoption wasn't inevitable. It required courage. Bukele had what the others lacked: the willingness to act on conviction."

The viral tweet and its responses had created an unexpected historical record. Scattered across the globe, Bitcoin advocates had tried to help their nations secure their financial futures. Most had failed, but their efforts weren't wasted. They'd planted seeds that would eventually bloom—just not in time to capture Bitcoin at $200.

The El Salvador news had transformed everything. We weren't selling a speculative asset anymore. We were building infrastructure for legal tender. The timing for our battles with the SEC and our public market ambitions couldn't have been more perfect.

Boiling the Oceans

The summer of 2021 brought unexpected challenges that threatened to derail not just our Cipher Mining plans, but the entire institutional adoption of Bitcoin. While we were deep in negotiations with the SEC, a new crisis emerged that demanded immediate attention: the environmental FUD claiming Bitcoin was "boiling the oceans."

The attack was coordinated and effective. Elon Musk suspended Tesla's Bitcoin purchases, citing concerns over the environmental impact of Bitcoin mining, particularly the use of fossil fuels like coal. The announcement sent shockwaves through the crypto community and gave ammunition to critics who had been looking for reasons to dismiss digital assets.

Shortly after the news hit, Saylor texted me: "We have to fix this FUD. Idea is to create a Bitcoin mining council that will transparently report the energy usage by industry."

"Love the idea. Tell us of the next steps," I replied immediately.

The environmental criticism of Bitcoin had become a coordinated attack that threatened to undermine years of institutional adoption progress. The narrative was both misleading and dangerous—misleading because it ignored Bitcoin mining's role in accelerating renewable energy development and grid stabilization, and dangerous because it gave regulators and institutions an excuse to retreat from digital asset adoption. For companies like ours that had built sustainable mining operations, the FUD represented an existential threat that required an immediate, coordinated response.

We moved quickly to establish a working group headed by the capable Taras Kulyuk, who began the meticulous process of collecting energy usage data from Bitcoin miners across the industry. We provided comprehensive information from Hut 8, our own operations, as well as projected data from our Cipher targets. Within weeks, the council published its first results and pledged to update them quarterly, bringing unprecedented transparency to an industry that critics claimed operated in the shadows.

Saylor also organized a crucial meeting between Elon and Bitcoin mining executives, which went a long way toward addressing the FUD and reopening dialogue about Bitcoin's actual environmental impact versus the sensationalized narratives.

The formation of the Bitcoin Mining Council represented a watershed moment for the industry's maturation. Rather than allowing critics to control the narrative about energy consumption, leading companies chose to proactively address environmental concerns through transparency and education. The council's emphasis on renewable energy usage and grid stabilization benefits helped counter the simplistic "Bitcoin boils oceans" narrative with data-driven analysis of mining's actual environmental impact.

No Further Comments

While we were fighting the environmental FUD, we simultaneously faced our most challenging regulatory battle yet: securing SEC approval for Cipher Mining's public listing. The summer of 2021 had been grueling—countless hours spent in protracted back-and-forth negotiations with an SEC team that, frankly speaking, simply didn't want to approve Cipher because they didn't like the crypto space.

We had always known the deal would push boundaries and attract heightened scrutiny from an SEC known to be crypto-skeptical at the time. But the intensity of the pushback that summer surprised everyone, including our seasoned advisers. The regulatory environment had shifted, and what might have been routine approvals in other sectors became battlegrounds when Bitcoin was involved.

The stakes couldn't have been higher. We needed this approval not just for Cipher, but to prove that legitimate Bitcoin mining companies could navigate the traditional financial system and operate within established regulatory frameworks. Failure would send a chilling message to other companies considering similar paths.

We mobilized our full arsenal of legal and lobbying resources, engaging the top legal minds at Latham & Watkins along with premier lobbying firms to help the SEC understand what we were trying to accomplish. The Latham SEC experts developed a comprehensive strategy, and Chris led the charge in formulating meticulous replies and arguments to address every single concern raised by the regulators.

The process was exhausting. Chris and the Latham team worked countless hours, crafting responses that had to be both legally bulletproof and educationally effective for regulators who often lacked a deep understanding of Bitcoin mining operations. Each round of comments required not just legal precision, but the patience to explain an entirely new industry to skeptical bureaucrats.

Finally, as we were flying to yet another strategy session with Bertrand in Ibiza, Chris called with the news we'd been waiting months to hear: the SEC had no further comments and the deal would go live. Subject to some minor deal conditions and shareholder votes, Cipher was set to start trading on Nasdaq.

The victory was a major business win as well as a validation that Bitcoin mining companies could operate within the traditional financial system while maintaining the innovative spirit that made the industry so compelling. We had proven that with enough persistence, legal expertise, and commitment to transparency, even the most skeptical regulators could be convinced of Bitcoin's legitimacy.

Having secured Cipher and actively pursuing Colossus listing, we landed in Ibiza for the meeting with Rajeev and Bertrand. During the meetings at Rajeev's villa, we had a candid discussion about the most optimal way to capitalize Bitfury. Was it spinning off subsidiaries and capitalizing them one by one? Or was it best to capitalize as a holding company where investors would get exposure to Bitfury as a full-stack technology company, including hardware R&D, chip production, data centers, immersion cooling, AI chips, and software platforms?

As discussions progressed, the arguments were leaning towards capitalizing Bitfury as a whole and having just Cipher Mining as the only other listed entity. And at the end of discussions, Rajeev commented: "I believe I have a great candidate for the opportunity to list Bitfury on US markets. Brian Brooks."

Within twenty-four hours, we were on Zoom with Brian to discuss him coming aboard as Bitfury CEO to lead the company for the US capital markets.

"Brian," Val said during our virtual meeting, "we need someone who can bridge traditional finance and crypto innovation. Your background at OCC gives you exactly the credibility we need."

"I've been watching what you guys have built," Brian replied. "The timing feels right to take this to the next level. When do we start?"

Bertrand chimed in: "We need to move fast. The window for crypto IPOs won't stay open forever."

We liked how Brian presented things, and he seemed like he could indeed be a very good candidate. So after a few back-and-forth and in-person meetings, we onboarded him and started the push for the US listing.

> Brian Brooks brought a unique combination of traditional financial services experience and crypto industry expertise. Having served as Acting Comptroller of the Currency under the Trump administration and later as CEO of Binance USA, he understood both regulatory frameworks and the operational challenges of scaling cryptocurrency businesses. His background provided exactly the kind of credibility that institutional investors would value—someone who could speak their language while understanding the technical and regulatory complexities of our industry.

Alongside starting the US listing project, we also had to make a painful decision to put Colossus on hold. The banks had been trying to secure cornerstone investors for weeks without success. It was becoming clear that European institutional capital interest simply wasn't as high as in the USA. Having both Cipher and Colossus listed in addition to the soon-to-be-listed Bitfury would be a major distraction. I initially did not agree with that position, but in the end, I went with the consensus. Boris also understood the arguments of the team and was happy to assume the role of a business developer for the holding.

Project Bullion Takes Shape

So with the new CEO in hand and a new course charted, we set up major strategy sessions for all executives in Istanbul, and everybody flew in for the meetings. It was October and the leaves were turning yellow, creating a golden backdrop as we looked out over the Bosphorus Strait. There was something poetic about gathering in this ancient city that had bridged civilizations for millennia, as we planned our own transformation from Eastern European startup to Western capital markets darling.

Istanbul's unique position as a bridge between Europe and Asia made it an ideal location for international business gatherings. The city's rich history of commercial exchange, combined with modern conference facilities and favorable visa policies for most nationalities, created an environment conducive to the kind of intensive strategic planning sessions that required full executive participation. Turkey's neutral stance in many geopolitical conflicts also made it a comfortable meeting ground for teams with diverse international backgrounds.

We had three intensive days of discussions where we covered every aspect of our business and future plans.

At this time, there was a major shortage of semiconductors globally, to the point where supply chains were affected and the manufacturing and automotive industries were severely impacted. Since our team was working on new chip development, we simply couldn't secure the supply. We were placing our bets with Samsung, but they had an eighteen-month wait time. We had to do something about this if we had any chance of making our IPO a success.

The global semiconductor shortage of 2021 to 2022 was triggered by a combination of pandemic-related supply chain disruptions, increased demand for consumer electronics, and automotive industry recovery. For Bitcoin mining companies, securing chip production capacity became as critical as securing energy contracts, as leading-edge semiconductors determined competitive positioning in an increasingly professional industry. The shortage had fundamentally altered the competitive landscape—companies with existing foundry relationships and production slots held massive advantages over newcomers trying to enter the market.

One of the key tasks we assigned to our contacts, new board members, and advisors was to secure chip production capacity. After countless meetings in Seoul and the UAE, we finally received positive news that Samsung had allocated several thousand wafers for new production, which was quite substantial and provided an adrenaline shock to the company.

On one of our calls, Bertrand was elated with joy: "George, Val, this changes everything! With Samsung's commitment, we can project meaningful chip production scaling. This gives us exactly the operational foundation we need for institutional credibility."

This good news arrived just a few weeks after the Istanbul gathering, and everybody was excited. The preliminary feedback from the market was that we could IPO at $4 to 5 billion valuation—a number that seemed almost surreal given where we'd been just eighteen months earlier. As we started putting things together, the plan was that Brian would work with Bertrand to create the Bitfury pitch deck, and we would start fundraising to raise $200–$250 million in a pre-IPO round, then proceed with listing the company on a US stock exchange within a twelve-month timeframe. We christened the initiative "Project Bullion," and Brian moved fast, retaining a top global investment bank that was ready to move quickly and close the deal for us.

As it turned out, 2021 was wrapping up to be a blockbuster year. We were back on top again, the Bitcoin market had recovered, and ended at $46,000 per coin. Following tradition, I was in the UAE with my family, raising glasses of champagne with Val, reflecting on how we had overcome yet another period of adversity.

With our new Western team in place, we were ready to capitalize on Bitfury itself to the tune of billions. The pieces were falling into place perfectly—experienced leadership, institutional backing, market momentum, and a compelling growth story.

But as always in our journey, fate would have different plans for us.

Standing on the terrace of our Palm Dubai villa, watching fireworks illuminate the sky as 2021 drew to a close, I felt the familiar mixture of satisfaction and anticipation that had defined our entrepreneurial journey. We had survived another cycle, adapted to new realities, and positioned ourselves for the next phase of growth.

The champagne tasted sweeter knowing how close we had come to losing everything once again. Now, with Cipher trading publicly and Bitfury having a Western CEO and preparing for its own IPO, we had proven that our vision of institutionalizing Bitcoin infrastructure wasn't just possible—it was inevitable.

"To victory," I toasted, raising my glass to Val against the backdrop of Dubai's glittering skyline.

"To victory," Val replied, his smile reflecting the confidence we both felt about our carefully laid plans.

Little did we know that yet another dramatic chapter of our story was about to come.

CHAPTER 18

FTXED

What lies behind us and what lies before us are
tiny matters compared to what lies within us.

—Ralph Waldo Emerson

January started strong with Bitcoin crossing $47,000.

The beginning of 2022 represented the apex of crypto's first institutional cycle. After years of being dismissed as digital tulips or rat poison, Bitcoin had achieved what seemed impossible just five years earlier—acceptance by Fortune 500 treasuries, integration into traditional banking, and recognition as a legitimate asset class. Major corporations were announcing Bitcoin treasury strategies, traditional banks were launching crypto services, and even central banks were exploring digital currencies. The infrastructure we'd spent a decade building was finally being validated by the very institutions that once mocked us.

Yet this moment of triumph would prove to be the calm before crypto's most devastating storm.

I found myself at Bruce Fenton's Satoshi Roundtable in Dubai. After years of scheduling conflicts where I couldn't attend the esteemed gatherings in North America—Bitfury had dispatched Sysman and Marat to represent us—I finally had no excuse. The event was being held in Dubai, practically in my backyard. As I walked into the Waldorf Astoria on the Palm, the marble floors reflecting the chandeliers overhead, memories of our early Bitcoin gatherings flooded back. Those cramped conference rooms in hotels seemed like another lifetime compared to this opulence.

"George!" Bruce greeted me warmly, his Boston accent still detectable despite years of international living. "It's great you've finally made it!"

"Better late than never," I replied with a grin, clasping his hand. "And it's brilliant you decided to hold it in my neighborhood. No excuses for missing it now."

Bruce was one of those rare individuals who bridged traditional finance and the crypto revolution with genuine credibility. With over thirty years in finance, he'd founded Atlantic Financial before becoming a full-time Bitcoin advocate in 2013. His Satoshi Roundtable, launched in 2014, had become the industry's most influential "unconference"— where real decisions were made under Chatham House rules, away from marketing pitches and public posturing. No PowerPoints, no sales decks, just honest conversations among people who moved markets.

The evolution of the Satoshi Roundtable mirrored Bitcoin's own journey from cypherpunk experiment to global financial phenomenon. What began as intimate gatherings of true believers arguing about protocol changes in mountain lodges had transformed into the crypto industry's top event—a convergence of Bitcoin OGs, billionaires, nation-state representatives, and the architects of a new financial system. The geographic shift from North America to Dubai itself told a story: crypto's center of gravity was moving eastward, following the money and the regulatory freedom.

I knew I was at the right place when I walked into the hotel's main lounge and, at first glance, saw half a dozen Bitcoin OGs. The air was thick with the energy of dealmaking and the subtle competition of who had the most impressive recent exit.

Gabriel from Bitt, who now wore the dual hats of crypto innovator and Ambassador of Barbados to the UAE—a testament to how crypto was reshaping diplomatic relations—was deep in conversation with Michael Cao. Michael had made his fortune in mining and EOS alongside Brock Pierce, riding multiple waves of the crypto boom with uncanny timing.

Bill Barhydt of Abra was holding court near the window, his latest pivot into crypto banking drawing a small crowd of interested investors. We'd invested in Abra earlier, and it was on a great trajectory. Bill had that rare combination of traditional finance pedigree and crypto vision that made him a bridge between worlds.

Adam Back and Samson Mow, our comrades who'd stood with us during the block size wars, were near the bar discussing Lightning with Sysman and Jameson Lopp, OG Bitcoin core contributor. Adam's Blockstream cap was his only concession to casual dress in a room full of designer labels.

Our Sheikh friends, Zayed and Ali, dressed in crisp white kanduras, were discussing a project with our old friend and Bitcoin OG, CZ, whose Binance had emerged to become the dominant global crypto exchange. CZ's characteristic humility couldn't hide the fact that he'd built one of the most valuable companies in crypto history in just a few years.

The gathering also included many new faces—crypto funds and investors from the Middle East and Asia, hungry for opportunities and connections. Young princes managing sovereign wealth funds mingled with Southeast Asian tech entrepreneurs and developers. It was a sign that the industry was evolving and expanding beyond its Western roots, finding fertile ground in regions where the combination of capital and regulatory flexibility created perfect conditions for innovation.

The conversations flowed from one table to another, ideas and opportunities crossing paths like the evening's gentle breeze. In one corner, a heated debate about stablecoin regulation. In another, whispered discussions of a new layer-two solution that could finally solve the scaling trilemma. Everywhere, the underlying current of opportunity flowed through the deals being structured, the partnerships formed, and the future being written one handshake at a time.

As the evenings progressed, the formal sessions gave way to the real business of the Roundtable—the informal connections that would shape the industry's next chapter. After the conference wrapped up, we gathered a small crew and celebrated CZ's birthday at Cipriani in DIFC, the restaurant's sophisticated ambiance a perfect match for the evening's mood.

Between perfectly grilled steaks and glasses of Brunello, we discussed Binance's incredible traction. CZ was characteristically thoughtful about the company's next moves, always thinking three steps ahead.

"We're looking for new places to expand," he said. "This regulatory arbitrage game is getting more complex. We need jurisdictions that understand crypto isn't going away."

I leaned forward, "Come to Georgia. The government is crypto-friendly. I think you'll like what you see."

CZ's eyes sharpened with interest, that look I'd seen before when he was evaluating a promising opportunity. "I'll definitely check it out," he said, raising his glass. "To new frontiers."

As we toasted, I couldn't help but reflect on how far we'd all come. From cypherpunk mailing lists to birthday parties with old friends, from arguing about block sizes to negotiating with nation-states. The revolution we'd dreamed of was becoming reality, one relationship at a time, one jurisdiction at a time.

The desert night was warm as we finally left Cipriani, the combination of excellent Brunello and better company creating that perfect buzz of possibility. As I watched CZ and Gabe head out into the Dubai night, I realized the importance of these get-togethers, especially for us OGs, to keep track of things. The industry was moving so fast that without these touchpoints, you could lose sight of the bigger picture.

The energy from Dubai carried forward into remarkable news. In February, just weeks after the Roundtable, we finally secured approval for our Sarnia facility in Ontario with power at an incredible three cents per kilowatt hour.

"George, it's official!" Vadym called, his voice electric with excitement. "Sarnia is a go. Twenty-eight megawatts to start, with expansion potential up to 200 MW."

I felt a surge of vindication. After months of navigating Canadian bureaucracy and energy negotiations, we'd secured one of the most competitive power rates in North America. The facility would be equipped with our latest blockchain infrastructure, positioning us for significant expansion.

The press release went out positioning Bitfury as continuing to lead the industry's expansion. Brian's quote captured our momentum perfectly: "As one of the industry's first and most established Bitcoin miners, we are pleased to continue to expand our operations with the launch of our state-of-the-art facility in Sarnia."

Little did we know this would be one of our last moments of pure optimism in 2022.

The False Prophet

In those heady early days of 2022, we had reason for optimism beyond just Bitcoin's price and our operational expansion. There was another source of hope—one that would prove to be our greatest disappointment. Gary Gensler, who had been sworn in as SEC Chair in April 2021, initially appeared to be aligned with us. Here was a man who'd taught "Blockchain and Money" at MIT, who understood the technology's transformative potential, who'd spoken respectfully—even admiringly—about Bitcoin's breakthrough in solving the double-spend problem.

"Finally," I'd told Val when Gensler's appointment was announced, "someone who actually understands what we're building."

I would direct many friends interested in Bitcoin to his MIT lectures, telling them, "If you want to understand Bitcoin and blockchain from someone who actually gets it, watch Gensler's course."

> How naive I was. I'd forgotten the oldest rule of Washington: power changes people. Or perhaps it merely reveals who they always were. The professor who'd taught Bitcoin's potential would become its most sophisticated enemy—not through ignorance, but through intimate knowledge of exactly where to strike.

By early 2022, the honeymoon was over. Gensler's SEC had launched what could only be described as a reign of terror against the crypto industry. His favorite phrase—"come in and register"—became a cruel joke, as company after company discovered there was no actual path to registration, no clarity on rules, only enforcement actions and Wells notices.

But the real betrayal was yet to come. Behind the scenes, Gensler was orchestrating something far more insidious than mere enforcement actions. Together with Senator Elizabeth Warren, he was laying the groundwork for what the industry would later call "Choke Point 2.0," a systematic campaign to cut crypto off from the banking system without ever passing a law or publishing a rule.

The pattern would become clear by 2023. Joint statements warning banks about crypto risks, sudden account closures, denied charter applications, and a coordinated squeeze would claim Silvergate, Signature Bank, and nearly strangle the entire industry. All orchestrated by the very man who once taught students about Bitcoin's innovation.

The irony was bitter as hemlock. The man who'd explained Bitcoin's innovation to MIT students was now determined to strangle it through regulatory pressure. The teacher had become the executioner.

War Comes to Europe

But regulatory betrayal would soon be overshadowed by a more immediate catastrophe. As we progressed with our Canadian expansion and watched Gensler's true colors emerge, worrying political developments were unfolding on the other side of the world. Reports emerged of Russian military exercises on Ukraine's border. Some analysts speculated about a potential invasion. Like most observers, we dismissed these as alarmist. Surely Russia wouldn't take such a catastrophic step.

The feeling was heavy, though. Between Gensler's mounting hostility and the geopolitical tensions, something felt fundamentally wrong about 2022. On the night of February 23, I fell asleep with deep unease. I woke early the next day, around 5:00 a.m., immediately checking my phone. Bitcoin had dropped nearly eight percent within hours, falling to around $34,300. Such dramatic movement meant something terrible had happened.

Then I saw it: Russian planes bombing Kyiv. Russian forces crossing the border. Full-scale invasion.

The Russian invasion of Ukraine marked a watershed moment for the global crypto community. For the first time, cryptocurrency would play a central role in a major geopolitical crisis—not as a speculative asset or technological curiosity, but as a lifeline for refugees, a funding mechanism for resistance, and a tool for circumventing financial warfare. The industry that had been built on abstract principles of decentralization and censorship resistance suddenly faced its most concrete test.

The shock was total. I quickly woke up fully and started checking every news source. We had dozens of developers in Ukraine, countless friends, and family members. We immediately began mobilizing, trying to understand how we could help.

Through our networks, we quickly connected with Ukrainian foundations. The unfolding refugee crisis required immediate action. I reached out to Laura Shin: "Laura, we are organizing a drive to help Ukrainian refugees."

Within minutes, Laura answered: "For sure, let me move some slots. I'm in!"

The crypto community's response was swift and overwhelming. CZ and Binance immediately stepped up, announcing a $10 million donation via Binance Charity's Ukraine Emergency Relief Fund—one of the largest private donations at that time.

I went on Laura's podcast *Unchained* with another Ukrainian crypto project leader—Ilya Polosukhin of NEAR—where we launched a major crypto drive that would end up raising over $100 million in crypto funds for the Ukrainian cause.

Our efforts quickly caught the attention of Ashton Kutcher through an unexpected connection. Dima Shvets, CEO of Reface and a Ukrainian entrepreneur, reached out to connect us. "My friend and investor Bill Tai and his friend George from Bitfury raised some $25 mln in BTC and ether," Dima wrote to Ashton. "Let's try to collaborate with your fundraising initiative and raise even more awareness."

Ashton responded immediately, and as I updated him in early March, "Approaching $15 mln! That's around where we are with our Bitcoin efforts."

Working with the Come Back Alive Foundation, we focused on what Ukraine needed most urgently—protective equipment and essential supplies. While humanitarian efforts were providing food and medicine, we prioritized protective gear, communication equipment like Starlink terminals, and other critical needs.

"We are about to break $10 [mln] of our $30 [mln] goal," Ashton messaged back. "Once we hit our goal, we will start to highlight and promote other efforts. Let's stay in touch."

The collaboration intensified as the crisis deepened. By April, we were working on securing twenty thousand protective vests. "Connected everyone with the right people in government," I updated Ashton. "Looks like we are making progress on the big order."

The speed and scale of the crypto community's response demonstrated something profound: within hours of the invasion, Bitcoin and other crypto were flowing into relief wallets from every corner of the globe. No bureaucracy, no wire delays, no government approvals needed. Within weeks, we had raised over $100 million in crypto, connected suppliers with Ukrainian organizations, and proven that when a crisis strikes, the crypto community can mobilize faster than any traditional aid mechanism. While banks were closed and SWIFT was weaponized, cryptocurrency became the lifeline that couldn't be shut down.

When Supercycle Meets Reality

Despite the geopolitical chaos, business had to continue. Goldman Sachs, which had been monitoring our progress, moved quickly. "Our committees have approved the assignment and we are prepared to move forward immediately," senior team members wrote.

The contrast with the world's chaos was stark. While we were helping evacuate refugees from a war zone, investment banks were competing for our business. Goldman's proposed timeline was aggressive: begin outreach within weeks, followed by first-round bids and a signed deal in the fall.

In retrospect, the timing of our Goldman Sachs process represented the last gasp of the bull market exuberance. Investment banks were still operating under the assumption that crypto's institutional adoption would continue its meteoric rise. Within weeks, that assumption would be shattered by the Terra Luna collapse, beginning a cascade that would freeze capital markets and destroy trillions in value. Our $5 billion valuation target, which seemed conservative in May, would soon appear delusional.

We couldn't have predicted what was coming. As we worked through Goldman's process, storm clouds were gathering. Terra Luna's collapse that same month would begin a cascade that would ultimately freeze capital markets. But for those few weeks in spring, with our Canadian expansion validated and Goldman orchestrating our process, it felt like we had finally broken through.

Terra Luna's collapse was the earthquake that brought everything crashing down. I was in Switzerland for an investor meeting when the news broke. My phone lit up with alerts as UST, the "stable" coin, lost its dollar peg.

"This is impossible," the investor next to me muttered, watching the price charts in disbelief. "Forty billion dollars can't just evaporate."

But it could, and it did. Do Kwon's algorithmic stablecoin experiment—which had seduced even sophisticated investors with promises of 20 percent yields through Anchor Protocol—unravelled spectacularly. Within seventy-two hours, both Luna and UST were essentially worthless. The carnage was staggering: over $45 billion in market cap vaporized, leaving a trail of institutional corpses in its wake.

The first major casualty was Three Arrows Capital. Su Zhu and Kyle Davies had bet everything on Luna, leveraging their $3.5 billion fund to the hilt. When UST depegged and Luna cratered to zero, their collateral evaporated overnight. Margin calls flooded in that they couldn't possibly meet.

On May 27, 2022, just days after the collapse, Su Zhu posted what would become an infamous epitaph for an era: "Supercycle price thesis was regrettably wrong." That blunt concession from someone who had championed an unshakeable belief in a never-ending bull market captured the shell-shocked reality hitting the entire industry. By July, 3AC had filed for bankruptcy, with the founders disappearing from public view like fugitives from a financial crime scene.

The contagion spread with terrifying speed. Celsius Network, which had hundreds of millions exposed through Anchor Protocol, froze withdrawals in June—the crypto equivalent of a bank run. Voyager Digital discovered that its $650 million loan to 3AC was essentially uncollateralized toilet paper. BlockFi required an emergency $250 million lifeline from FTX just to stay afloat.

Galaxy Digital lost an estimated $300 million. Korean VC firm Hashed saw over $3 billion disappear, one of the largest VC losses in crypto history. Even Jump Crypto, which had backstopped Terra's peg with its own reserves, suffered massive losses and reputational damage.

The Terra Luna collapse revealed the crypto industry's fatal flaw: the recursive nature of leverage built on leverage, all ultimately backed by nothing but confidence. When that confidence evaporated, the unwinding was swift and merciless. What made this crash different from previous crypto winters was its systemic nature—this wasn't just speculators getting burned, but supposedly sophisticated institutional players who had borrowed billions against tokens whose value proposition they never truly understood.

The collapse shattered several myths simultaneously. Algorithmic stablecoins weren't stable. Twenty percent "risk-free" yields were neither risk-free nor sustainable—they were simply Ponzi economics dressed up in DeFi terminology. The entire edifice of crypto lending was built on circular dependencies: platforms lending to each other, using the same collateral multiple times, all while pretending the music would never stop.

At our next board meeting, Bertrand, a veteran of numerous financial crises, delivered an ominous prediction: "This is going to trigger a cascade. When leverage unwinds, it happens at light speed."

He was prophetically correct. The Terra collapse was crypto's Lehman moment, exposing the interconnected fragility of an entire financial system built on sand. Do Kwon, once crypto's wunderkind, became a fugitive with an Interpol red notice. South Korea issued arrest warrants. Regulators worldwide suddenly woke up to the systemic risks that had been building in plain sight.

The real tragedy was in the details. Retail investors had poured life savings into Anchor Protocol, seduced by yields that traditional finance couldn't match. They didn't understand they were the exit liquidity for a system that could only sustain itself by attracting ever more capital. When the music stopped, they were left holding worthless tokens.

Amid the market carnage, there were still signs of life in our portfolio. In October, I received welcome news from one of our most promising ventures. Axelera AI, which we had incubated within Bitfury before spinning out, had just closed a $27 million Series A round.

"George, you need to see this," Val said, forwarding the announcement. "They're getting tremendous traction."

I read through with growing pride. In just fourteen months, the team had grown to over eighty people across Europe, successfully taped out their first test chip, and attracted tier-one investors including Innovation Industries and IMEC.

The timing was bittersweet. Here was proof that our strategy of diversifying beyond pure crypto plays was working—Axelera's AI edge computing technology represented exactly the kind of breakthrough that could thrive regardless of Bitcoin's price.

The FTX Apocalypse

If Terra Luna was an earthquake, FTX's collapse in November was complete Armageddon. I was back in Dubai when the first domino fell: a CoinDesk article about Alameda Research's balance sheet. Knowing that our old friend Mike Casey was overseeing the editorial, I was 100 percent confident in the quality of the reporting. The moment I read it, I knew this wasn't just smoke—it was the spark that would burn the house down.

I rubbed my eyes, trying to process what I was reading. The trading firm's assets consisted largely of FTT tokens—essentially Sam Bankman-Fried's IOUs to himself. Billions of dollars in "assets" that were illiquid at best, worthless at worst.

> The FTX collapse represented more than just another crypto exchange failure—it was the shattering of crypto's carefully constructed narrative of maturation and legitimacy. Sam Bankman-Fried had become the industry's golden boy, the MIT graduate who spoke Congress's language, who donated to the right causes, who promised to give away his billions. His fraud wasn't just financial; it was a betrayal of the trust that the entire industry had worked to build. In stealing customer funds to cover trading losses, SBF didn't just destroy FTX—he validated every skeptic who had ever called crypto a scam.

Within hours, the crypto Twitter sphere was in full meltdown mode. When CZ announced Binance would sell its FTT holdings, it triggered a bank run on FTX. Sam's increasingly desperate tweets trying to reassure users only accelerated the panic.

I was having dinner with CZ in Tbilisi when the full scope became clear. He had just finished meetings with the Georgian Prime Minister about Binance's expansion plans, but our conversation was dominated by FTX's implosion.

"I had to act," CZ explained, his normally composed demeanor showing strain, "when I saw that balance sheet. It was a disaster."

By November 11, FTX had filed for bankruptcy. But the real horror was just beginning to emerge. Customer funds—supposedly segregated and safe—had been illegally lent to Alameda to cover trading losses. The scale was breathtaking: $8 billion missing.

As FTX's collapse sent shockwaves through the industry, we faced our own moment of truth. Bitcoin had plummeted below $20,000, mining economics were brutal, and our chip development program was hemorrhaging cash. The perfect storm had arrived.

We gathered for an emergency board meeting that would determine Bitfury's future. The Zoom call had none of the optimism from earlier in the year. Faces were grim, voices tense.

Brian Brooks laid out the situation with characteristic directness. "We have two options. Invest another $50 million in chip development for a potential next-generation breakthrough, or mothball the program and wait for better times."

The context was particularly painful. Our first-generation 5-nanometer chip had come out with average results—definitely not the breakthrough we'd anticipated. The chip team was asking for additional capital for a second tapeout, convinced they could achieve the performance leap we needed. But we were caught in a vise: Bitcoin prices collapsing, chip pricing down across the board, and resources becoming increasingly scarce.

> The decision to abandon chip development marked the end of an era for Bitfury. Since 2011, our identity had been inextricably linked to our silicon innovation. But the brutal economics of chip development in a bear market forced a reckoning: would we cling to our identity and risk everything, or adapt to survive?

The debate raged for hours. Engineers pleaded for one more chance, arguing that giving up now would waste years of accumulated knowledge. They pointed to learnings from the 5 nm tapeout that could inform a more successful second attempt. Finance presented brutal projections of cash burn against Bitcoin's crashed price. Sales showed the reality of trying to compete without breakthrough technology—we'd be at the mercy of Bitmain and others for hardware supply.

Finally, Val made the call. There was no dramatic metaphor or literary reference—just the cold calculation of risks and benefits. He'd weighed every angle: the mediocre 5 nm results, the massive capital requirements for a second tapeout, the collapsed Bitcoin price, the tightening market for chip development resources. The math was unforgiving.

"It's time to mothball the project. The economics don't work," he said simply.

I agreed. Sometimes it takes even bigger courage to stop doing something rather than continue. We live to fight another day—instead, we would end up allocating funds into a new, groundbreaking technology. It's in stealth mode now, but if everything aligns, the world will hear again about the new Bitfury chips. Only time will tell.

The vote was painful but unanimous: we would wind down chip development, closing a defining chapter in Bitfury's history.

$2 Trillion in Ashes

I was at the Namos Dubai having lunch on December 12th when the news broke: Sam Bankman-Fried had been arrested in the Bahamas. The boy genius who had graced magazine covers and testified before Congress was now in handcuffs.

Val messaged immediately. "Did you see the indictment? Wire fraud, conspiracy, campaign finance violations. They're throwing the book at him."

"That was fast," I replied. "He destroyed billions in value and set the industry back years."

The charges were staggering. The next day, December 13, federal prosecutors unsealed an eight-count indictment that read like a financial crimes greatest hits: wire fraud conspiracy, securities fraud, commodities fraud, money laundering, and campaign finance violations. The SEC piled on with a civil complaint, accusing SBF of defrauding equity investors by diverting over $1.8 billion in customer deposits to Alameda Research while falsely representing FTX's risk management systems.

This was one of the largest fraud and money-laundering cases in US history, involving billions in missing customer funds. The timing was particularly dramatic: his arrest came right before he was scheduled to testify before Congress, preventing him from spinning his narrative to lawmakers.

After ten days in Bahamian custody, SBF agreed to extradition. On December 22, he was released on a historic $250 million bail package—the largest pretrial bail ever set. The conditions were stringent: house arrest at his parents' Palo Alto home, ankle monitor, and surrendered passport. The former billionaire who had flown private jets around the world was now confined to his childhood bedroom.

The saga continued into 2023. On January 3, he pleaded not guilty to all charges, maintaining his innocence even as his inner circle flipped. By February, his bail conditions were tightened after alleged witness-tampering attempts—he'd tried to contact his ex-girlfriend Caroline Ellison and FTX counsel. The judge had seen enough. On August 11, bail was revoked entirely, and SBF was sent to the Metropolitan Detention Center in Brooklyn, trading his parents' comfortable home for a federal jail cell.

The details that emerged were increasingly damning. Customer funds used to buy luxury real estate in the Bahamas. Political donations made with stolen money. A corporate culture of drugs and polyamory that read more like a cautionary tale than a tech startup. The entire FTX empire had been built on lies, enabled by a complicit inner circle and a media eager to anoint the next tech visionary.

The arrest sent shockwaves through both crypto and regulatory circles. For those of us who had been in the industry since the beginning, watching regulators struggle to understand Bitcoin while giving SBF a free pass, there was a bitter irony. The "responsible" face of crypto, the one who called for regulation and donated millions to politicians, turned out to be running the biggest fraud in the space. Meanwhile, the "outlaws" and "anarchists" who had built Bitcoin were still here, still building, still fighting for a decentralized future.

As 2022 drew to a close, I found myself on a family vacation to Mauritius on New Year's Eve, watching fireworks light up the Indian Ocean. The contrast with the previous year's celebration was stark. Then, we had been drunk on possibility, Bitcoin at $47,000, institutions lining up to invest.

Now, Bitcoin limped along at $16,000, massively down sixty-five percent from the year before. FTX was bankrupt. Three Arrows was liquidated. Celsius had collapsed. BlockFi was gone. The crypto industry had lost over $2 trillion in value. We had shuttered our chip program, our core identity, for over a decade.

The crypto winter of 2022 was different from all that had come before. Previous bear markets had been about price—speculators getting washed out, weak hands folding. This was about trust. The industry's attempt to build bridges to traditional finance had been sabotaged from within. Every institution that had taken a chance on crypto was now questioning that decision. The very foundations we'd spent a decade building—custody, lending, trading—had been revealed as houses of cards. Recovery wouldn't just require higher prices; it would require rebuilding faith itself.

But we were still here. Bloodied, humbled, but still standing.

"What does not kill you makes you stronger," I said, raising my glass over Zoom.

"To the next chapter," Val replied.

The champagne tasted different this year—less like victory, more like survival. But sometimes, in the depths of winter, survival is its own form of victory.

CHAPTER 19

THE DRAGON RISES

In the midst of winter, I found there was,
within me, an invincible summer.

—Albert Camus

The Emirates flight back to Dubai in January 2023 felt different from any I'd taken before. Below, the desert stretched endlessly—a fitting metaphor for the crypto winter we were traversing. I pressed my forehead against the window and whispered the words that had become my lifeline: "This too shall pass." Some days, they rang hollow. Today, they felt like a prayer.

Bitcoin had stabilized around $16,000, a number that would have thrilled us in 2017 but now felt like a monument to collective delusion. The Dubai skyline appeared through the haze, its ambitious towers reaching toward promises that suddenly seemed naive. I thought of Icarus, wings melting, plummeting toward an unforgiving sea.

But perhaps that's the wrong myth. Perhaps we were more like Sisyphus, condemned to push our boulder up the mountain again and again. The difference was, each time we pushed, we changed the mountain itself. Every cycle carved new paths, and each crash created new foundations. We weren't just repeating; we were iterating.

Bruce's Satoshi Roundtable that February was a study in contrasts. Gone were the yacht parties where champagne flowed like water and every conversation ended with "when we hit a million." The Waldorf's opulent halls now hosted a different breed of gathering: survivors comparing scars.

"Here we go again," Bruce said, finding me by the coffee station on the first morning. "Another correction, another exodus."

"No worries, Bruce," I replied, taking a sip of coffee. "We've seen this rodeo before. All shall be well."

Bruce smiled wearily. "How many of these cycles have we been through now?"

"Enough to know they always end," I said. "The tourists leave, the builders stay. Same story, different year."

But regardless, as tradition would have it, I ran my chess games with Sysman on the terrace overlooking the gulf, joined this time by Galaxy co-founder David Namdar, who was an adept chess player. Little did they know that during COVID, I had hired a grandmaster and was confidently approaching an ELO 2000 rating.

"Your opening game has improved dramatically," Sysman observed after I executed a particularly sharp Sicilian Defense. "Where did you study this variation?"

"Lockdown had its benefits," I replied with a grin. "While everyone else was watching Netflix, I was perfecting my game."

"Check," I announced, sliding my queen across the board with satisfaction.

Sysman studied the position intently, his cybersecurity background making him methodical in crisis situations. "You've been sandbagging us this whole time, haven't you?"

"A magician never reveals his secrets," I laughed. "But let's just say I had excellent coaching during the pandemic."

When David sat down for his game, his confidence was already shaken. "I saw what you did to Sysman," he said, arranging his pieces carefully. "But I've been playing since I was eight."

"Experience is valuable," I agreed, opening with my favorite King's pawn. "But so is recent study."

Twenty-five moves later, he was staring at mate in three.

"Impressive," David said, extending his hand. "Looks like COVID has had its benefits for you."

The attendees weren't the fair-weather evangelists who'd flooded in during the bull run. These were the battle-tested veterans who understood that crypto's promise transcended price charts. In the muted conversations over Arabic coffee, I heard the real work being done—protocols being refined, infrastructure being built, foundations being laid for the next cycle.

> Bear markets reveal character the way audit reports reveal fraud—completely and without mercy. The tulip traders, the momentum chasers, the keynote speakers who'd never actually built anything—they evaporated like morning dew in the desert. What remained were the engineers who coded through the crash, the entrepreneurs who hired during the hysteria, the believers who saw winter not as death but as dormancy. Seeds planted in snow grow the strongest roots.

"Building in a bear market is like dating someone at their worst," one developer quipped during a panel. "If you can love the technology when it's down eighty percent, you might actually deserve the gains."

On the final night, the survivors gathered in a penthouse suite overlooking the Arabian Gulf. The mood was somber but not defeated—more like soldiers sharing a drink after a brutal battle, knowing more lay ahead. A poker game materialized, as they always did, becoming our informal therapy session.

"Know what I learned this year?" an investor mused, pushing all-in with pocket aces. "The difference between being early and being wrong is just surviving long enough to find out."

A lucky flush cracked his aces. The table erupted in bitter laughter. Even here, 2022's cruel lessons persisted—sometimes the best hand still loses.

When Dignity Faces the Storm

As the evening wound down, CZ pulled me aside on the terrace. The desert wind carried the scent of approaching rain—unusual for Dubai, ominous in its timing.

"George," he said, his trademark confidence replaced by something I'd never seen before—vulnerability. "This year will be difficult for me."

I studied his face in the amber light. "The FTX fallout?"

He nodded, gripping the railing. "The establishment needs a villain. They want to prove the whole industry is rotten." He paused, choosing his words carefully. "Binance's perceived role in FTX's collapse... refusing to bail out a fraud somehow makes us complicit."

"That's insane," I said. "You saved people from losing even more."

His premonition would prove devastatingly accurate. By November, Binance and CZ would plead guilty to anti-money laundering violations. The fine: $4.3 billion, one of the largest corporate penalties in U.S. history. CZ personally would forfeit $50 million and step down from the empire he'd built from nothing.

When sentencing arrived in April 2024, our industry rallied. Character letters flooded Judge Richard Jones's desk—from employees whose families CZ had lifted from poverty, from users in countries where Binance was their only financial lifeline, from industry OGs who respected his integrity and what he had done for the industry.

In the days leading up to CZ's sentencing, I made my position clear. I sent Judge Jones my letter of support, and on April 25th, I posted a message on X:

> Sincerely hoping that the US Justice System shall prevail and CZ will be sentenced to probation next week. CZ has acknowledged his mistakes, voluntarily travelled to the US to face the Justice System, and paid a massive $4.3 billion fine. He has been convicted of AML compliance failure—but has not pleaded guilty, nor has the government alleged any crime involving money laundering, fraud, theft, or market manipulation. There has been no misappropriation of customer funds. Many of us know how much he's done for the crypto community and for the world. Sending good karma.

The post resonated deeply. Within hours, it reached hundreds of thousands, and the outpouring of support was overwhelming—not just from anonymous accounts, but from crypto builders, influencers, and long-time industry allies.

CZ himself responded with a humble 🙏.

These weren't just hashtags or comments. They were statements of identity. The crypto industry, fragmented and cynical as it can often be, was rallying behind one of its own.

That moment reminded me of something we too often forget: behind the charts, code, and compliance battles are humans—builders with vision, grit, and flaws. And when the pressure peaks, the real community shows up.

The judge acknowledged the "extraordinary" support but remained unmoved. Four months in federal prison. Less than the DOJ's vindictive three-year recommendation, but prison nonetheless. For building the infrastructure that brought financial services to millions of unbanked. For the crime of moving too fast in an industry Washington didn't understand.

As CZ prepared to serve his sentence, I thought back to that night on the Dubai terrace when he'd predicted this outcome. He'd known what was coming and faced it with dignity. That's what separated the true builders from the opportunists—the willingness to pay the price for changing the world.

Yet even as the crypto establishment burned, something remarkable was happening with our non-crypto ventures. Joe, the CEO of our immersion cooling company, LiquidStack, messaged with news that made me smile.

"George, I got great news. We're closing our Series B. The lead investor is a global industry giant. Thirty-five billion market cap. They're putting in fifteen million dollars and want to integrate our tech into their global operations."

I felt a smile crack across my face—the first genuine one in months. "Joe, that's incredible. You did it."

"We did it," he corrected. "The shift to building immersion technology for AI. That vision is finally paying off."

The irony wasn't lost on me. Our flight to safety during crypto's darkest hour had led us to opportunities we never would have seen from the summit. Sometimes you need to descend into the valley to find the hidden paths up the next mountain.

> Success blinds as surely as staring at the sun. When Bitcoin was soaring, we could only see crypto opportunities. Every conversation led to tokens, and every innovation needed a blockchain. But the crisis restored our peripheral vision. Suddenly, we saw all the problems crypto thinking could solve outside crypto: cooling systems, energy optimization, and AI infrastructure. The bear market didn't limit our options; it revealed them. Sometimes you have to lose your religion to find your faith.

The Overhang Problem

By March, Bitcoin had crawled back above $20,000—not a recovery, but at least a pulse. It was during this period of cautious optimism that we confronted our Cipher Mining position. The trigger came from none other than Howard Lutnick.

Howard was a banker and a force of nature with a thick New York accent that could cut through any boardroom. But Howard Lutnick carried a gravity few on Wall Street could match. On September 11, 2001, Cantor Fitzgerald lost 658 employees—including his own brother—in the World Trade Center attacks. Howard survived only because he was taking his son to his first day of kindergarten. In the aftermath, he pledged profits and healthcare to victims' families and willed Cantor back from the brink of collapse. That mix of tragedy, resilience, and relentless drive shaped the man we came to know: blunt, fast-talking, and impossible to ignore.

As Chairman and CEO of Cantor Fitzgerald, he embodied Wall Street's unflinching confidence—razor-sharp, and always five moves ahead. He didn't waste time on pleasantries; every conversation felt like a deal in motion, his words delivered with machine-gun precision.

"There's an overhang issue," Howard explained during our call. "Large institutional investors see your massive stake and freeze. They're concerned one day you may have to liquidate the position for whatever reason."

"In addition," he continued, "given your large holding, the free float is not that large and hence low liquidity. Serious investors look at this, and it scares them off." Then came his recommendation: "You guys have a great deal of share overhang in Cipher. It may make sense to distribute shares."

We'd looked at several deals with Howard before and had come to value his opinion highly—so much so that we'd brought his perspectives to board consideration. When someone of his caliber and market experience raises a concern, you listen.

I thought his advice made tons of sense and reached out to a few Cipher investors. One of the investors I contacted was Mike Alfred, who ran a successful investment firm and sat on the board of another Bitcoin miner, Iris Energy. Mike was also a large investor in Cipher himself and was one of the most knowledgeable people in the mining space, understanding both the operational complexities and the public market dynamics.

"Mike, we're considering something radical," I texted him one evening. "Distributing our Cipher shares pro rata to all Bitfury investors to increase free float and drive liquidity. Thoughts?"

My phone rang within seconds. "George, that's a great idea," Mike said without preamble.

"You don't think it signals a lack of confidence?" I asked.

"The opposite," Mike insisted, his voice energized even through the phone. "It signals maturity. You're saying Cipher can stand on its own. You're rewarding the investors who backed you through the years. And you're removing the concentrated ownership sword hanging over the stock price. Plus, you'll increase liquidity, and that's key."

Free float and daily trading volume are the lifeblood of public markets. Institutional investors won't touch a stock with limited liquidity. They need to know they can exit positions without moving the market. Our concentrated ownership had inadvertently created a liquidity trap: low free float meant minimal daily volume, which scared off the very institutional capital that could drive Cipher's valuation higher. By distributing our shares, we wouldn't just increase the free float—we'd create the trading depth that attracts index funds, enables options markets, and allows serious investors to build meaningful positions. It was Public Markets 101: liquidity begets liquidity, and broader ownership creates higher valuations.

Digital Monkeys for Good

Yet even as we wrestled with public market mechanics, the bear market continued to reveal which projects had substance beneath the speculation. It was during this period that Bill Tai called with another opportunity.

"George, I've got something for you," Bill said, his characteristic intensity that surfaced when he'd identified a signal in the noise. "It's about monkeys."

"OnChainMonkeys," Bill explained. "Danny Yang and Amanda Terry. You know them. Real team, real vision. NFTs as a force for good. We are closing an oversubscribed investment round, and I want you guys in."

The markets were collapsing in 2022. Bitcoin was down 70 percent, and lenders were blowing up. Yet here was Bill, spotting an opportunity. Amanda was my Wharton classmate—sharp, relentless, media-savvy. Danny, a Stanford PhD, had built MaiCoin into Taiwan's top exchange and was one of the Bitcoin OGs running Stanford meetups. Both had a great deal of credibility.

So when Bill put their names together, Val and I didn't hear "NFT project." We heard track record and depth.

And then I remembered back in 2021, Amanda had sent a note to us: "Support OnChainMonkeys (OCM) auction—100 percent proceeds to Giga Connect." A member donated their NFT; the proceeds were wired to rural schools to help bring internet access. The donor and winner were both acknowledged through "Metagood Moment NFTs." Clever, simple, impactful. Bill amplified it through UNICEF ties. Amanda called it "profit with purpose." It set the tone: OCM was about alignment, not hype.

I was intrigued.

On a subsequent call with Danny, he put it plainly: "NFTs bring people into crypto. Missions create a new gig economy—like Uber, but community-owned."

Non-Fungible Tokens (NFTs) are unique digital certificates of ownership stored on a blockchain. Unlike cryptocurrencies, where each coin is identical and interchangeable, NFTs are one-of-a-kind digital assets that can represent ownership of art, music, videos, or any digital content. Think of an NFT as a digital deed or certificate of authenticity—it proves you own a specific digital item, even though copies of that item might exist elsewhere. The technology enables creators to sell digital works directly to collectors while maintaining provenance and scarcity in the digital realm.

And so we invested. OCM would go on to prove that substance could survive speculation.

The team's philosophy drew inspiration from Yves Klein, the French conceptual artist who pioneered performance pieces involving destruction as transformation. Klein believed that to truly possess something, you had to be willing to sacrifice its current form—an idea that would prove central to OCM's most audacious move.

In 2023, OCM migrated to Bitcoin via Ordinals—a new protocol that allowed inscribing data directly onto individual satoshis, creating native Bitcoin NFTs. Metagood spent $1M inscribing assets directly onto the Bitcoin blockchain. Holders could burn their Ethereum versions to resurrect them on Bitcoin, embodying Klein's ritual of destructio,n enabling transcendence.

The migration was both a technical upgrade and a philosophical statement about permanence. OCM Genesis rose into the top Ordinals collections by market cap, attracting holders who valued Bitcoin's long-term durability over Ethereum's flexibility. The success attracted established artists who saw Bitcoin's permanence as the ideal foundation for digital art. Danny Yang created open-source code libraries from the OCM Dimensions collection, the first 3D generative art collection on Bitcoin, embedding tools that other artists subsequently used to create their own works. OCM helped artists, including Bryan Brinkman and Alexis André, put their art on Bitcoin, while Michael Hafftka, whose works have been in the Metropolitan Museum of Art, collaborated with OCM to create pieces only possible on Bitcoin. Meanwhile, Amanda and Bill presented at Davos while Danny spoke in Tokyo, positioning OCM as a driver of the emerging

"Art on Bitcoin" movement. Former Sotheby's CEO Tad Smith spoke about how "OnChainMonkey community has a vital role to play in the future of digital art."

At Sora Summit, Danny articulated their core insight: Bitcoin NFTs were like Klein's rituals—burn to truly own. Ownership as belief, destruction, permanence. "If you care about 100 years from now," Danny said, "Bitcoin is the chain most likely to endure. Art belongs there."

This investment taught me something crucial about surviving crypto winters: the projects that endure aren't necessarily the ones with the highest valuations or the loudest marketing. They're the ones that create genuine community, authentic value, and long-term vision. Bill's credibility, Amanda's drive, Danny's rigor—a community with purpose that built culture while others obsessed over technical debates.

Amanda and the OCM community always signed off with !RISE, which stands for their values: Respect (treat everyone with respect), Integrity (operate with the highest integrity), Sustainability (build for the future), and Enrichment (create value that helps make a better world).

With those monkeys rising on-chain, you could glimpse a higher purpose: climbing together, lifting everyone.

The BlackRock Earthquake

With Cipher's decision bagged, the next watershed moment for the industry came on June 15, 2023. I was playing tennis at my local club when my phone exploded with notifications. Between games, I glanced at the messages, and my heart stopped. I stood there unable to process what I was reading.

BlackRock had filed for a Bitcoin ETF.

"You alright?" my opponent called from across the net. "Should we take a break?"

I couldn't answer. I couldn't move. I certainly couldn't continue playing tennis after that. Larry Fink—the man who'd called Bitcoin "an index of money laundering"—had just validated everything we'd been building for a decade.

My racquet dangled uselessly at my side as I scrolled through the messages. This wasn't just another ETF filing. This was BlackRock.

$10 trillion BlackRock. The world's largest asset manager had just bent the knee to Bitcoin.

"I have to go," I managed to say, already heading for my bag. The match didn't matter anymore. Nothing mattered except what this meant for our industry, for Bitfury, for the future we'd sacrificed so much to build.

I called Val immediately. "Are you seeing this?"

"Yes. Amazing," he said. "He's calling Bitcoin 'digital gold.'"

"Now the entire financial world will follow," I mused.

The conversion of Larry Fink was our Constantine moment. When the Roman Emperor embraced Christianity, it didn't matter whether his faith was genuine—what mattered was that persecution ended and construction began. Fink's blessing transformed Bitcoin from a barbarian at the gates to an invited guest at the feast. The revolution hadn't stormed the citadel. The citadel had decided the revolution was profitable.

Within days, Bitcoin surged past $30,000. More importantly, the narrative had fundamentally shifted. We weren't defending crypto's right to exist anymore—we were building infrastructure for an asset class that the world's largest asset manager was racing to offer their clients.

When Larry Fink changed his mind about Bitcoin, he changed the permission structure for an entire generation of financial professionals. Suddenly, believing in Bitcoin wasn't career suicide; it was career insurance. The revolutionaries hadn't stormed the castle; the castle had opened its gates and invited them to dinner.

The applications flooded in—Fidelity, Invesco, WisdomTree. Each filing was another pillar supporting the new reality. Bitcoin wasn't going away. It was going mainstream.

But if BlackRock's embrace marked Wall Street's capitulation, the crypto industry still faced an existential threat from Washington. The financial establishment might have bent the knee, but the regulatory establishment was doubling down on its war against crypto. What we needed wasn't just institutional adoption—we needed political revolution.

By late 2023, the American crypto community had endured enough. After years of regulatory persecution, debanking, and watching legitimate businesses get destroyed by Operation Chokepoint 2.0, they finally did what Americans have always done when pushed too far—they organized, mobilized, and fought back through the political process.

The transformation was remarkable. An industry that had prided itself on being apolitical, on building outside the system, suddenly realized that ignoring politics meant politics wouldn't ignore you.

The intellectual ammunition came from those who'd documented the persecution. Balaji Srinivasan, who'd coined the term "Choke Point 2.0," rallied the industry through social media. Nic Carter's detailed exposés in Castle Island Ventures's newsletters became required reading, documenting every debanking, every regulatory overreach. Ryan Selkis turned Messari into a war room, his Twitter feed a daily chronicle of anti-crypto policy actions.

Fairshake PAC emerged as the spear tip, raising over $85 million from Coinbase, a16z, Circle, and Kraken. This wasn't just another Super PAC. It was crypto's declaration of war against those who'd tried to strangle the industry through regulatory persecution.

The crypto voting bloc had arrived with unprecedented coordination. Brian Armstrong at Coinbase launched "Stand With Crypto," transforming his company from an exchange to a political force. Chris Dixon at a16z brought Silicon Valley's sophistication to crypto advocacy. Jesse Powell funded litigation efforts from Kraken's treasury. Every major player understood: engage politically or die quietly.

Throughout 2023 and into 2024, the legal and policy front became a crucial battleground. The Global Blockchain Business Council, which we had helped establish years earlier, became a crucial voice for the industry. When Caitlin Long's Custodia Bank sued the Fed directly after being denied a master account, the Council stepped up, filing a joint amicus brief alongside the Digital Chamber, arguing that the rejection was politically motivated and part of the Choke Point 2.0 squeeze.

The debanking wasn't limited to new ventures like Custodia. Even our publicly-traded companies—Cipher Mining and Hut 8—began facing challenges opening accounts to receive Bitcoin payouts. Banks that had once eagerly courted their business now demanded excessive disclosures or simply refused service, citing "regulatory pressure" and reputational risk. Here were Nasdaq-listed companies with full regulatory compliance being treated like pariahs.

The irony was bitter: we'd gone public to gain legitimacy, only to find that legitimacy meant nothing when regulators decided to strangle an entire industry. Both companies joined the broader crypto-industry coalition calls for Congressional hearings on Operation Choke Point 2.0, citing their debanking as evidence that this wasn't about risk management—it was about systematic exclusion. They supported and amplified House and Senate hearings throughout that time, standing as proof that even the most compliant, transparent crypto companies weren't safe from the financial blockade.

GBBC's policy engagement went beyond legal battles. Through position papers like the Global Standards Mapping Initiative, they helped lawmakers understand the evolving industry norms and terminology. Their US Blockchain Coalition and regular events like Blockchain Central DC created direct channels to regulators at the Fed, SEC, and OCC, consistently highlighting how debanking was harming innovation and consumer access. It was gratifying to see the organization we'd helped birth now fighting on the front lines of regulatory clarity.

Coinbase sued the SEC, demanding clarity on rules that didn't exist. The Blockchain Association coordinated federal outreach, while state-level groups like the Crypto Freedom Alliance of Texas leveraged crypto-friendly jurisdictions. Coin Center, the nonprofit think tank, provided constitutional arguments that even skeptics couldn't dismiss.

The strategy was multi-pronged: targeted ad campaigns in swing districts exposed anti-crypto voting records. Endorsement scorecards from Stand With Crypto turned crypto stance into a litmus test for candidates. Lobbying efforts pushed pro-innovation bills like FIT21 and the Clarity for Payment Stablecoins Act. For the first time, crypto wasn't asking for permission. It was demanding representation.

Orange-Pilling the President

The turning point came on July 27, 2024, when former President Trump headlined Bitcoin 2024 in Nashville—the largest Bitcoin conference globally, organized by our old friend David Bailey. David, a Bitcoin OG who'd been in the space nearly as long as we had, had built the Bitcoin Conference into the industry's premier gathering. I remembered our early conversations at various Bitcoin meetups, when the entire conference could fit in a hotel ballroom. Now he was hosting former presidents and ten thousand attendees.

Watching the livestream from Italy, I witnessed something unprecedented: a former US president addressing over ten thousand Bitcoiners, many sporting "Make Bitcoin Great Again" hats. David had pulled off what seemed impossible just years earlier—orange-pilling the President of the United States.

The crowd erupted in standing ovations when Trump made three key promises: fire SEC Chair Gary Gensler on day one, pardon Ross Ulbricht, and position the US as the "crypto capital of the planet." The energy was electric, even through the screen.

"If Bitcoin is going to the moon," Trump declared, "I want America to be the nation that leads the way."

This was a seismic shift. The man who'd once dismissed crypto as a scam was now promising to create a strategic Bitcoin reserve from government holdings, including seized Silk Road coins. He vowed to make America a "Bitcoin mining powerhouse" while rejecting CBDCs entirely. The transformation from crypto skeptic to crypto champion was complete. David Bailey had orchestrated a conference to create the stage where Bitcoin entered American politics at the highest level.

November 2024 delivered the results the crypto industry had fought for. Anti-crypto politicians who'd treated the industry as an easy target discovered it had teeth. Some lost primaries to crypto-friendly challengers backed by Fairshake's war chest. Others suddenly found religion and softened their stances. Elizabeth Warren's "anti-crypto army" rhetoric, which had once seemed politically savvy, now looked like a liability as constituents demanded innovation, not strangulation.

Trump's return to the White House in November 2024 came with explicit promises to make America "the crypto capital of the world." For an industry that had spent years being targeted by Operation Chokepoint 2.0, the reversal was whiplash-inducing. Suddenly, the regulatory clarity we'd begged for wasn't just possible—it was policy.

The contrast between administrations was stark. While Biden had overseen Chokepoint 2.0 and Gensler's reign of terror, Trump promised regulatory clarity and respect for innovation. For an industry that had been persecuted for years, it felt like potential salvation.

By late 2024, Bitcoin's response was volcanic. $80,000. $90,000. Each new high was a rebuke to everyone who'd written us off.

If BlackRock marked the financial establishment's capitulation, the November 2024 elections delivered the political knockout punch. The two earthquakes—first financial, then political—had reshaped the landscape completely. Wall Street and Washington had both bent the knee to Bitcoin.

In that instant, I observed with fascination as the American crypto community learned the hard way that building great technology wasn't enough. You needed political power to protect innovation from those who feared it. The coordinated response—from Armstrong's grassroots mobilization to the industry's checkbook diplomacy, from Long's legal challenges to Balaji's intellectual warfare, from GBBC's policy engagement to David Bailey's conference platform—showed an industry that had matured from cypherpunk experiment to political force. They'd moved from "then they fight you" to fighting back and winning.

"The war on crypto is over," Val said during our strategy call. "We won."

"The war is over," I agreed. "Now the floodgates will open up. Let's get ready."

Saylor's Cabana

On that very optimistic note, I arrived in Miami in December for Art Basel, where art, money, and ambition collide in that intoxicating way only Miami can orchestrate. The SLS Hotel hummed with energy as jet-lagged collectors and dealers moved between exhibitions, each searching for their next revelation.

That's when I found them—Jiha Moon's dragon sculptures. Five pieces that stopped me cold in the gallery's white-washed space. As someone born in the Year of the Dragon, the symbolism felt almost predestined. In Eastern mythology, dragons don't hoard gold in caves like their Western counterparts. They soar through clouds, bringing rain and prosperity, representing transformation and wisdom gained through trials.

Standing before these creatures, I saw our journey reflected. We'd become dragons ourselves—not through conquering markets, but through surviving them, transforming with each cycle, bringing prosperity not just to ourselves but to an entire ecosystem.

"I'll take all five," I told the artist. "And could you inscribe each with the Bitcoin symbol?"

The next day, before flying to Costa Rica for Marat's forty-fifth birthday, Val and I visited Michael Saylor at his Miami compound.

We'd come to discuss his treasury strategy and the state of the industry going forward—conversations that had become increasingly important as MicroStrategy blazed new trails in corporate Bitcoin adoption.

"Gentlemen," Michael said, greeting us in his cabana surrounded by palm trees and three of his favorite parrots, one of which was named Bitcoin. "Bitcoin isn't just an asset anymore. It's becoming the global denominator for value itself."

We discussed MicroStrategy's transformation into a Bitcoin treasury company—a model that turned traditional corporate finance on its head.

"The beauty is," Michael explained, his eyes alight with the fervor of true belief, "once you understand Bitcoin's power law, everything else becomes obvious. We're not buying Bitcoin—we're selling fiat. There's a difference."

As we prepared to leave, we reminisced about the good old days—the formation of the Bitcoin Mining Council, those intense Zoom calls during the energy FUD, watching the industry evolve from the fringes to the mainstream.

I couldn't resist: "I just wish you'd come to Bitcoin earlier, Michael."

Michael's eyes lit up. "George, I wish that as well. But what matters is that we're here now, building the future."

> Michael had discovered what every convert knows: the fervor of the latecomer exceeds the faith of the founder. Those of us who'd been in Bitcoin since the beginning had been worn smooth by cycles, our enthusiasm tempered by experience. But Michael brought the fresh zeal of someone who'd found religion in his middle age. His certainty wasn't naïve—it was necessary. Every movement needs its prophets, especially the ones who arrive just as the founders grow weary.

The $100K Moment

Costa Rica greeted us with warm rain and that particular green that only exists in the tropics. Marat had assembled fifty friends from around the world at a boutique hotel in Santa Teresa, where jungle meets ocean in a way that makes you question why humans ever invented cities.

"Forty-five years old," Marat mused over welcome cocktails. "Two decades of chasing the next big thing, and Bitcoin's still the most interesting technology I've ever seen."

The party flowed from sunset into starlight, stories and laughter mixing with the sound of waves. Fire show dancers moved like liquid flame against the tropical night, their torches casting dancing shadows across the gathering. Then, near midnight, our friend Inga Hofmann, co-founder of Musical.ly that would later become TikTok, approached me and Val with jubilation: "Look! $100,000!"

Everything stopped. On her phone screen: Bitcoin at $100,000.

The eruption was primal—cheers, tears, embraces that tried to capture fourteen years of struggle in a single moment. Marat found us in the chaos, eyes glistening.

> There are moments when time folds in on itself, when past and future collapse into a single point of pure present. Seeing $100,000 on that screen, surrounded by friends in the Costa Rican night, I felt every moment of the journey simultaneously—every crash, every sleepless night, every breakthrough, every betrayal. We were celebrating our own transformation. The price was proof, but the proof was of something deeper than profit: that a group of dreamers could bend reality to their will.

"Ten dollars to a hundred thousand," Marat said. "We actually did it."

"I always knew it was a matter of when, not if," Val added. "Next stop is one million."

As the celebration continued, I found myself walking down the beach, needing space to process the moment. Two hundred meters from the party, I lay down on the sand, still warm from the day's sun.

Above, the moon hung like a silver Bitcoin in the sky, its light turning the waves to molten silver. I thought of all the wins and losses, of all the sleepless nights, of all the meetings where investors laughed us out, of all the skeptics and doubters who'd told us we were chasing digital fool's gold.

"We've won," I said to the moon, to the stars, to the ocean that had seen empires rise and fall. "We've really won."

But even as I said it, I knew the truth. In Bitcoin, you never really win—you just survive to build another day. And tomorrow, we'd wake up and build again, because that's what dragons do. They don't rest on their hoards. They soar through clouds, bringing rain to those below, transforming the landscape with each pass.

Victory in revolutionary technology isn't a destination—it's a transformation. We'd won not because Bitcoin hit $100,000, but because we were no longer the same people who'd started this journey. The market had been our crucible, each cycle burning away what wasn't essential, revealing what was. We'd sought to master the market and instead discovered it had mastered us—shaped us, refined us, prepared us for challenges we couldn't yet imagine.

The sound of distant laughter drifted down the beach. My phone buzzed—probably someone wanting to celebrate, to plan, to dream about what came next. I silenced it and lay there a moment longer, letting the magnitude sink in.

One hundred thousand dollars. A number that had once seemed impossible. Now it was just another waypoint on a journey that had no real destination, only the next mountain to climb, the next transformation to undergo, the next generation to guide.

I stood, brushing sand from my clothes, and walked back toward the lights and laughter. The dragon had risen. Time to spread its wings.

CHAPTER 20
AND THEN YOU WIN

*First they ignore you, then they laugh at you,
then they fight you, then you win.*

—Mahatma Gandhi

New Year's Day, 2025. The Maldives stretched before me like a promise kept—endless blue meeting endless possibility. I'd woken before dawn in our beach villa, drawn to witness the first sunrise of a year that felt less like a new beginning and more like a coronation.

My family slept peacefully nearby, joined by Chris Allen and his wife, Julia, for our annual celebration. Through the glass floor of our villa, I watched reef sharks glide through crystal waters—apex predators moving with the confidence of those who know their place in the ecosystem. I smiled at the metaphor. We'd become sharks ourselves, not through predation but through adaptation.

Just weeks ago in Costa Rica, Bitcoin had crossed $100,000 during Marat's forty-fifth birthday. The same Marat who'd pestered me about "magic Internet money" at $10 had witnessed its ascent to six figures on the very night of his celebration. As I'd lain on that beach, the moon casting silver Bitcoin shadows on the waves, I'd whispered into the tropical night: "We've won."

Now, watching the sun paint the Indian Ocean gold, I understood that victory in revolutionary technology isn't measured in price points—it's measured in transformation. And by that metric, we hadn't just won. We'd helped rewrite the rules of the game itself.

> The ancient alchemists sought to turn lead into gold, never realizing the real transformation happened within themselves. We'd sought to mine digital gold, only to discover we were mining something far more valuable: resilience, wisdom, the ability to see opportunity in catastrophe. Every bear market had been a teacher, every failure a hidden gift. The gold was never the point; the quest was.

Later that morning, I walked the island's circumference, each step a meditation on the journey. The question that visitors to success always ask surfaced: What if we'd done things differently? What if we'd simply held those three hundred thousand bitcoins from 2015?

I let the math wash over me like the waves at my feet. Three hundred thousand bitcoins at $100,000. Thirty billion dollars. The numbers were seductive in their simplicity.

But then another what-if emerged, perhaps even more tantalizing: What if our 16 nm chip had worked as advertised? We'd had a real shot at becoming the undisputed industry leader with an 80 percent market share. The dominant position in what's estimated as a $10 billion annual sales industry, with solid margins. Latest rumors have put Bitmain's valuation at $50 billion. This could have been us.

Yet as I continued walking, I thought of what we'd actually built. Cipher Mining and Hut 8, now valued at a few billion, accelerating Bitcoin mining and AI infrastructure in America. Axelera, pushing the boundaries of AI chip technology and making artificial intelligence more efficient. Crystal Blockchain, keeping the ecosystem clean and compliant. LiquidStack, revolutionizing how the world cools its computation. The scores of companies we'd incubated, the dozens of entrepreneurs we'd mentored, the hundreds of jobs we'd created.

We could have been a thirty-billion-dollar Bitcoin fund, doing some sort of MicroStrategy-similar play on capital markets with that many coins. Or we could have been a fifty-billion-dollar chip giant, dominating mining hardware globally. Instead, we went through many setbacks and learning experiences, adapted and pivoted to incubate successful companies, and capitalized to the tune of billions.

As I like to say: "Shoot for the moon, but even if you miss, you'll end up amongst the stars."

Each failure taught us something crucial. Each pivot opened doors we didn't know existed. We'd aimed for chip dominance and ended up as ecosystem builders. The setbacks weren't detours—they were the journey itself, transforming us from hardware manufacturers into architects of the Bitcoin ecosystem.

> There's a Zen koan that goes, "Before enlightenment, chop wood, carry water. After enlightenment, chop wood, carry water." Before Bitcoin mooned, we built infrastructure. After Bitcoin mooned, we built infrastructure. The price was never the revelation—the building was. Those who understood this survived. Those who didn't become footnotes in someone else's success story.

Success, I've learned, is not the absence of failure—it's the transformation of failure into wisdom. Our 16-nanometer chip debacle could have been our epitaph. Should have been, by all rights. A 99 percent yield in testing that mysteriously collapsed to 1 percent in production? It defied explanation, defied logic, defied everything we knew about semiconductor manufacturing.

The stakes had been enormous. Success would have meant market dominance on a scale that dwarfed our wildest dreams. With working 16 nm chips, we were positioned to control eighty percent of a rapidly expanding industry. The same industry that would eventually crown Bitmain as an undisputed king. That crown should have been ours.

Some nights, I still wonder: Was it sabotage? A competitor's industrial espionage? Or were we simply too far ahead, our low-voltage design pushing beyond what even TSMC could reliably produce? Perhaps we shouldn't have showcased the chip all over the world in December 2015, right before its production, and stayed in stealth mode! The mystery may never be solved, but the lesson is crystal clear: sometimes your greatest strength becomes your greatest vulnerability. Our technical excellence had made us rigid. The failure forced us to become fluid.

Like a master judoka using an opponent's force against them, we transformed our catastrophic setback into a catalytic change. Unable to dominate through chips, we learned to succeed through ecosystems. Unable to control through hardware, we learned to influence through investments. The very disaster that should have destroyed us instead revealed our true nature: we weren't a mining company that happened to innovate. We were an innovation company that happened to mine.

The Paradise Perspective

That evening, as Chris and I watched the sunset paint the sky in impossible colors, our families' laughter drifting across the water, he posed the question that had been hovering all day.

"Any regrets?" he asked.

I considered my answer carefully. "Regrets are for people who think the past could have been different. Everything we did, every decision we made, was the best we could do with what we knew then. The chip failure, the market crashes, the betrayals and breakthroughs—they weren't detours from our destiny. They were the road itself."

Chris smiled. "You know what separates us from everyone who didn't make it?"

"What's that?"

"We never confused activity with progress. When mining stopped working, we didn't mine harder. We evolved."

He was right. The cryptocurrency graveyard is full of companies that perfected obsolete strategies. We'd survived by accepting a fundamental truth: in exponential technologies, adaptation beats optimization every time.

Darwin never said "survival of the fittest"—that was Herbert Spencer's interpretation. Darwin spoke of the survival of the most adaptable. In crypto's Cambrian explosion, the apex predators weren't those with the sharpest teeth or the strongest armor. They were the shapeshifters, the ones who could be miners on Monday, investors on Tuesday, incubators on Wednesday. The market didn't select for strength; it selected for metamorphosis.

The Infinite Game

As midnight approached on that first day of 2025, I found myself back on the beach, this time with my entire family. My sons played in the phosphorescent waves, their laughter mixing with the eternal rhythm of the sea. We were pointing out constellations to the boys, while Chris and my eldest were deep in conversation about the history of Britain.

This—this moment of connection, of possibility, of multiple generations united in wonder—this was wealth beyond any crypto fortune.

"Dad," my son called out, "look at the water! It's glowing!"

The bioluminescence transformed every wave into liquid starlight. Each movement created new patterns of brilliance. It was a perfect metaphor for our journey—agitation creating illumination, disturbance generating beauty.

Gandhi's progression had proved prophetic, but incomplete. Yes, they had ignored us when Bitcoin was just a cypherpunk curiosity. Yes, they had laughed when we said it would transform finance. Yes, they had fought us with regulations, with competition, with every weapon at their disposal.

And yes, we had won.

But here's what I understood now, standing in the glow of the waves: the victory wasn't Bitcoin hitting $100,000. That was just a number on a screen, a milestone that meant everything and nothing. The real victory was that we were still here to see it.

The true triumph wasn't measured in price points but in persistence. Every morning, when we'd chosen to continue when quitting would have been logical. Every pivot, when the path forward vanished. Every brutal decision to let people go, every sleepless night wondering if we'd make payroll, every moment of crushing doubt followed by the choice to keep building—those were the victories that mattered.

Bitcoin at $100,000 wasn't our achievement. Our achievement was conquering ten thousand hard things to be standing here when it happened. The price was just the scoreboard. The game had been played in conference rooms and data centers, in missed family dinners and predawn flights, in choosing to evolve when evolution seemed impossible.

Winning, I realized, was never an event. It was the accumulated result of facing down every hard thing, day after day, year after year, until what once seemed impossible became inevitable.

Standing there in the Maldivian night, surrounded by family and friends, watching bioluminescence turn the ocean into a galaxy, I understood something fundamental: We had survived crypto winter, and in doing so, we'd discovered that within us burned an invincible summer—one that no market crash could extinguish, no chip failure could dim, no setback could freeze.

The adventure that began with Marat showing me a Bitcoin white paper had evolved into something neither of us could have imagined. From a garage in San Francisco to the halls of Congress, from chip design to ecosystem architecture, from fighting for survival to nurturing the next generation—every chapter had prepared us for this moment.

But this moment, glorious as it was, was not a conclusion. It was a comma in a sentence that would outlive us all. The dragon had risen, spreading its wings across a sky that suddenly seemed too small for our ambitions. New startups to incubate. AI frontiers to explore. Financial systems to reimagine. Human potential to unlock.

> The paradox of achievement is that it only reveals how much remains undone. We'd climbed Everest only to discover it was a foothill. But that's the gift of success in revolutionary technology—it doesn't satisfy ambition; it amplifies it. Every problem solved reveals ten problems worth solving. Every summit reached shows a hundred peaks beyond. The journey doesn't end with victory; victory simply upgrades the journey.

"Come on," I called to everyone. "Let's go celebrate."

As we walked back toward the lights of our villa, the phosphorescence fading behind us but somehow still glowing in our eyes, I knew with crystalline certainty: the best chapters weren't behind us. They were waiting to be written, in code and companies, in mentor sessions and board meetings, in every entrepreneur we'd lift and every innovation we'd enable.

We'd shot for the moon and landed among the stars. But the view from here revealed something amazing—there were galaxies beyond, each one waiting for explorers brave enough to venture into the unknown.

The Bitfury story, which began with questioning whether digital scarcity was possible, had become proof that transformation was inevitable for those who refused to quit. We'd started as miners, became builders, and evolved into enablers. The next evolution was already beginning.

First, they ignore you. Then they laugh at you. Then they fight you. Then you win.

And then—if you're doing it right—you help others win too.

But remember this: the win itself is just punctuation in a story written by endurance. Every hard thing conquered, every impossible day survived, every choice to continue when stopping made sense—that's where victory lives. Not in the price of Bitcoin or the valuation of companies, but in the brutal, beautiful journey of becoming someone who could handle whatever the universe threw at them.

The dragon rises not because the market finally recognized our value, but because we never stopped climbing, especially when the mountain seemed infinite.

The adventure continues. The hard things await. And we wouldn't have it any other way.

To the moon and beyond—one conquered challenge at a time.

CHAPTER 21

21 LESSONS FOR TOMORROW'S BUILDERS

It's your road and yours alone. Others may walk it with you,
but no one can walk it for you.

—Rumi

As I reflect on this wild journey—from a curious meeting in a Kyiv café to watching Bitcoin cross $100,000 on a Costa Rican beach—I'm struck by how many lessons crystallized through trial by fire. The path from discovering Bitcoin to helping build a global technology enterprise has taught me insights that no Ivy League could impart.

In keeping with Bitcoin's sacred number—21—as the embodiment of scarcity and value, I share 21 hard-won insights from our odyssey. These are battle-tested principles, each paid for in sleepless nights, near-bankruptcies, and moments of transcendent victory.

Lesson #1: Shoot for the Moon, and If You Miss, You Will Still Be Among the Stars

You have limited time in this world. Spend it on big ideas and ambitious projects rather than something small. When you pursue a moonshot, the universe seems to conspire to make it happen.

When Val and I first discussed transforming Bitfury from a Ukrainian-Latvian-Finnish startup into a global force, many called us delusional. The idea of institutional adoption seemed like science fiction. Yet we aimed for nothing less than revolutionizing global finance.

This moonshot mentality attracted extraordinary people. It's why engineers worked through the nights to solve impossible problems. It's why investors took chances when logic said run. The audacity of your vision becomes a gravitational force, pulling resources and talent into your orbit.

Even our apparent failures proved this principle. We could have built a conservative mining operation, but instead, we aimed to revolutionize the entire Bitcoin ecosystem. When our chip leadership dreams were shattered, we didn't retreat—we evolved into ecosystem builders, incubating companies worth billions. Always remember: "Nothing big ever came out of something small."

Lesson #2: Start with the End in Sight

I love the analogy of Steven Spielberg always envisioning the end of his movies first, then building everything toward that conclusion. We adopted this philosophy, always knowing our destination: capitalizing Bitfury in Western markets, bringing institutional legitimacy to a technology born in cypherpunk forums.

This approach fundamentally changed how we made decisions. Every potential partnership, every product development roadmap, and every hiring decision was evaluated against this end goal. This clarity meant saying no to lucrative consulting contracts that would have distracted us, declining partnerships that offered immediate revenue but long-term limitations. We resisted the temptation to establish mining operations in geographies that, while operationally efficient, would complicate our eventual Western market story.

For any project, have a clear vision and specific goals, then determine what essential foundations you need to place to make it happen. Everything else will fall into place.

Lesson #3: Make Sure to Climb the Right Mountain

Have a clear vision of where you're going. Resources are limited, and time pressure is constant. What's truly devastating is spending all your time and resources climbing a mountain only to realize it's the wrong one.

We faced countless crossroads where we could have pivoted: become a cryptocurrency exchange, a blockchain consultancy, or chase every emerging token trend. We chose our mountain carefully: building the infrastructure for Bitcoin's future. This meant watching competitors raise easy money in ICOs while we ground through the unglamorous work of chip design and data center operations. But when the ICO bubble burst, we remained standing.

Be diligent in analyzing your market and understanding that you're climbing the right mountain—that there's a genuine opportunity to connect the dots and make something significant. Sometimes wisdom means admitting you've chosen the wrong mountain and finding a better one while you still have energy to climb.

Lesson #4: Accept the Hard Reality of Entrepreneurship

Entrepreneurship is hard. It's lonely. It's often thankless, and the journey is always full of peril and adversity. People think entrepreneurship is glamorous and enjoyable, but you must be prepared to be like a swan—everyone sees how beautifully it glides across the water, but no one sees how hard it paddles beneath the surface.

During our chip crisis, when months of work yielded one percent production success, I remember standing in my Hong Kong hotel room, knowing we were weeks from bankruptcy. The weight of hundreds of employees' futures, of investors' trust, of our own dreams was crushing.

Prepare to work hard. Prepare to sacrifice. Prepare to "eat glass" if necessary. Prepare for sleepless nights, junk food, red-eye flights—all for the sake of that vision. Have this reality check from the start: entrepreneurship isn't for everyone, and you should understand this.

Lesson #5: Learn to Say No

In a world full of distractions, learning to say no is crucial because time is your most valuable resource. As an entrepreneur, you're constantly bombarded with competing priorities. Practice ruthless prioritization.

Success brings a tsunami of opportunities. Conference keynotes, partnership proposals, investment pitches—each seemingly important, all collectively fatal. We learned that saying no to good opportunities was essential to achieving great ones.

I like to tell the story of a man with a jar, big stones, pebbles, and sand. He asks his child to fill it up, and the child starts with sand, then pebbles. The man stops him and says, "No, put the big stones in first, then the pebbles, then the sand. If you put the sand in first, there won't be room for the big stones." Identify your organization's big stones and ruthlessly prioritize them over the pebbles and sand. Always.

Lesson #6: Surround Yourself with Complementary Brilliance

You cannot be a genius at everything. A key trait of leadership is surrounding yourself with smart people. Understand everyone's strengths and weaknesses. Don't fear having people smarter than you—thrive on it.

Val could spend eighteen hours analyzing chip specifications with otherworldly focus. I couldn't sit still for eighteen minutes without thinking up three new deals or partnerships. Marat saw market patterns before they emerged, but couldn't remember to check his email. Ever.

These complementary strengths made us powerful together.

Too many founders recruit mirrors of themselves, creating echo chambers of similar thinking. We actively sought our opposites. When I wanted to move fast, Val insisted on a detailed analysis. When Val dove deep into technical minutiae, I pulled us back to market realities.

Lesson #7: Bring in People of Impact

Fill your team with initiators—people who are proactive and make things happen. Give them accountability in a decentralized way, and they'll perform and deliver.

Promote meritocracy in your organization. Everyone's idea and impact are valuable, but when they step up to the plate, they ought to know to give their best. Create an environment where performance and results matter more than hierarchy or politics.

Some of our greatest breakthroughs at Bitfury came from team members who took initiative without waiting for perfect instructions. Our expansion into Kazakhstan happened because Timur saw opportunities and moved decisively. Our spinning out of successful companies like Axelera and LiquidStack occurred because Fabrizio and Joe identified potential and acted on it.

Ensure you have these impact-makers in your organization, and quickly remove those who hide behind corporate facades as you grow. Otherwise, these "weeds" will eventually overtake your garden and damage the "roses."

Lesson #8: Be a Person of Your Word

Your word is everything. My father taught me that you only have one chance to establish credibility and trust. That's it.

During the 2018 crash, we owed tens of millions for chips ordered during the boom. Facing the challenges, we gave our counterparts our word that it would be solved and worked day and night to restructure everything into win-win agreements with the mentality of making things right, not screwing anyone over.

Every time we sold our block box solutions for mining, if there was a delay in putting in equipment, we always compensated clients with computing power from our pool. We never left anyone hanging.

Later on, when we desperately needed payment terms during our darkest period, those same suppliers extended credit that helped save our company.

At our organization, we could have taken shortcuts or gone "sideways," but we always kept our word. This was one of the foundational pillars that attracted me to Val's energy—that unwritten rule that your word is your bond.

Your reputation is about approaching every relationship with integrity. Treasure it.

Lesson #9: Give Credit Where It's Due

In a rapidly growing organization, recognition can be overlooked. Step up and ensure praise is given where deserved—both publicly and with tangible rewards.

We often provided incentives and bonuses for good performance, but more importantly, we always had an "outstanding bonus" component—a substantial reward for those who "moved mountains." When our chip designers were ahead of schedule on the 55 nm chip, they received substantial bonuses. When our engineering team performed the miracle of building a twenty-megawatt facility in twenty-eight days, their bonus was substantial, but the companywide recognition was priceless.

Create a culture where achievement is impossible to ignore. The cost of generous recognition is nothing compared to the value of a team that believes miracles are possible.

Lesson #10: Create a Culture Where Bad News Travels Fast

When mistakes happen, ensure they're acknowledged, analyzed, and that you move forward quickly. It's vital that mistakes aren't punished in your organization. We had a saying at our company: "Bad news must travel fast." Nothing should be swept under the carpet.

We held accountable those who hid problems and gave credit to those who brought issues to light. You must analyze situations, implement solutions, and move on. You cannot allow issues to remain hidden, growing into cancer cells.

This culture saved us millions of dollars when a team member identified a potential flaw in a chip design before it went to manufacturing. Because they knew they wouldn't be punished for delivering bad news, they immediately escalated the concern. Heck, this culture saved us from bankruptcy over and over again.

Lesson #11: Eradicate Negative Thinking

Negative thinking attracts more negativity and leads to a downward spiral. In our organization, we fought negative thinking like cancer cells, never allowing it to spread.

If we found someone spreading negativity, they were removed from the organization. We never tolerated negative thinking. There was always a solution to every problem, and we expected people to bring both problems and potential solutions—never just complaints.

This wasn't about suppressing legitimate concerns, but rather about maintaining a solutions-oriented mindset. When facing the 2018 to 2019 crypto winter, one approach would have been to focus on how impossible the situation was. Instead, we channeled our energy into creative solutions: spinning out companies, pivoting business models, and finding new revenue streams.

Lesson #12: Think Outside the Box

Creativity is paramount. Linear thinking abounds, but entrepreneurs must embrace exponential thinking. This approach enables you to leapfrog competition and pivot when necessary.

When most blockchain companies were focusing solely on cryptocurrency applications, we were already envisioning how the technology could revolutionize land registries, intellectual property management, and supply chain verification. This outside-the-box thinking positioned us years ahead of the market.

We took this same approach to hardware: designing full custom chips and boards from scratch, obsessing over how to squeeze maximum compute power from minimal energy. While others bought off-the-shelf components, we reimagined the entire architecture.

Our decision to spin out companies during the bear market seemed crazy. Why give away valuable assets? But this unconventional thinking allowed those companies to thrive independently and increase their capitalizations.

Thinking outside conventional boundaries isn't just helpful for entrepreneurial success; it's essential. The biggest breakthroughs come from questioning assumptions everyone else takes for granted.

Lesson #13: Cultivate Resilience

Nothing will work out as planned. Things will go awry. Circumstances will change. Situations will become incredibly difficult. But staying the course and continuing to push forward is vital.

I was struck by Idealab's Bill Gross and his research showing that timing is the most important factor in entrepreneurial success—more than the team, funding, or even the idea itself. Yet if you persevere enough, if you stay prepared, sooner or later you'll catch that perfect wave. As our angel investor Bill Tai would say, "Entrepreneurship is all about finally catching the wave and then riding it."

Our resilience was tested during multiple crises: the 2014 to 2015 cryptocurrency bear market, the 2016 TSMC yield disaster, the 2018 to 2019 crypto winter, and the 2022 FTX collapse. Each time, competitors folded while we adapted. When markets eventually recovered, we emerged stronger because we'd used downturns to improve our technology, diversify our business model, and strengthen our team.

Lesson #14: Master Adaptability

Understand that change is constant. Be ready to adapt and adapt calmly. As Marcus Aurelius taught in his *Meditations*, you can only control how you react to things. When you understand that change is constant, you embrace it.

Bitfury began primarily as a mining hardware manufacturer, but we recognized early that we needed to evolve with the market. We adapted our business model to include mining operations, then blockchain software solutions, and eventually a comprehensive security and analytics platform. Each evolution required letting go of old assumptions and embracing new realities.

The most dramatic adaptation came when we had to abandon our chip development program—our core identity for over a decade. Instead of clinging to the past, we pivoted toward building AI infrastructure and supporting next-generation technologies. We went into AI chip design, embracing the future, as well as seeing the bottleneck in data cooling and developing immersion cooling solutions.

Lesson #15: Remember "This Too Shall Pass"

King Solomon's famous saying holds true in entrepreneurship. Everything passes—both the bad news and, to some extent, the good news too. Having the mindset that no matter how difficult a situation becomes, it will eventually pass gives you perspective and strength.

During our darkest moments—when Bitcoin hit $3,700 and we were down to less than half a million dollars—this principle kept me centered. I knew the difficulty was temporary, that markets change, that sentiment evolves. This perspective prevented panic decisions and allowed us to maintain our strategy until conditions improved.

The same principle applied during euphoric times. When Bitcoin hit $60,000 in 2021 and everyone was declaring permanent victory, remembering that "this too shall pass" kept us preparing for the next downturn.

Lesson #16: Treat Your Journey as a Marathon with Strategic Sprints

Startups are a journey of rhythm. As my good friend and Wharton classmate Dan Zilberman likes to say: "There are times when you need to hustle intensely, and times when you should slow down, pause, reflect, and conserve your energy for the next surge. Know when to walk and when to sprint."

Building our Georgian facility in less than a month nearly killed our team. But we followed it with deliberate deceleration—time to document learnings, optimize processes, and restore human energy. This rhythm became our secret weapon.

Our Cipher Mining SPAC process required an intense sprint—three months of sixteen-hour days to complete one of the largest Bitcoin mining deals in history. After closing, we deliberately stepped back to integrate operations and plan strategically rather than immediately chasing the next transaction.

The entrepreneurs who burn out are those who only know one speed: maximum effort. The ones who succeed understand that sustainable growth requires cycles of intense focus followed by strategic reflection. Sprint when the opportunity demands it, but always build in time to recover and recalibrate.

Lesson #17: Have Fun Along the Way

When you truly love what you're doing and the impact you're making, it transforms your experience. Despite hunger or exhaustion, your passion keeps you jumping up every morning. Work and life become intertwined in the best way.

We held board meetings on Necker Island and strategy sessions in Kyiv banyas. We celebrated victories with Georgian feasts and processed defeats through chess matches with Sir Richard. Work became play, play became work.

We never had "down days" because we loved our work so much. We'd have meetings on Sundays, Saturdays, holidays—it didn't matter because we genuinely enjoyed what we were doing. This was our blessing and our key to success.

Lesson #18: Practice Self-Reflection

As an entrepreneur building a company amid constant noise, it's crucial to make time for self-reflection. Find your space—early mornings were my favorite, when everything was quiet. I would meditate, sit, and think deeply about our vision, our priorities, and our "big stones."

I made it a practice to spend one weekend every quarter in complete solitude, away from technology and business demands. These periods of reflection often provided clarity that was impossible to achieve in the day-to-day hustle.

The companionship of books proved vital to this practice. James Allen's classic, *As a Man Thinketh,* and Marcus Aurelius's *Meditations* became my constant companions. I would reread these books regularly—in the morning on beaches, during long plane flights, or in the evening before bed. Returning to these timeless works infused me with perspective and made a huge difference in my decision-making.

Lesson #19: Do Good and Good Things Will Happen to You

You cannot fake genuine intentions. If you're truly there to make an impact, help people, and do good, the universe will respond in kind. Always be conscious of this principle, and you shall prevail.

We built Bitfury with a commitment to ethical practices and prioritized responsibility in our operations, transparency in our dealings, and positive social impact through our technology applications. These decisions occasionally came with short-term costs, but the reputation and relationships they built created long-term value that far exceeded any immediate sacrifice.

Our contributions to Virgin Unite, Coin Center, Blockchain Trust Accelerator, and various educational initiatives exemplified this principle. We supported entrepreneurship programs and technology education in underserved communities—not for publicity or business advantage, but because it was right.

Lesson #20: Always Maintain an "I Can" Attitude

Remember: Attitude is everything. "I can, I can, I can"—you can do anything in this life. It's just a matter of attitude, focus, and execution.

One of my favorite sayings was "Those that think I can and I cannot are equally right," and I would often repeat it. This mindset became our greatest asset through countless challenges. When competitors raised more funding, when technical problems seemed insurmountable, when market conditions turned against us, the "I can" attitude kept us moving forward. It's not blind optimism, but rather an unshakable belief in your ability to find a way, to adapt, to overcome whatever obstacles appear.

When our 16 nm chips failed spectacularly and threatened our existence, this mindset helped us find alternative solutions and survive. When we launched Cipher Mining SPAC with just energy LOI letters and no one believed us, the "I can" attitude made the impossible possible.

The difference between entrepreneurs who succeed and those who don't often comes down to one simple belief: "I can figure this out." This attitude becomes self-fulfilling—it attracts people who want to be part of something ambitious, opens doors that seemed permanently closed, and creates momentum even when logic suggests you should quit.

Lesson #21: Believe that Impossible Is Nothing

This was truly in Bitfury's DNA: Impossible is nothing. While we always did thorough preparation and analysis, when the moment came, we committed fully and moved forward.

I love the story of the Columbia math PhD student who fell asleep during class and woke to see two problems on the blackboard. Thinking they were homework, he spent all night solving one of them.

The next day, he apologized to the professor for only completing one problem—not realizing he had just solved a centuries-old mathematical mystery that had stumped geniuses for generations.

When we decided to build our own ASIC chips despite having no prior experience in semiconductor design, many said it was impossible for a startup. We embraced the challenge, assembled a team of brilliant engineers, and went on to create some of the most efficient chips in the industry. What seemed impossible became our reality because we refused to accept conventional limitations.

When all the large banks said no one would fund a company with only energy letters of intent, we went on to raise hundreds of millions and capitalized on the opportunity to the tune of billions. Sometimes the greatest breakthroughs come from not knowing what's supposed to be impossible.

Where Are They Now: The Ecosystem Thrives

As I write these final words, the companies we incubated during our journey continue to validate our core belief: that building an ecosystem creates more lasting value than any single product. Here's where our "children" stand today:

Cipher Mining and Hut 8 have both achieved what once seemed impossible: they are publicly traded on NASDAQ with valuations in the billions. Together, they've secured thousands of megawatts in energy capacity in North America and expanded beyond Bitcoin mining into the exploding AI data center market, proving that infrastructure built for one revolution can power the next. Their future is very bright.

LiquidStack has become NVIDIA's official partner, securing strategic funding from Tiger Capital and Trane Technologies, a $100 billion industry behemoth. As the AI boom drives unprecedented demand for efficient cooling solutions, Joe and his team are perfectly positioned at the intersection of two exponential trends.

Axelera AI has grown into Europe's leading AI chip company, successfully launching their METIS chip and approaching unicorn valuation. Fabrizio's vision of democratizing AI computing is becoming a reality, one efficient chip at a time.

Crystal Blockchain continues its steady ascent, recently securing a strategic investment from industry giant Tether and positioning itself to capitalize on the stablecoin and real-world asset (RWA) boom that's digitizing traditional finance.

Each success validated our approach: that true entrepreneurship isn't about creating one perfect product, but about nurturing an environment where innovation can compound. Sometimes the greatest victory isn't dominating one market, but creating the conditions for multiple breakthroughs to flourish. We learned that letting go—spinning out promising ventures when they outgrew us—was actually the highest form of value creation.

Your Time Is Now

As this journey concludes, Bitcoin has crossed $100,000. The experimental technology we championed when it was worth less than a dinner is now held by nation-states. The impossible has become inevitable.

But this isn't about Bitcoin—it's about belief. Every transformative technology begins with someone foolish enough to challenge conventional wisdom. Every great company starts with founders naive enough to think they can change the world.

These 21 lessons are tools, not rules. Use what serves you, discard what doesn't, and discover your own along the way. The entrepreneurial journey isn't about following someone else's map but creating your own territory.

The world doesn't need another entrepreneur waiting for perfect conditions. It needs builders who will start with what they have, where they are, with the knowledge they possess today. Every moment you delay beginning is a moment the universe must wait for your contribution.

Stop waiting for permission. Stop waiting for perfect timing. Stop waiting for someone else to solve the problems you see. The world needs your moonshot, and it needs it now.

Now go forth. Build something extraordinary. Make your own impossible possible.

And remember—when they ignore you, laugh at you, fight you, that's when you know you're on the right path.

Your time is now. Begin today.

ENDNOTES

1   Advisory Board. Internet Way Back Machine. Accessed August 13, 2025. https://web.archive.org/web/20010405174328/http://www.eyefrog.com/advisory.html.

2   "Nokia Unveils New Partnerships and Acquisitions; Outlines Plans for the Future." *SPGlobal*, December 4, 2007. https://www.spglobal.com/marketintelligence/en/mi/country-industry-forecasting.html?id=106597381. Accessed August 18, 2025.

3   Tai, Bill. November 24, 2010. Comment on Bitcoin. https://x.com/KiteVC/status/7601056028561408.

4   Huang, Vicky Ge. "The Trump Family Advances Its All-Out Crypto Blitz, This Time With Bitcoin Mining." *The Wall Street Journal.* March 31, 2025. https://www.wsj.com/finance/currencies/the-trump-family-advances-its-all-out-crypto-blitz-this-time-with-bitcoin-mining-86a1e8d9. Accessed August 19, 2025.

5   Vigna, Paul and Michael J. Casey. *The Age of Cryptocurrency, How Bitcoin and the Blockchain Are Challenging the Global Economic Order.* New York: Picador: 2016.

6   Antonopoulos, Andreas M. *Mastering Bitcoin: Unlocking Digital Cryptocurrencies.* Sebastopol, CA: O'Reilly Media Inc., 2015.

7   Weiss, Mitchell and Elena Corsi. "Bitfury: Blockchain for Government." *Harvard Business School Case 818-031*, October 2017. https://www.hbs.edu/faculty/Pages/item.aspx?num=53445. Accessed July 31, 2025.

8   Mikitani, Hiroshi and Ryoichi Mikitani. *The Power to Compete: An Economist and an Entrepreneur on Revitalizing Japan in the Global Economy.* Hoboken, NJ: John Wiley & Sons, 2014.

9   Ammous, Saifedean. *The Bitcoin Standard: The Decentralized Alternative to Central Banking.* Hoboken, NJ: Wiley, 2018.

10   Lansing, Alfred. *Endurance: Shackleton's Incredible Voyage.* New York: Carroll & Graf, 1986.

ABOUT THE AUTHOR

George Kikvadze is the Founder of Cryptic8 VC, investing at the intersection of technology and longevity. He serves as Vice Chairman and early backer of Bitfury Group, the Bitcoin and blockchain technology company at the heart of this book.

A Bitcoin pioneer since 2013, George was privileged to be behind three tech unicorns—Bitfury, Cipher Mining, and Hut 8—and is currently advising several promising companies on their path to unicorn status.

George is a member of YPO Europe One Chapter and holds degrees from Wharton and Johns Hopkins. Beyond his professional achievements, he enjoys tennis and chess and remains a lifelong learner who continues to seek knowledge across diverse fields. Most importantly, he is a dedicated father to his two sons, Luca and David, instilling in them that nothing is impossible—the philosophy that has guided his entrepreneurial journey and life.

CONNECT WITH GEORGE

Follow him on social media today.

@BitfuryGeorge

THIS BOOK IS PROTECTED INTELLECTUAL PROPERTY

Instant IP [IP]

The author of this book values Intellectual Property. The book you just read is protected by Instant IP[IP], a proprietary process, which integrates blockchain technology giving Intellectual Property "Global Protection." By creating a "Time-Stamped" smart contract that can never be tampered with or changed, we establish "First Use" that tracks back to the author.

Instant IP [IP] functions much like a Pre-Patent since it provides an immutable "First Use" of the Intellectual Property. This is achieved through our proprietary process of leveraging blockchain technology and smart contracts. As a result, proving "First Use" is simple through a global and verifiable smart contract. By protecting intellectual property with blockchain technology and smart contracts, we establish a "First to File" event.

Protected by Instant IP [IP]

LEARN MORE AT INSTANTIP.TODAY